Andrew Linn

Sheffield 2000

SOUND

THE DARWIN COLLEGE LECTURES

SOUND

Edited by *Patricia Kruth and Henry Stobart*

CAMBRIDGE
UNIVERSITY PRESS

PUBLISHED BY THE PRESS SYNDICATE OF THE UNIVERSITY OF CAMBRIDGE
The Pitt Building, Trumpington Street, Cambridge, United Kingdom

CAMBRIDGE UNIVERSITY PRESS
The Edinburgh Building, Cambridge CB2 2RU, UK   www.cup.cam.ac.uk
40 West 20th Street, New York, NY 10011-4211, USA   www.cup.org
10 Stamford Road, Oakleigh, Melbourne 3166, Australia
Ruiz de Alarcón 13, 28014 Madrid, Spain

First published 2000

Printed in the United Kingdom at the University Press, Cambridge

Typeset in Linotron 300 Iridium 10/14pt

A catalogue record for this book is available from the British Library

Library of Congress Cataloguing in Publication data
Sound / edited by Henry Stobart and Patricia Kruth.
    p.   cm. – (The Darwin College lectures)
  Includes index.
  ISBN 0 521 57209 6
    1. Sound.   I. Stobart, Henry, 1958–   .   II. Kruth, Patricia, 1954–   .   III. Series.
QC225.6.S68   2000
534 – dc21   99–15819 CIP

  ISBN 0 521 57209 6 hardback

Contents

Introduction

PATRICIA KRUTH and HENRY STOBART

> When the sun was about to rise for the very first time, God and his brother Supay made a bet. The one whose cockerel crowed first would be the winner. As the sun climbed into the sky God's black rooster triumphantly cried out KUKURUKU! Suddenly, with a resounding KUN! the defeated Supay and his red rooster vanished. They entered certain large rocks and deep into the earth, where they remain to this day. This is why these rocks ring like bells when struck with a stone and cry out of their own accord during nights of the full moon. They are the bells of the inner earth.

This tale from the high Andes was told to one of us to explain the origin of the resonant boulders that perch high on the mountainside above the narrator's home, rocks that literally ring like bells when struck (Figure 1). The story focuses on the juxtaposition between sound (the cock crow) and silence (failure to crow). A world order is created through this encounter, where God rules the external world into which sounds are released, disperse and decay, and Supay governs the inner world – animating the resonant rocks and the earth in which he is enclosed. The sound of God's black rooster has long faded, but the failure of Supay's red rooster to crow now presents itself as potential sound. It is no coincidence that in several parts of the Andes musicians invoke or even sacrifice a red cockerel before an important performance.

In this story, the 'live' (resonant) quality of ringing rocks is treated in terms of a living body; both are animated by a mysterious inner presence. Indeed, the ability to emit sound is a principal way we recognise a 'live' body, whilst 'dead' also means unresonant. Unlike the ringing rocks, which have maintained eternal resonance, living bodies – like sounds – emerge, exude energy, grow, fade away and eventually decay. Such parallels between the temporality of sound and life are evident in a variety of contexts and built into many languages. From this perspective the shaping of sound might be equated with the shaping of life, and the journeys of sounds with those undertaken by living beings.

FIGURE 1. The narrator playing a bell stone in the Bolivian Andes.

This book is the fruit of a series of lectures, each accompanied by a sound event, the sounds of which have now evaporated and transformed into memories and the visual traces in this volume. This reminds us of the ephemeral and transitory nature of sound – no sound is more than a few moments old. Sounds are simultaneously present and absent; we perceive them but they are no more than the moving and intangible shadow of the source or the object that created them. When we perceive them, they have already departed. Sound moves through time and space and it both literally and metaphorically moves us. It wraps around and contains us but, unlike an image, cannot itself be contained.

Communication is a primary function of sound. Likewise, through bringing together and orchestrating perspectives on sound from a variety of disciplines, communication is the underlying principle and a primary concern of this volume. Even though the chapters and approaches are very different from one another, many motifs recur through the book, harmonising together within a rich interdisciplinary counterpoint.

How singular is sound? Should we talk of hearing as separated from the other senses? Sensory perceptions may be combined in a multiplicity of ways. For example, in poetic synaesthesias perfumes, colours, sounds and/or tastes are perceived in harmony; in the unforgettable words of the poet Milosz, 'The smell of silence is so old . . .'. On the other hand, senses may be understood in a 'scientific' way, as purely physical mechanisms; in Jean-Luc Godard's *Pierrot le fou* (1965), Ferdinand, in a state of confusion, complains that he has a machine for seeing called the eyes, another for listening (the ears), and yet another for talking (the mouth). He feels they are separate machines. There is no unity.

The tendency in Western culture, since Aristotle, has been to place sight first in a hierarchy of the senses, followed by hearing and the other senses. This primacy of the visual, however, has not always been constant; in medieval Europe, for instance, hearing as the sense through which the word of God was perceived often displaced sight, and the ranking of the senses itself was a popular literary theme. In Alain de Lille's allegorical epic *Anticlaudianus* (1183), as related by Constance Classen, the senses are represented by five horses that pull a carriage carrying Prudence to Heaven. 'Sight is first in the shafts as the swiftest of the horses, followed by Hearing, Smell (enveloped in the fragrance of flowers), Taste and Touch. The coach is unable to reach Heaven, however, so Prudence, persuaded by Theology, unharnesses Hearing and rides on to Heaven with him alone.' More recently, in *Notes sur le cinématographe* (1975), the film-maker Robert Bresson writes, 'The eye (in general) superficial, the ear profound and inventive. The whistle of a train engine imprints in us the vision of an entire station.' For Bresson, as for Michel Chion as we shall discover, sound is as 'cinematic' as image.

Whatever the order within this shifting hierarchy, the danger when studying the senses is to decontextualise them from one another – for instance by essentialising vision as a characteristic of the West, as opposed to sound, smell and taste as that of non-Western cultures, or by reifying a visual/auditory divide. Indeed, when we focus on the sounds of a CD, this does not mean that our other senses have ceased to function; however, as Bresson stresses, 'The eye solicited alone makes the ear impatient, the ear solicited alone makes the eye impatient. *Use these impatiences.*' Many of the contributors to this volume are clearly aware of this issue. For example, Christopher Page uses Holbein's painting *The Ambassadors* and the sight of the magnificent Turkish rug to turn our attention to how the ambassadors would have reacted to Ottoman sounds (p. 138). In the foreground of the painting is a curious, distorted and almost spectral shape – an anamorphosis. This enigmatic presence suggests a vivid parallel with Page's endeavour to reconstruct ancestral voices. The solving of both these mysteries relies on the necessity of a distance between the 'detective' and the object, and of a movement – respectively of the eye in space and the ear in time. In both cases we start from an illusion – Page points out that 'any modern performance of a medieval piece must be a phantasy' – and end with a denial, an awareness that there is nothing absolute but only relativity. However, whereas the spectator of the painting can find the right *point of view* from which the anamorphosis will reveal its enigma – in this case, the skull which brings out the vanity of the picture – the scholar of medieval music realises that his or her reconstruction of sounds can only be approximate. There is no perfect *point of hearing*; only interpretations. This may be precisely one of the seductive properties of music that allows for what Brian Ferneyhough refers to as 'the spiritual power of creative misunderstanding'.

We have chosen to begin this series of essays with silence, not because we imply an evolutionary sequence from silence to sound, as some might assume, but rather because it seemed necessary to create and define silence to give meaning to sound. Similarly, in placing speech before music we do not imply an evolutionary approach. Indeed, Darwin was convinced that musical instinct evolved 'low down in the animal series' and long before articulate speech, which he describes as one of the latest and certainly the highest of the arts acquired by human beings – a controversial view, which brings into question what is meant by 'musical instinct'. Rather than on evolution, our focus is upon sound itself.

We move from silence, via the physical properties of sound and its perception by the ear, to sound as a medium of communication in birdsong and speech. From these uses of sound we then turn to music, passing from the Middle Ages, via twentieth century transformations in Western Art Music, to World Music – the local and the global in a Papua New Guinea rainforest society. Finally, we explore the interplay of sound and image in the context of cinema.

The anthropologist **Philip Peek**, a specialist on African divination systems with a long interest in sound and silence, addresses the issue of **Re-sounding Silences** from a cross-cultural perspective. For this daunting task, Peek uses a wide range of references to compare Native American, Asian, African and European-American cultures. For example, he notes how the respectful and reticent silences of Native Americans have often been interpreted by outsiders as sullenness, stupidity or hostility, and how certain Asian societies, who statistically speak much less than European-Americans, consider verbally communicative individuals to be offensive. In particular, Peek develops a wealth of ethnographic material from Africa, and points to the widespread use of usually silent creatures as divinatory agents in cross-world communications (between this world and the spirit world). He also describes the silence of divine kings who do not speak in public nor must be spoken to directly. Their mouths are typically shielded with veils and fans and they are accompanied by spokesmen who speak both 'for' and 'as' the king. These various references to silence are portrayed by Peek as culturally meaningful and linked to wisdom, and contrasted by what he presents as a European-American fear of silence. Echoing a point made by Robert Murray Schafer in *The Tuning of the World* (1977), Peek's central argument is that European and European-American cultures are characterised by negative attitudes towards silence, whereas the other cultures to which he refers find silence meaningful and 'positive'. However, reading this chapter we are left to wonder whether the ambiguity and complexity of silence is not to some degree shared by most, if not all, cultures.

Whereas Peek approaches silence primarily in relation to speech, **Charles Taylor** includes a musical dimension to **The Physics of Sound**. He begins by explaining that sound is vibration involving changes in air pressure, and that it requires a medium for its transmission. Regularity of changes in air pressure tend to give the sensation of musical pitch, whilst random ones give that of noise. However, as Taylor is at pains to point out and is evident in later chapters, the distinction between music and noise is intensely subjective. After defining amplitude, frequency and hearing ranges, a theme to which Jonathan Ashmore returns, he explains how sound transmission varies according to temperature and why, for example, on a warm day, sounds travel far greater distances over water than over dry land. The issue of sound reflection, and the effects this has on architectural acoustics and the various soundscapes we inhabit, is of special significance to later chapters. Communication using sound would be extremely difficult if we simply floated in space without any form of sound reflection. Conversely excessive reflection (reverberation), causing each syllable to be repeated many times, can make speech almost unintelligible. After considering anti-sound – an exciting new branch of research dedicated to, for instance, aircraft noise reduction – Taylor focuses on a variety of musical sounds and the issue of resonance. His discussion of the problems of early attempts to electronically synthesise instrument timbres and how these have been overcome serves as a helpful background to the chapter by Brian Ferneyhough. In his text, as in his lecture demonstration, Taylor exhibits a remarkable ability to make complex physics highly accessible and enjoyable. This chapter serves both as an excellent introduction to the physics of sound ... and as a guide to playing the musical saw!

To appreciate the charms of the musical saw, amongst other reasons, humans and certain other species have evolved floppy appendages on the sides of their heads – the ears. Although the physiology of the outer and middle ear have been well understood for a long time, the precise workings of the inner ear have remained a challenge. In the last few years, a number of groundbreaking advances have been made in this area, especially thanks to the application of new biochemical and biophysical techniques. **Jonathan Ashmore** is at the forefront of this exciting new field of research and his chapter focuses on the physiology of the cochlea of the inner ear – the main organ of **Hearing**. This extraordinary and tiny organ is able to detect and analyse disturbances in air pressure of as little as 2/10 000 000 000. In particular, Ashmore examines the basilar membrane, which acts like a sound spectrum analyser, and whose role is vital in allowing distinct incoming sound frequencies to be separated. Ashmore studies how, at a molecular level, the so-called hair cells, which are the most important cells in the cochlea, detect and amplify sound. Finally, he shows how, through the process of transduction – whereby the shape of the hair cells is distorted – sound information is transmitted to the nervous system and then on to the brain. The molecular biology of hearing, Ashmore stresses, includes potentially enormous areas that are just about to open up. Reading this chapter, one cannot but marvel at the very miracle of hearing and the complexity of the body; it is, for example, quite astonishing to realise that, as well as amplifying sound, the cochlea also produces minute quantities of sound, or in other words that the ear emits sound. Understanding how the hearing system functions is indispensable if we are to detect and even possibly prevent deafness, but also to compensate for the hearing losses that may affect all of us with ageing. This understanding has also made possible amazing pioneering operations whereby people who suffer from some kinds of deafness (for example, as a result of meningitis turning their cochlea to bone) have recently been given cochlear implants – consisting of electrodes implanted in the cochlea – allowing them to re-emerge into the world of sound.

One sound that has continued to inspire us through the centuries, as manifested in the works of countless poets and musicians, is that of bird song. Why do birds use sound to communicate? What are the functions of songs? How do birds learn to sing and how do they build up their repertoires of songs? These are just a few of the questions **Peter Slater** addresses in his fascinating chapter **Sounds Natural: The Song of Birds**. He describes how sound is by far the most practical medium for communication, and reveals how the syrinx – the sound-producing organ of birds – is able to create two separate sounds simultaneously. (Indeed, during the Sound Event following the lecture, a slowed-down recording of a lyre bird was played singing simultaneously two different popular songs it had copied – one from each side of the syrinx.) This chapter also highlights the complex repertoire of certain species and the interactive way in which birds learn to sing from one another, leading to the sharing of songs by male birds from the same neighbourhood. Songs that are not copied tend to become extinct, whilst inaccurate copying may give rise to new songs, which in turn spread through the population. Song learning, it has been suggested, might help to match the song to the bird's habitat, where over many 'cultural generations' songs become more suited to a particular environment. Although not to be taken literally, this idea resonates richly with Steven Feld's chapter, in which he shows how the music of the Kaluli (Papua New Guinea) reflects and maps their rainforest habitat. Incidentally, Feld's 1982 book *Sound and Sentiment* focuses specifically on the intimate relationship between Kaluli music and bird song, where the voices of the rainforest birds, imitated in music, are interpreted as those of the spirits of their dead – bird song as ancestral voices.

As Slater points out, research into bird song has developed considerably over the past decades, largely thanks to the development of the sonograph in the 1950s and more recent computer technology, enabling visual representations of sound to be compared. This was not available to Charles Darwin, who betrays his fascination with bird song in *The Descent of Man*. He was particularly struck by the variation in the power and inclination of different male birds of the same species to sing. Indeed, at that time in England a birdcatcher would sell an ordinary male chaffinch for sixpence whereas an excellent singer could be sold for as much as £3; 'the test of a really good singer being that it will continue to sing whilst the cage is swung around the owner's head'.

Humans' ability to communicate through language and speech has often been invoked as a primary characteristic differentiating human beings from other species. However, perhaps we should not lose sight – sound? – of Peter Slater's approach to bird song and, as Steven Pinker has suggested, think of language more as a biological adaptation to communicate information rather than as the 'ineffable essence of human uniqueness'. In approaching the diversity of the world's languages and the way they are shaped in **The Sounds of Speech**, **Peter Ladefoged** demonstrates some of the parameters influencing such adaptation. There are some 7000 mutually unintelligible languages in the world and the use of sound is subject to three main constraints: the ease with which specific sounds can be created, the readiness with which they can be recognised, and our cognitive capacity to organise and remember them. After considering the significance of pitch to convey emotion, and nuances of meaning both within phrases and in the syllable structure in tonal languages, he goes on to discuss vowels. Vowel sounds are distinguished by different combinations of overtones or resonances in the vocal tract; these are called formants and their number varies considerably in different languages, for example there are as many as 26 in Austrian German dialects. It is silence rather than sound that characterises the consonants p, t and k (voiceless stops), which are found in almost all languages. Less common, however, are the ejectives of, for example, the Andean language Quechua, and the clicks of the African Bushmen, which uniquely are produced by sucking air into the mouth. Ladefoged observes that 'learning to sing is like learning a language, easier to pick up and do with perfection if you are a child, but more difficult when older'. Nobody, he suggests, is completely tone deaf. Is music then as intuitive to humans as speaking a language?

Concern with sustaining and patterning sounds has occupied the creativity of humans for millennia. Whilst the utility of this is evident for language, the evolutionary advantages are much less clear in the case of music, a point also made by Darwin. 'As neither the enjoyment nor the capacity of producing musical notes are faculties of the least use to man in reference to his daily habits of life, they must be ranked among the most mysterious with which he is endowed.' The following three chapters are dedicated to this enigma, the first is by the scholar, broadcaster and director of Gothic Voices **Christopher Page**. We chose the title **Ancestral Voices** both to evoke sounds from the past and to pay homage to David Munrow (1942–76), who, during the final years of his tragically brief career, made a series of television programmes of the same name. The role of Munrow, as the founder of the London Early Music Consort and a tireless performer and broadcaster, has been of paramount importance to the immense popularity and relevance Early Music enjoys today. As Page elegantly puts it in his thought provoking chapter, 'to reconstruct ancestral voices we must boldly fashion the music according to our desires, but our desires can be discreetly fashioned by our discoveries'. The crucial point, and one also very much brought out by Munrow, is that for music to communicate, whether in the Middle Ages or today, it must be shaped by both knowledge and desire.

Near the start of his chapter, Christopher Page asks the question 'What did the medieval three-part song *Novus miles sequitur* – today preserved as a manuscript – sound like in 1173?' We will never know for sure, but in part it is this very enigma and the tantalising intimacy of the text that compels us to attempt to recreate the sounds. To address the issue of how we might approximate the sounds of *Novus miles sequitur*, Page dramatically sets out from twelfth century Canterbury Cathedral, the scene of Thomas Beckett's murder, and skillfully negotiates the sound shifts of the intervening centuries. Two of the most vital periods he pinpoints are the generations leading up to 1500 when the psaltery was developed into the harpsichord, and those following 1800 when the harpsichord was eclipsed by the piano. We discover from Page that, although the medieval world recedes ever more into the distance, paradoxically, we have come closer to approximating its musical sounds. This would never have been possible, Page argues, at the dawn of this century, a time redolent of the lushness of Victorian aesthetics. Is this, we are left to wonder, a quirk of history where medieval and twentieth century modernist aesthetics have fortuitously fallen into tune with one another, or does it reflect a wistful urge to reclaim a lost, pre-industrial past? Also, to what degree has our discovery of this music been fuelling and shaping contemporary aesthetics and musical practices?

According to the composer **Brian Ferneyhough** at least, the recent flourishing of the Early Music Movement has greatly contributed to the liberation of our generation's new music from its former institutional rigidity. In his essay **Shaping Sound** on the expansion of sound resources in twentieth century Western Art Music, he also observes that 'music conspicuously lacks any obvious referent external to itself and it is thus largely constrained to enter into conversation with its own past'. The enticing complexity of Ferneyhough's beautifully composed text is, quite appropriately, almost beyond words. He starts by demonstrating the profound impact of percussion on twentieth century composers, showing how a sense of permanent transformation set free from any ultimate need for resolution is achieved through its use in *Ionisation* (1934) by Edgar Varèse, and how pitched and unpitched instruments are delicately combined in Pierre Boulez's *Le Marteau sans Maître* (1954). To shape sound, Ferneyhough insists, is to enunciate musical idea. The ear's ability to perceive the structuring of unfamiliar sounds as music was further stretched by the introduction of unconventional instrumental techniques and sounds not hitherto considered musical, such as those resulting from dragging a number of chairs from one place to another (John Cage) or a microphone across the surface of a tamtam (Karlheinz Stockhausen).

The so-called 'advancement' of musical thinking, as advocated by Theodor Adorno in terms of the sedimentation of tradition, came to mean precisely the opposite, as composers' desires for liberation from the constraints of serialism led them to explore alternative instrumental techniques. In many cases, this took the form of a direct attack on conventional assumptions, as in Helmut Lachenmann's *Pression* (1969) for solo cellist, which uses little by way of standard technique or notational practice, and reduces the instrument to its bare bones, enabling new sonic concepts to emerge. In the same way, in his piece *Atemzüge*, Dieter Schnebel used the science of phonetics to dissect and then recombine the sounds (resulting from specific positions of the vocal organs) usually employed intuitively in acts of human speech. Finally, Ferneyhough briefly considers the impact of computer analysis on musical composition. Thanks to more recent technological developments, the 'irritating artificiality' of early electronically synthesised sounds has given way to the fusion of sampled natural sounds and digital editing as in the piece *Mortuos Plango Vivos Voco* (1980) by Jonathan Harvey, where a boy's voice is superimposed on the main partials of a tolling bell. Digital analysis of complex sound spectra has also served as the basis of instrumental compositions by, among others, Tristan Murail and Gérard Grisey.

According to Darwin, 'So different is the taste of the several races, that our music gives no pleasure to savages, and their music is to us in most cases hideous and unmeaning'. Such language and the implied cultural assumptions cannot be accepted today, but Darwin's point concerning the non-universality of musical taste will be recognised by many. Oddly, however, today such descriptions as 'hideous and unmeaning' are more likely to be applied to certain forms of 'contemporary' Western Art Music or genres of Popular Music than to the music of other cultures. Such a situation probably tells us more about the social and cultural processes, resulting in part from technological developments, than about the sounds of the music itself.

Darwin was writing before the invention of the phonograph and before the advent of ethnomusicological studies based on extended field work such as that by **Steven Feld** among the Kaluli of the Papua New Guinea rainforest. The stretching of the ear's capacity to appreciate unfamiliar sounds, described by Ferneyhough, is superbly demonstrated in today's widespread enjoyment of 'world music'. Feld's recent collaboration with Micky Hart of the Grateful Dead in the production of a CD of Kaluli music and forest sounds, *Voices of the Rainforest*, has catapulted him into the world music arena – a position which for him, as an academic, is deeply ambivalent. Kaluli music, which for Darwin and his contemporaries might have been 'hideous and unmeaning', is now enjoyed and, thanks to Feld's research, at least in part understood, by a mass audience. In his evocative, far-reaching and moving chapter **Sound Worlds**, Steven Feld explores the complex musical interactions between local and global sounds. He begins with a history of the term 'world music', showing its passage from academia – to mark 'ethnically other' musics and as substitute for the more cumbersome term 'ethnomusicology' – to the commercial world as a sales tracking category for 'danceable ethnicity'. This is followed by a discussion of the ambivalent responses to the global commercialisation of local musics, which Feld describes in terms of anxious and celebratory narratives, thus leading him to focus on his research with the Kaluli. Feld has been working with the Kaluli for over 20 years and he describes both the cultural and ecological changes that have transformed the lives of these people, and the development of his own approaches to research.

Recently, Feld has coined the term 'acoustemology' (drawing together acoustics and epistemology) to focus our attention on 'the primacy of sound as a modality of knowing and being in the world'. Puzzling though this idea may seem at first, on reflection it is highly engaging and was evoked in Feld's lecture itself, which was given to a background of rainforest sounds, thereby transporting us to the Kaluli sound world. Feld relates a number of musical metaphors directly to the Kaluli's ways of poetically mapping out their environment. These include: 'lift-up-over sounding', where the overlapping rather than synchronic sounds of the rainforest are evoked in music; and 'flowing' where the omnipresent and resounding movement of water shaping the body of the landscape is expressed in the circulatory and repeating motion of song. Finally, the evolving interactions between the local and global are explored in vivid descriptions of three very different song performances recorded between 1971 and 1994. Each in its own way demonstrates how 'local knowledge' is articulated as 'vocal knowledge'.

In Kaluli musical discourse, and in Feld's choice of the expression 'poetic cartography' as the sung evocation of places and the paths that connect them, we frequently encounter a visual dimension. The visual and the aural are not presented as separate entities but constantly interact with one another, and it is to this interplay in the context of cinema that we now turn.

The book includes an extra chapter, **Audio-Vision and Sound**, by the theoretician, composer and film-maker **Michel Chion**. This essay is a synthesis and introduction to his important research on the audiovisual relationship in sound cinema. The product of the fusion of sound and image is usually perceived in terms of image: historically, films were 'silent' for the first 30 years before sound was 'added', and ontologically cinema is a visual medium. However, in his essay, Chion argues that we 'audio-view' a film and that in audiovisual combination hearing and seeing constantly influence and transform one another. He demonstrates that there is no such thing as an audiovisual redundancy: although sound may seem to duplicate the meaning of an image, the two are in fact independent. Moreover, there is a lack of symmetry between sound and image because whereas there is 'a visual frame for images' there is 'no sound frame for sounds'. Instead, we tend to perceive sounds as emanating from the visual image – the screen (even, for example, when the sound of a film is heard through headphones on an aeroplane).

Among a variety of audiovisual effects Chion discusses, is that of *synchresis* (from 'synchronism' and 'synthesis'), whereby a sound and an image that coincide are perceived as belonging together even if actually unrelated. For instance, almost any sound can convincingly be synchronised with human footsteps (from ping-pong balls to glass objects), thereby freeing sound from the need to mimic reality. Indeed, sounds in cinema often do not attempt to reproduce reality so much as to '*render* (i.e. convey, express) the feelings associated with the situation'. Chion observes that conscious hearing attention is voice-centred and coins the term *audio(logo)visual* to emphasise the primacy of speech in cinema. After exploring ways in which sound is used to construct and/or structure filmic time, Chion points out that audiovisual relations may also be based on shortcomings where sound makes us aware of what is missing in the image, and vice versa – a situation which he calls *audio-division*.

The new terminology forged by Chion requires that we stretch our eye as well as our ear and our brain's capacity but also – more significantly – by being named, these effects, which had hitherto been intuitive, acquire an identity.

The chapters in this volume cover an immense range of themes and approaches to sound; yet they are by no means comprehensive. Neither was it our intention to provide a complete account of the aural world – a vain endeav-our, which would go against the recalcitrant nature of sound.

We end, as we began, with a contemporary story about another mythic figure. We find ourselves in the Sculpture Garden of the Museum of Modern Art in New York, it is 10 July 1992. The noise of midtown Manhattan rush-hour traffic rumbles beneath ebullient bird song. At a desk lit by a table lamp, on which are placed sheets of paper, microphones and an alarm clock, sits an eld-erly gentleman dressed in denim shirt and jeans. At what seem randomly pre-cise intervals, he interrupts the otherwise constant traffic noise from beyond the walls of the garden and the singing of the birds by chanting unintelligible speech sounds. After an hour and 15 minutes, the gentleman stands, and from the many rows of seats facing him applause errupts, marking the end of the performance.

Many in the audience had spent the 75 minutes reading books or the 'Week-End Section' of *The New York Times* whilst others appeared meditative. This was a performance by John Cage, a month before his death, of part of *Empty Words* (1973–8), a work which, in its entirety, would last from evening until the chorus of bird song at dawn. For many people, the noise of traffic would be classed as sound pollution, yet for Cage, 'the sound of traffic' was silence – his preferred sound, never the same, always different. He liked the sound of traffic because, in contrast to music, it did not create the impression that someone was talking to him, expressing his or her feelings or ideas. The sound of traffic was not talking to him, it was just 'acting' and Cage liked its activity. Silence as traffic noise was clearly an integral part of the concert, so much so that one was led to wonder where the locus of the concert was placed. The unobtrusive figure of Cage and the few sounds he uttered led one's attention beyond the walls of the Sculpture Garden. Had the performance merely been interrupting the silent sounds? If the concert was located beyond the Garden's walls, did it actu-ally begin or end?

Our opening tale from the Andes made *present* the contrast between sound and silence, a *certainty* that we must feel in order to act and be emplaced in the world. This final story leaves us with a sense of *absence* and *uncertainty* about place, time, and the very nature of the sounds – words, music, noise or silence? From these securely intangible **Sound** perspectives, we turn to the chapters of this volume, which we now invite you to read with a listening eye.

FURTHER READING

Bresson, R., *Notes sur le cinématographe*, Paris: Gallimard, 1975.

Classen, C., *Worlds of Sense*, London: Routledge, 1993.

Darwin, C., *The Descent of Man*, London: John Murray, 1871 (second edition, 1877).

Le Breton, D., *Du Silence*, Paris: Éditions Métailié, 1997.

Pinker, S., *The Language Instinct*, London: Routledge, 1994.

Weis, E. and Belton, J. (eds.), *Film Sound: Theory and Practice*, New York: Columbia University Press, 1985.

1 Re-Sounding Silences

PHILIP PEEK

To begin this collection of essays on our acoustic world with the topic of silence suggests that we 'naturally' move from silence to sound. It is assumed that there is a shift from inchoate silence to meaningful sound. This portrayal of human development has it that first there is absence, no human speech or song, but only later do significant utterances and sounds occur. In reality, many world cultures move from sound to silence, most easily demonstrated in religious contexts. But as well we can quickly realize that neither sound nor silence is comprehensible without the other.

From those disciplines devoted to the evolution of human phonation and communication, we learn that we are 'hard-wired' for sound and apparently programmed for speech. We cannot not learn a language. Perhaps reflecting that primacy of speech, many origin myths around the world have speech as the first of human accomplishments. We are also programmed for hearing. Cultural systems can be properly considered as extra-somatic systems of survival. In other words, to compensate for our lack of sharp senses and physical abilities we have the means to call out a warning to others or shout for help. Surely signing can do much of this and obviously writing serves such functions, but the point is that it is speech that allows us to live as we do. Therefore, when humans choose silence, one must listen carefully.

I begin, selfconsciously, with what brought me to the topic of silence – and that was sound. For many years, I have studied the sounds of African cultures to be heard in historical narratives, sacred prayers, music, verbal arts and so on. Yet, over and over, I encountered significant silences. While researching the primacy of speech in African societies, I wondered about the significance of the absence of this essential element – if words have literal power, what does it mean to choose not to speak? Why is it that divine kings throughout Africa seldom speak publicly? In the huge corpus of sacred and secular narratives told

FIGURE 1. Anansi the Spider as depicted on a linguist's staff of the Ashanti of Ghana.

FIGURE 2. Spider divination among the Kaka Tikar of Cameroon: the oracular message is read by the diviner from the cards as rearranged by the spider.

by African peoples, there are many characters, notably trickster figures, who are silent creatures in the natural world yet they play very important communicative roles. For example, in Ghana there are many Ashante tales about Anansi the Spider, a very quick witted and often sacred character (Figure 1). Spiders are not known as noisy, yet in a world where words are acts and soundscapes underlie all else, they serve as spokesmen and are a source of tales. One also wonders why the silent Tortoise is so often an emblem of wisdom? And what of that wily Hare (Bugs Bunny's African trickster ancestor)? In Africa, these characters survive and triumph by their wits, usually expressed through clever words, yet they are essentially silent creatures in the 'real' world.

In African divination systems, where cross-world communications (between this world and the 'spirit world') are literally life-giving, we find an extraordinary number of silent or voiceless creatures involved. In Central Africa, pangolins (scaly anteaters) are linked to diviners, while in West Africa we find spiders (Figure 2) and land crabs serving as divinatory agents. One may always argue that these creatures may well be selected for other culture-specific reasons, but it remains that silent creatures are chosen and often the absence of vocal communication is emphasized. Thus, among the Dogon of Mali, their divinatory agent the 'Pale Fox' is said to be totally speechless and can use only his paw

FIGURE 3. Guro mouse divination from Côte d'Ivoire: the mouse will walk over the chicken bones in the tortoise shell; the resultant arrangement is interpreted by the diviner.

prints tracked across a diviner's carefully prepared grid to communicate life-guiding messages to human beings. Having lost their original ability to speak, the mice used by the Guro and Yohure of the Côte d'Ivoire for divination can communicate only through the divination apparatus (Figure 3). Nearby, the Lobi of Ghana and Burkina Faso seek oracular messages from specific spirits who are known to have no tongues and can communicate only by causing the joined hands of diviner and client to move up or down.

Further research confirms that 'normally' silent creatures are chosen for a range of significant communicative cultural functions in the arts as well as in religion. Why, for example, would one choose to 'cool' a heated head, to calm a person down, as the Nigerian Yoruba do, with the liquid of a snail? And why would the Isoko of the Niger Delta cure stuttering by having a child drink the water in which a snail has been boiled? Why, unless this absolutely silent creature has something very important to do with proper speech?

Thus, from a variety of contexts, we have evidence that an auditory criterion was being employed for the selection of significant creatures. Many of these creatures, such as the pangolin and bat, have other anomalous features to recommend them, but so many of these creatures seem to share an acoustic dimension of voicelessness and silence. Why should 'normally' silent animals be chosen for such critical communicative roles? Everything from representing the king, to divinatory agents and messengers to God – small, silent creatures have been entrusted with so much. Why are not the large, loud creatures used?

Properly we will find our answers in those very African cultures, but first it will be informative for our broader study of human beings' acoustic realms to consider silence among other world cultures. We will turn first to the Americas and Asia, then, briefly, Europe and European-America before returning to Africa.

Native Americans and the silence of propriety

Part of an old Navajo song goes,

> The mole, his hunting place is darkness.
> The mole, his hunting song is silence.

Studies of Native Americans have noted how quickly Europeans will judge negatively their reticence and attribute a range of negative stereotypes, such as sullenness, passivity, stupidity, and hostility. On the other hand, within those same Native American groups, silence is positively valued and one finds in silence the essence of good character and evidence of another's courage, self-control and dignity. One who speaks quickly, loudly, and directly gains only disrespect. According to Keith Basso, the Western Apache 'give up on words' when they are faced with uncertainty in social relations. For example, when one is with kin of the recently deceased or even with one's own children returned from college (or in other very explicit situations), silence is considered the appropriate action. Rather than commit an error by speaking inappropriately, one's wisdom and thoughtfulness are demonstrated by silence.

Even more generally speaking, we find that in South American religions deities often have associations with sonic forms, some of which may be silence, just as their visual forms might be invisibility. Among shamans, silent curing via magical blowing on the ailing may be used rather than healing songs. During initiation ceremonies, periods of silence mark a variety of key stages, initiates' 'senselessness' or the presence of sacred entities. Among Native American peoples there are very different meanings for silence, yet all are essential and respectful; silences pervade ritual acts and intensify significant actions. From these few examples, we find that silence has curative functions. Saying 'nothing' can aid in smoothing over awkward social situations. In the apparent silence of religious ceremonies, we learn that much of significance has been conveyed and the ailing client is once again in harmony with the larger social world. Such social and spiritual harmonies are heard in silence among Asian peoples as well.

Asia and the search for silence

Europeans have stereotyped Asians as speaking less, as being quieter than Europeans, and often they add those same negative evaluations as I just noted for Native Americans. In actual fact, research has demonstrated that Asian peoples really do speak less than Europeans. Europeans speak almost twice as much as the Japanese and the latter have more proverbs valuing silence (and devaluing speech) than do Europeans. The Japanese gave us such expressions as 'Speech is silver, silence is golden', 'Those who know do not speak; those who speak do not know', 'A flower does not speak', and 'Out of the mouth comes evil'. There are even reports of South Asian peoples for whom verbally communicative individuals are considered quite offensive. Asian children are taught to listen as much to silence as to sounds.

Clearly, very different worldviews are involved. This is also demonstrated by the acceptance of essential space and silence, the integrity of the interval. The Japanese make a distinction between *ma*, a determinate interval (in time or space), 'space between', and *kukan*, an indeterminate interval, 'empty space'. This perspective finds intriguing continuity with the presence and functions of the physical world of the vacuole. This is a space in a cell that appears to be empty and functionless but, as each cell type is investigated, the critical roles of vacuoles in different organisms are revealed. Thus, as with silence in much human communication, this is not purposeless 'empty' space, any more than the spaces that were used in Morse Code were purposeless.

That there are absolutely meaningful, sacred silences is abundantly demonstrated in Asian religions where silence is equated with the holy and is sought through various meditative techniques. There is a fundamental distrust of the obvious, the superficial, the easily heard: 'What is real is, and when it is spoken it becomes unreal.' During meditation, for self-realization through introspection, Europeans tend to close their eyes, whereas Asians tend to close their ears. There is no question that during silence, hearing becomes highly acute, which reminds us of the yin/yang nature of sound and silence.

The question 'What is the sound of one hand clapping?' has become a caricature of the Zen *koan* (intentionally puzzling teaching questions) and the alleged 'inscrutability' to Europeans of Asian thought; but, nevertheless, it is an informative cliché. Where else would we find silence as such an instructive reference? The literature on Asian philosophies is full of references to the 'deafening silence' of the Master's response to some error in the monastery, to the interior voice of silence when meditating, to the silences in Noh drama, and so on.

The Japanese carry the importance of silence into their written literature also. There is a 'silence marker' often used in writing. The attitude of the Japanese towards silence is also reflected in their most important poetry. *Haiku* frequently treat the topic of silence:

> A voiceless flower
>> speaks
>>> to the obedient
>> In-listening ear.

(Onitsura, 17th–18th cent.)

> Thinking comfortable
>> thoughts
>>> with a friend in silence
>>>> in the cool evening . . .

(Hyakuchi, 18th–19th cent.)

In fact, silence is so important and powerful that the Japanese know to guard against being seduced by it. We are all familiar with Japanese gardens as sites of contemplation and great serenity. But, as if to demonstrate the power of silence, there is a device in many gardens to prevent absolute silence. A small bamboo tube slowly fills from a trickle of water and then *clacks* down loudly as it empties. Then it rises to be filled again. This device ensures that we hear the silence. In Japanese culture not only is silence clearly not nothing, but it usually indicates a desired state of mind or status of being.

Africa, where 'silence is also speech'

As I have noted, there are numerous instances of cultural silences in African societies. It appears that they cluster in two basic, and not unrelated, areas. Ritual uses of silence seem to refer fundamentally to the Other ('normally' silent) World of deities, spirits and ancestors. Although in full experience the Other World is not 'really' silent, it cannot be heard easily. The other basic realm of significant meaning is that of wisdom and respect. For cultures throughout Africa, the absence of speech is commonly understood to convey respect, sagacity, esoteric knowledge and serenity.

We should also observe that silence can be the manifestation of social power, where the control of others is demonstrated by silencing them. Those in power, be they elders, men or rulers, can prevent others from speaking – they can cause silence. But these instances often overlap with situations of ritual, sacred uses of silence and/or situations where respect or wisdom is evidenced in not speaking.

African religious beliefs and practices provide numerous instances of the roles of silence. Many times during my research on Isoko religion in the Niger Delta, priests would speak of the awesome 'deep' silence that indicated the presence of a deity. Such a silence might surround a shrine or be temporary, marking the arrival of the deity for ceremonies. Silence may also be used by a deity to demonstrate its power by not answering prayers or responding to sacrifices. The Yoruba of Nigeria have proverbs about the phenomenon of the deity who is so powerful that it does not have to acknowledge our puny existence; for example, '*Akii je nii gb'orisa niyi*,' [It is the silence of the deity that confers dignity on it.]

Throughout Africa, silence and death are linked in a variety of ways. Silence is usually observed during aspects of burial and funeral ceremonies at least as a matter of respect for the deceased if not representing more fundamental associations. This silence may indicate beliefs about communication and the Other World, as the recently deceased (and thereby silenced) individual returns to that other, silent world. This association of kinds of silence seems probable and correlates with prohibitions of speech during the birth process, thereby reminding us of the cyclical nature of birth and death here being equivalent to death and birth in the Other World.

An analogous phenomenon occurs with some of the silences of initiation rituals. As one moves from one status to another, 'dying' in one role in order to be reborn in another, one then must relearn all human skills, including speaking. Silence as well as speechlessness often figures in initiation ceremonies. The loss and then relearning of speech and language effectively stand for death and rebirth.

African masquerade traditions often include fearsome silent masks who are non-speaking, non-sounding, and in their silence reveal even more potency than if they were noisy and loud. Sometimes masks may have no mouths depicted at all. We also know that masks which do 'speak' seldom do so in normal voices, using instead instrumental means or voice disguisers to communicate. Others may use exclusively visual languages of gesture and sign language to communicate. While the treatment of masqueraders' voices may comment on the fearsomeness of spirit speech, a closed or absent mouth may demonstrate the wisdom of silence. One who could speak wisely chooses silence instead. Some scholars have speculated that the accented (enlarged, decorated) ears and eyes of some African mask styles signals the importance of listening and looking rather than speaking.

Because musical instruments are most often heard in performance contexts with masqueraders and dancers, we might note here how often 'silent' animals are employed in the construction of musical instruments. We find pangolin skins used for the spectacular harp-lutes of the Mangbetu (Figure 4). Accounts recorded among numerous African peoples indicate that reptiles are significant creatures in part because of their sounds, or lack thereof. While we know many reptiles can hiss loudly, most are considered by Africans to be silent. Thus, we might understand such instruments as giving voice to the voiceless, as when a drum head is made from a snake's skin. Significantly, we find tortoise shells used widely both as percussive instruments (Figure 5) and as containers for divinatory apparatus or the diviner's materials.

Certain instances of the denial of speech seem to participate in both demonstrations of sacredness and of secular wisdom (indeed, one can hardly maintain a strict separation of those two areas). Silence can be associated with specific actions in the sense that by refusing to speak one demonstrates something. For

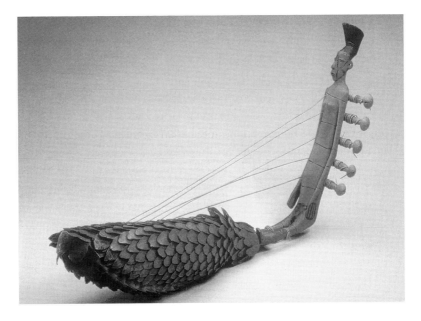

FIGURE 4. Mangbetu harp with pangolin skin.

FIGURE 5. Isoko Oworu masquerader with attendants striking tortoise shells.

25

example, among the Isoko of the Niger Delta, a warrior will place a certain leaf in his mouth to indicate his resolve that he will not speak until a specific action is completed (usually the killing of some individual). Silence may be required in certain ritual acts in relation to certain highly potent and dangerous forces, such as smallpox and strangers. If, as many African cultures have it, to speak is to act, then to not say something is to prevent its actualization. A taboo might exist where speech at certain times in certain places is prohibited.

Similarly, silence indicates certain avoidance patterns, classically of mothers- and sons-in-law but also between those who might marry. But here we seem to be moving into the areas of respect and proper behavior, as demonstrated by restrictions on speech and sound. Relations between juniors and seniors may be revealed by some restrictions on speech. The Tutsi of Burundi emphatically employ silence in their speech behaviors. Upper caste girls are carefully trained to be respectfully silent, while Tutsi elders dramatically use silence to control their juniors. The silence of an elder can effectively stifle all social inferiors and end the proceedings – there is no recourse.

Among the Mende of Sierra Leone, a person's silence is understood to demonstrate one's composure and quality of judgment. Thus, just as wise persons seldom open their mouth and the chief is quietly aloof and the proper woman is discreetly silent, so the masks are depicted with small, pursed mouths as appropriate for their exalted status. The images of ideal, perfect silence permeate the society, occurring in all possible contexts to continually remind people how to behave as a proper Mende woman or man. The chaste girl is silent, while the promiscuous woman is talkative. Here, as elsewhere, the study of esthetics among African peoples usually reveals their most fundamental philosophical tenets.

Silence also 'reveals' secrets. Absolute secrecy through complete silence is neither possible nor effective because secrecy survives only with partial information, some sounds but not with complete silence. In other words, one must be aware that one is not receiving all or sufficient information; complete ignorance is simply that and nothing more.

We could also study the presence of silence in folk tales and proverbs. Indicative of the importance of silence, the Kuranko of Sierra Leone have an ideophone for silence when it occurs in tales. In the verbal arts we easily find a variety of paths to pursue. Many narratives told by African peoples comment on the loss of speech by animals, usually as punishment for, strikingly, communication errors such as a garbled message from God to humans which looses death into the world. Narratives often caution against loose talk and many proverbs laud silence and the silent person. In Mali, the Bamana say that 'Silence reveals paths, speech confuses them.' Among the Hausa of northern Nigeria, the silence of the dove is frequently praised and rewarded in tales. And in southern Nigeria, we find the tortoise's silence and wisdom cited in numerous contexts. The complexity and subtlety of allusions and metaphorical references are impressive. The Ashanti say 'Precious beads don't speak.' This refers to the waist beads all women wear, which are fairly snug. Therefore, they do not rattle, or 'speak', and cannot tell us what they have seen of the woman's private life.

A wonderful example of meta-communication on cross-cultural differences is provided by the Yoruba and Igbo of southern Nigeria. In several of their masquerade traditions, Europeans are depicted not only by masks of expected skin color and clothing, but by their silence. They do not speak, but they continually write on everything and everyone. This is intended as a comment on the Europeans' poor speaking abilities, their virtual silence, rather than an observation about their literacy. This form of silence *is not* an indication of wisdom but of a degree of non-humanness.

There is overwhelming evidence that African peoples value silence. Their social behavior, their arts, their religions all demonstrate this; but do they directly discuss the issue? Is there discourse on silence? What few studies we have of African philosophies and systems of thought provide further support. Among the Bamana and others in the Western Sudan, silence is valued as the supreme virtue of the wise, prudent, courageous man and it defines the elder of true moral character. On the other side of the continent, we find similar comments from the Fipa in eastern Africa. Here quiet speech is associated with careful thought and wise expression. Wherever we find reference to human discourse, the values of considered and careful speech are always cited, while the dangers of loose talk are cautioned against. These attitudes correlate with the firm conviction that true knowledge is secret knowledge – not all should know all things and surely not all should speak of all things.

The distinction between (relatively) secular and sacred realms is seldom easily maintained in analyzing African cultures and the separation of types of silence seems to converge in practices surrounding divine kingship. Divine kings in Africa seem to be surrounded by silence. There are restrictions on all

27

speech in and around palaces, but what is especially striking is the muteness of the divine king. Not only does the king not speak in public but commoners are not supposed to see the king's mouth move. Among the Yoruba, kings wear crowns with beaded veils and some still carry small fans to shield their mouths further. The Ashantehene of the Ashanti Federation in Ghana carries a gold object in his mouth during public outings, which signals his non-speaking and reminds others not speak to him. Most divine kings have spokesmen who not only speak 'for' the king but 'as' the king. These traditions remain very much alive and well in Africa today, as I learned during a visit in 1996 to the Ashantehene in Kumasi, Ghana. He has at least five *okeyame* with him during audiences and no one ever speaks directly to him.

An extraordinarily poignant tale from the Yoruba of western Nigeria brings forth the subtlety of thought on these matters, in regard to both divine kings and the concepts of silence.

> The king invited the animals to a great feast, and offered a prize to the best dancer. The animals danced energetically before him, each showing off its own most striking qualities – the elephant its grave dignity, the leopard its beautiful coat and sinuous agility, the gazelle its spectacular leaps and so forth. When, at the end of the dance, they gathered around the king to hear his judgment, to their surprise and displeasure he awarded the prize to the tortoise. Answering their complaints, the king asked them who had provided the feast, and who was giving the prize, to which they could only reply 'It is you, O king!'. 'And so it is that I awarded the prize to the tortoise,' said the king, 'for it is only I who can see the dance of the tortoise: his dance is entirely inside him!'
>
> (G. Leinhardt in *The Category of Person*, 1985)

What an exceptional testimony for the importance of the unstated, for the superior quality of the inner state! This seems to correlate as well with the frequently encountered comment among African carvers that they seek to represent interior states of being, states of high moral character, not simply exterior, perhaps false, surface features that are easily apparent to all.

The comments are extended here in order to demonstrate that we are dealing with a larger worldview, not a few isolated instances that highlight silence. If we are correct in finding positive associations for silence in African cultures, we would expect to find continuity with African peoples in the Americas. Just as Asian-Americans and Native Americans have maintained their cultural values, so we find African-Americans have retained their most sacred precepts.

In these cultures where the dominant figure is almost always the 'Man of Words', from bluesman to preacher, rapper to politician, one would not immediately expect to find wise words about silence – but we do.

An essential area of this African heritage is that of the verbal arts, from what have now become 'All-American' folk tales, such as that of Brer Rabbit, to the more personalized narratives of the Signifying Monkey. Here again, we find the constant African caution against the dangers of loose talk. When tricksters are tricked, it is usually because they have talked too much. The Monkey never seems to know when to quit and, as he tries to trick the elephant or lion one more time, he gets into trouble. Strikingly, the most silent of creatures, the rabbit and spider, are the most popular survivers in the trans-Atlantic move. That central figure of speech from the Akan peoples, Anansi, who now appears throughout the Caribbean as Anansi, Buh Nansi, Boy Nasty, Compe Anansi, and even Aunt Nancy, is still the same irrepressible talker, always trying to get the better of others.

Another critical area of expression is musical. I have always believed that the significant difference between Black blues performers and White blues performers is the former's use of silence. Acoustic spacing, affective silence and suspended beats can be found in all forms of African-American music, from contemporary gospel to urban rap. Older African-American musicians often council younger performers to leave spaces so the audience can better hear what is (and isn't!) played. In fact, one can argue that other aspects of African-American culture, even textiles, are 'rhythmized' in these same ways and depend on 'silence' for their sense. Certainly effective sermons are punctuated dramatically with carefully crafted silences as part of the call and response exchange between the preacher and the congregation.

Europeans and European-Americans – Nature abhors a vacuum

This survey of non-European cultures and their uses of silence demonstrates that for them silence is meaningful, it is potent yet positive; while it can be fearful, it is usually a portent of wisdom rather than evil. But when we turn to cultural practices among Europeans and Euro-Americans we find dramatically different assumptions.

One traditional starting point for Western scholarship on any topic is to look to the classical world to find the roots for contemporary terminology. Terms for, and references to, silence in Greek and Roman traditions are usually pejorative and, thereby, set the tone for subsequent understandings. The silent person is excluded for some 'inglorious act' or for being a stranger. While European cultures often trace their roots through Greece and Rome, it seems this dislike of silence is common to other Mediterranean cultures because silence is not cherished in Jewish or Arab cultures either.

The physical impossibility of absolute silence provides another point from which to study Western attitudes. Composer John Cage is often cited for his observations about the internal noises of the human body stemming from the nervous system and the circulation of blood. He as well as many others have commented on the impossibility of absolute silence, because of these bodily noises as well as the perpetual nature of ambient sound. There are always vibrations of some sort in the world around us as well as within us. In fact, it appears that, if the brain is deprived of sound, the mind will supply its own 'hallucinatory' sounds, as those who have used isolation tanks have discovered.

This could lead us to a discussion of deafness and whether or not absolute silence is experienced by those who cannot hear normally, but we already sense the enormous possible scope of this topic and realize we cannot pursue every lead. Nevertheless, we must note the vehemence with which the (dominant) hearing community discriminates against the non-hearing population as a clear signal of the negative attitudes towards silence in European and European-American cultures. The debate between the use of signing and the struggle to imitate unheard speech by the deaf continues, as was recently revealed when a non-hearing woman won the Miss USA beauty contest.

It is certainly possible to find culturally sanctioned, even desired, conditions of silence in European cultures. But even where one finds sacred silence, the bearers of this silence are waiting to be fulfilled with God's voice, to become one with the Holy Ghost, and so on. The condition of silence is a prerequisite for sound, not the goal as we find in Asian traditions. Vows of silence are punishments, attempts to sacrifice human sound to demonstrate piety. To give up speech is as religiously significant as giving up eating or sexual intercourse. Some Christian faiths use silence to expel the transgressor, as with the Amish people and their 'shunning'. Silence is not sought as a positive state in and of itself but as a condition awaiting correction or fulfillment by spiritual forces.

Shifting from sacred to secular contexts, we find some ambiguities in responses to silence, but the associations are largely negative. Certainly silence is not desirable in legal settings. Several years ago there was heated discussion in England whether to permit the courts to assume 'legally' that a defendant's silence was an admission of wrongdoing (as is already true in France). Although such refusal to testify is often portrayed suspiciously by the popular mind in the USA, we still do maintain that legally one does not have to speak if that might be self-incriminating, i.e. in the USA we are still protected by the Fifth Amendment. Nevertheless, it is safe to say that the popular impression is that one is avoiding truth or hiding something by taking such a position. This follows logically or we would not have formally to protect the act of silence in the courtroom. Witness recent reports about dramatic cases of murder and politics in the USA – the less said, the greater the negative speculation. Studies by legal experts and psychologists reveal that this is exactly how most people interpret silence in the courtroom. It is commonly believed that an honest person speaks forthrightly, and quickly, because it takes time to lie; that is why the dishonest person speaks slowly. Certainly lawyers must successfully negotiate those issues as they defend and prosecute in front of judges and juries who are making private decisions about guilt and innocence based not on facts but on perceived courtroom behaviors.

In popular entertainment, silence remains one of the most durable means of terrifying an audience. We scare ourselves with performative silence. Throughout Europe and the USA there are traditions of celebratory mumming when neighbors visit each other while carefully disguised by costumes and silence. These masked 'strangers' are mute and present a mock threat to their hosts. But this practice finds more modern forms also. How often do we observe that the little seen or unheard monster, the non-speaking 'psycho' or murderer in a film, is the more frightening? Is it not a sure sign of impending doom when the birds stop singing? Clearly, we scare ourselves with additional silence, not more noise. The silent, telepathic communication of alien invaders from outer space is usually one of their most sinister characteristics.

Whatever the discipline or perspective, it is abundantly clear that Europeans worry about silence. Where we hear nothing, we project sound. The 'Nature' of European cultures definitely abhors a vacuum and, at least in the USA, that vacuum will be filled with speech. There is concern at social gatherings about 'dead air' and 'awkward silences'. Such moments of quiet could never be understood as a time of comfort for the participants. European-Americans are often told they are very loud and are continually chattering. But is not the sign of a well-running machine a nice steady hum? Surely, then, a silent machine is a broken machine. Talk is good – silence is bad.

Conclusion

The natural world that cultural beings inhabit is one of sound. Noise is natural. It is silence that must be created. Humans are genetically programmed to speak, and to hear. Normally, we cannot not speak; therefore, to choose silence is a significant act of humanness. This act is as significant in distinguishing ourselves from other animals as is the act of human language. The cessation of sound, the stopping of speech, the choice of silence is always noteworthy. This condition is generally understood to be one of respect and wisdom among African, American and Asian cultures.

At this point we can briefly return to my query about the choice of 'naturally' silent animals for critical communicative functions in African cultures. After reviewing the evidence for the values not only of careful and cautious speech but of silence itself, the choice of those often small but definitely voiceless creatures, such as spiders and tortoises, is totally logical. By their very reticence and by their protection of true knowledge by seldom voicing it, these beings serve to remind us of the power of words and significance of sound, as well as the wisdom of listening to Other-Worldly sounds that might otherwise go unheard.

In approximate African fashion, I will end with a tale, a tale that must be listened to carefully for it reminds us of the value of silence. It is also notable that not only is this tale found throughout the continent of Africa but it is still told throughout the Americas by African descendants.

> A hunter found a human skull in the forest and asked, 'What brought you here?' The skull answered, 'Talking brought me here.' The hunter ran and told the king that he had found a skull that talked. The king did not believe him and sent a guard to see if his story was true, with orders to kill him if it was not. All day long the hunter begged the skull to speak, but it remained silent and the hunter was killed. When the guard had left, the skull asked, 'What brought you here?' The hunter's head replied, 'Talking brought me here'.

(W. Bascom, 'The talking skull', 1992)

FURTHER READING

Bascom, W., 'The talking skull', in *African Folktales in the New World*, p. 24, Bloomington, IN: Indiana University Press, 1992.

Basso, K., ' "To give up on words": Silence in Western Apache Culture', in *Language and Social Context*, ed. P. P. Giglioli, pp. 67–86, Middlesex, UK: Pelican Harmondsworth, 1985.

Bauman, R., *Let Your Words Be Few*, Cambridge: Cambridge University Press, 1983.

Cage, J., *Silence*, Middleton, CT: Wesleyan University Press, 1961.

Fawcett, C., 'Tokyo's silent space', in *Tokyo: Form and Spirit*, ed. M. Friedman, p. 182, Minneapolis: Walker Art Center; New York: H. Abrams, 1986.

Howes, D. and Classen, C., 'Sounding sensory profiles', in *The Varieties of Sensory Experience*, ed. D. Howes, pp. 257–88, Toronto: University of Toronto Press, 1991.

Hunter, L., 'Silence is also language: Hausa attitudes about speech and language', *Anthropological Linguistics*, **24** (1982), 389–409.

Ishii, S. and Bruneau, T., 'Silence and silences in cross-cultural perspective: Japan and the United States', in *Intercultural Communication: A Reader*, 6th edition, eds. L. A. Samovar and R. E. Porter, pp. 314–19, Belmont, CA: Wadsworth Publishing, 1991.

Lienhardt, G., 'Self: public, private. Some African representations', in *The Category of Person*, ed. M. Carrithers, S. Collins and S. Lukas, p. 143, Cambridge: Cambridge University Press, 1985.

Peek, P. M., 'The power of words in African verbal arts', *Journal of American Folklore*, **94** (1981), 19–43.

Peek, P. M., 'The sounds of silence: cross-world communication and the auditory arts in African societies', *American Ethnologist*, **21** (1994), 474–94.

Samarin, W. J., 'Language of silence', *Practical Anthropology*, **12** (1965), 115–19.

Sontag, S., 'The aesthetics of silence', in *Styles of Radical Will*, pp. 3–34, London: Secker and Warburg, 1969.

Sullivan, L. E., *Icanchu's Drum*, New York: Macmillan, 1988.

Tannen, D. and Saville-Troike, M. (eds.), *Perspectives on Silence*, Norwood, NJ: Ablex Publishing, 1985.

Zahan, D., *The Religion, Spirituality and Thought of Traditional Africa*, transl. K. Ezra and L. M. Martin, Chicago: University of Chicago Press, 1979.

2　The Physics of Sound

CHARLES TAYLOR

Sound is one of the five principal means that we use in communicating with our surroundings, but it is unique in that it needs a medium for its transmission. Light can travel in empty space; touch, taste and smell need physical contact; but sound travels as waves in the air, or some other medium. My intention in this chapter is to lay down some of the fundamental principles of the physics involved in the study of sound.

As a London University student evacuated to King's College Cambridge, I was privileged to attend lectures on sound by Dr Alexander Wood. His demonstrations impressed me so much that I have been a devotee of lecture demonstration ever since. All sounds involve changes in the pressure of the air. A quiet human voice, for example, involves changes in the pressure of the air immediately outside the mouth of the speaker of about one or two parts per million. The changes need to be rapid; a change of pressure of about 1 part per million can be produced by pressing the point of a blunt pencil about 1 mm into a balloon inflated to about 30 cm diameter. But no sound is heard. However, if a pressure change is made rapidly with a sharp point, a very loud sound can be heard. When a pressure change occurs at a particular point it is passed on to the immediately adjacent point, and so on, in the form of a longitudinal compression wave. (Longitudinal because the displacement of the air occurs in the same direction as that in which the wave is travelling.) The sequence of pressure changes may be extremely complex.

Different kinds of sound

Broadly speaking, sounds can be divided into noise and music; but that distinction is open to many interpretations. Clearly, a very musical sound can be regarded as noise if it is distracting the listener from some other more important sound. Thus, the beautiful performance of a Debussy prelude in the room next door may be regarded as intolerable noise by someone trying to write programme notes on a Beethoven sonata. In its simplest scientific terms, noise is usually regarded as a completely random collection of pulses producing a sound like that of steam escaping from a valve, or the background noise of a radio set. Any kind of regularity in the pressure changes can lead to a sensation of musical pitch. Figure 1*a* represents the waveform shown on a cathode ray oscilloscope for what scientists would describe as white noise. Figure 1*b* represents the waveform of a rather reedy musical sound and Figure 1*c* is for a pure musical tone.

Pure tones

The wave trace for a pure musical tone is that of a sine wave and it requires two numbers to specify it. The first is the frequency (the number of repetitions in one second, measured in Hertz (Hz)), and the second is the amplitude, or size of the wave. Musically, the frequency is related to the pitch of the note – the higher the frequency, the higher the pitch. The amplitude is related to the loudness of the sound – the larger the amplitude, the louder the sound – although the relationship is quite complicated.

Most textbooks in the past have indicated that pitch and loudness are unrelated, but in fact this is not strictly true. If a note of about 440 Hz (A above middle C) is sounded quietly and then suddenly made louder, some listeners will sense a lowering of the pitch, some a rise in pitch, and some will not notice any change. This is a dynamic effect that occurs only with pure tones when the amplitude changes suddenly. For much lower notes, most people sense a lowering of pitch and for much higher notes everyone senses a rise.

This is one of the many complications that occur as a result of the extraordinarily complex mechanism of perception by the ear–brain system.

Range of frequencies

Table 1 shows some examples of the range of frequencies of sound produced by various instruments and animals. Broadly speaking, the human ear–brain

(a)

(b)

(c)

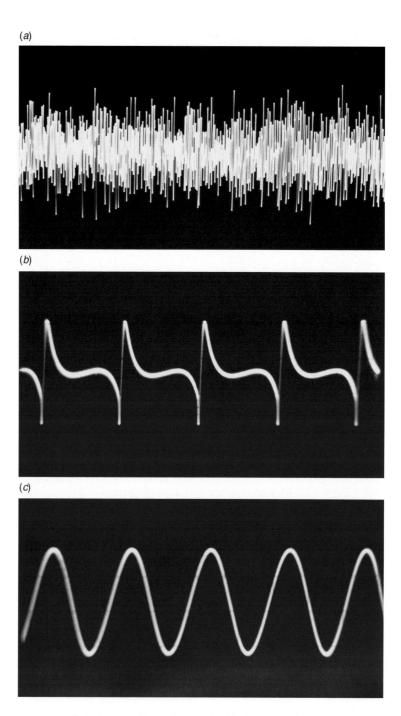

FIGURE 1. Cathode ray oscillograph traces for: (a) white noise, (b) 'reedy' musical tone, and (c) a pure tone of approximately the same frequency as (b).

Table 1. *A comparison of sound frequency ranges used by certain animals and musical instruments*

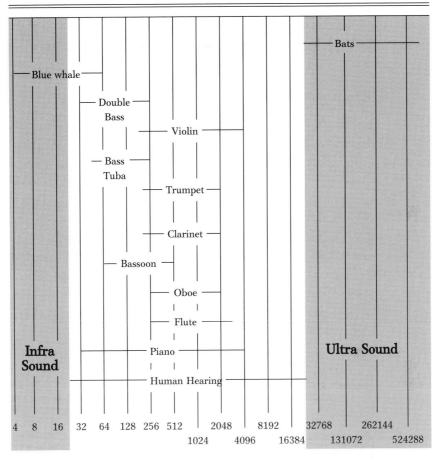

Frequency in Hertz

system can detect frequencies between about 33 Hz and about 16 700 Hz (a range of about nine octaves). These limits vary enormously from person to person and are particularly dependent on age. They can also be dependent on the history of the individual. Long exposure to high levels of sound can very quickly alter the response. The upper limit in particular can come down to 6000 Hz or so in those whose age is over 70 years. Most people have their highest sensitivity in the region of 1000–2000 Hz.

One of the many astonishing features of the ear–brain system is its range of sensitivity to loudness. Pressure variations of as little as a few parts per 100 000 000 can give detectable sounds and variations of up to 1 part per 1000 begin to cause pain or damage. No fabricated instruments are capable of such a wide sensitivity range.

Infra- and ultrasound

Sounds of frequencies below about 30 Hz are known as infrasound. They are produced by some very large animals, such as the blue whale, but cannot be heard by the human ear–brain system. Sounds of frequency about 16 Hz can, however, be 'felt'. The 32 ft (c. 10 m) pipes on some cathedral organs produce notes in this region and the whole building seems to vibrate when they are sounded.

Sounds of frequencies above about 20 000 are described as ultrasonic. Bats use these and higher frequencies to perform echolocation to enable them to fly in the dark without hitting objects and also to locate insects. Professor David Pye of Queen Mary College, London, has made a special study of these mechanisms and has developed instruments that record and play back the sounds produced by bats with the frequencies scaled down so that they can be heard by the human ear–brain system. Using such devices it is possible to show that there are many sources of ultrasound of which we are usually unaware. For example, dropping a pin produces quite a high intensity of ultrasound, as does shaking a bunch of keys.

Imaging with ultrasound

One well-known use of ultrasound is to produce medical images from inside the body. Frequencies into millions of Hertz can be used and the waves are reflected by different kinds of tissue within the body. The most familiar use is in examining pregnant women. Ultrasound is much less damaging than X-rays and can reveal extraordinarily vivid pictures of a baby in the womb.

Table 2. *Velocity of sound travelling through various media*

Medium	Velocity in m/s
Mild steel	5900
Oak	3850
Sea water	1531
Dry air	330
Hydrogen	1284
Helium	965

Transmission of sound

We have already seen that sound is transmitted in the form of longitudinal compression waves in the air. But it also travels in a similar manner through many other media. The principal differences that occur between one medium and another are in the velocity of propagation. Table 2 shows a comparison between the velocities in different media. The velocity of sound in air is dependent on the temperature and increases as the temperature rises. This increase in velocity is the cause of abnormal transmission over water surfaces. Figure 2*b* shows how this occurs. The air in immediate contact with the cool surface of a lake is obviously cooler than the air a little higher up. There is therefore a velocity gradient that causes sound waves to curve down towards the surface. Over a hot land surface the reverse is true (Figure 2*c*) and the sound waves are dispersed upwards. This gives rise to the muffled effect sometimes noticed on a hot summer day.

Diffraction of sound occurs very widely but we are usually unaware of it. It is obvious, however, that it must occur. If you walk past a row of detached houses and there is a band playing in the park behind them you do not experience sound 'shadows' as you walk by. Clearly the sound is diffracted through the spaces between the houses (Figure 3).

Reflection of sound

Perhaps one of the most important properties of sound is reflection. Specific echo is one of the consequences of reflection. But far more common is the effect described as reverberation.

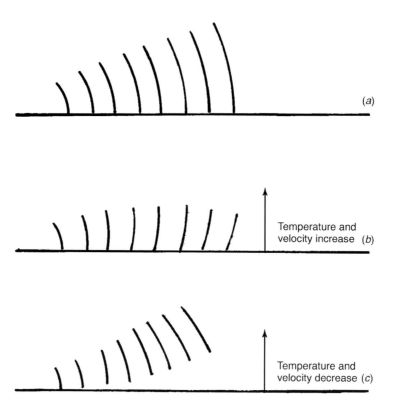

FIGURE 2. (*a*) Normal transmission. (*b*) Transmission over a lake in summer; the air temperature (and hence the velocity of sound) is lower at the surface and increases with height. (*c*) Over land the temperature gradient is reversed and the decrease of temperature (and hence velocity of sound) with height causes the sound to rise.

If we were floating in the air without any solid surfaces near by (Figure 4) we should find it very difficult to communicate at distances greater than a few metres. Usually, however, we at least have our feet on the ground (Figure 5), and possibly, our backs to the wall. The sound reflected from these hard surfaces then reinforces the direct sound and we can hear at much greater distances. However, if the source of sound is completely surrounded by hard walls as in a room, then the reflections may become extremely troublesome (Figure 6). Each syllable, for example, is heard several times and in the extreme case intelligibility is completely lost. A good example of this effect is the noise produced by a small number of children in an indoor swimming pool. The surfaces of the

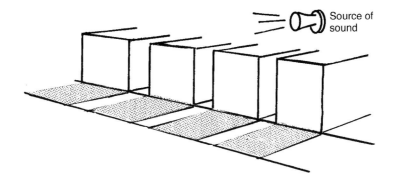

FIGURE 3. A sound source behind a row of houses does not produce sound
'shadows' for a passer-by as would happen with a light source (indicated by shading).

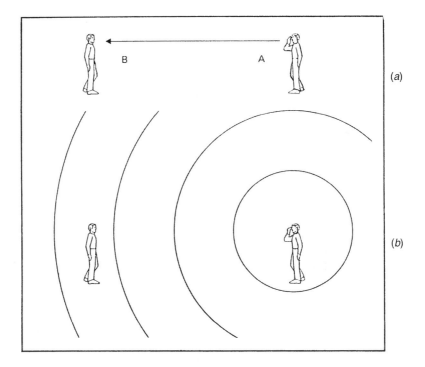

FIGURE 4. Two people isolated, e.g. floating free, (a) would find difficulty in
communicating because the sound waves spread out (b).

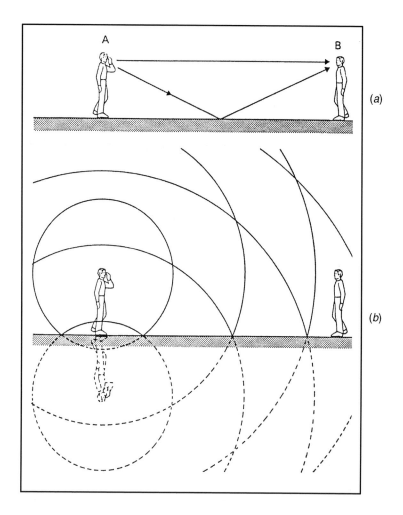

FIGURE 5. Communication is a little easier when one is standing on a flat surface (*a*). The reflected waves and the sound image are shown at (*b*).

water, walls, roof, etc. are all reflective and the sound waves go round and round for some time. This is, in essence, the problem of architectural acoustics.

Architectural acoustics

When one designs a building to have good architectural acoustics, the first problem is to obtain a clear idea of the purpose that is to be served. It is very

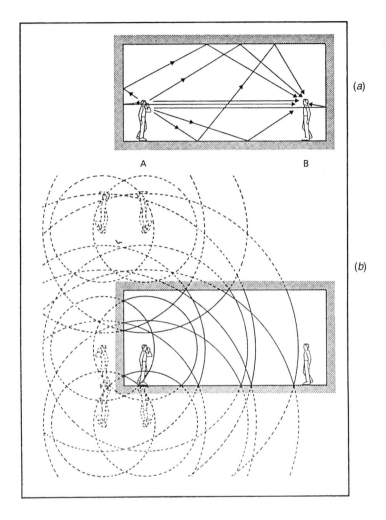

FIGURE 6. In a room the sound bounces round (*a*) and many sound images are formed (*b*).

difficult to create a building that will work well with a solo musician and also with a full chorus and orchestra or a public meeting. Yet this is sometimes the problem that is set. The solution is always a compromise between getting enough reflections from the walls to keep the sound level up, while at the same time not producing blurring of the sounds because of excessive reverberation. Fortunately the ear–brain system does provide some assistance. It seems to have a formula that says, 'If you hear the same sound several times in rapid

(a)

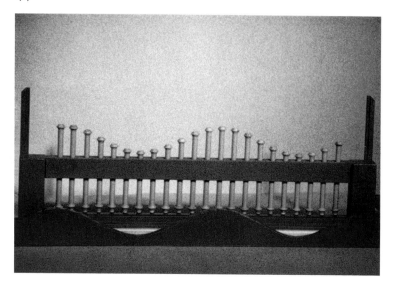

FIGURE 7. Model to illustrate addition of waves in and out of phase. (*a*) The two parts of the model. (*b*) The plastic wave is inserted in phase with the wave indicated by the rods. (*c*) Here, the insert is out of phase.

succession (i.e. successive reflections) then you are probably only meant to hear it once'. The successive reflections are blended together to give the reverberant effect. The ear–brain system is, however, aware of all the time delays involved for the different reflections and this is how, for example, a blind person can tell almost immediately, just by listening, the size and shape of a room.

The design and building of concert halls has developed enormously through the use of computer-assisted design and it is now possible to incorporate adjustments so that the acoustic properties can be varied to suit different applications. One of the best recent examples of the success of these techniques is Symphony Hall in Birmingham.

Anti-sound

It is well known that if two identical waves are added together and are in phase (i.e. in step) then the result will be a wave of twice the amplitude. But if the waves are exactly out of step the two waves will cancel out and there will be no resultant (Figure 7). A very simple demonstration of this can be performed with

(*b*)

(*c*)

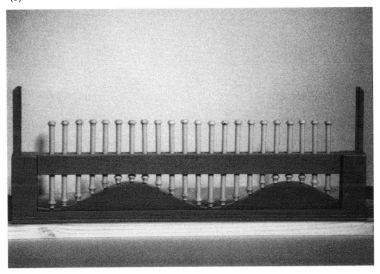

FIGURE 7. (*cont.*)

a tuning fork. The fork is struck and then held close to one ear. If the fork is then rotated about the axis of its stem the level of sound is heard to rise and fall. The air between the prongs is compressed when the air outside the prongs is expanding, so if the fork is held with the prongs in line with the ear or at right angles to the ear, a sound will be heard. But if the plane of vibration of the prongs is at 45° to the ear, the two waves will be out of step and no sound is heard. The effect can also be demonstrated by feeding an electronically produced pure tone simultaneously to two loud speakers that face each other. If the two speakers are fed in phase then a loud sound is produced, but if they are out of phase then the loudness is very much reduced. This principle has now been extended to sounds that are not pure tones. For example, the sound of an aircraft's engines can be sampled by a microphone and then processed by a computer so that a waveform is generated that is the exact opposite. This is then fed to loudspeakers inside the aircraft and this 'anti-sound' when added to the original engine noise can reduce the level very considerably. Research in this field is still in its infancy but there are some very promising possibilities. One of these is to prevent the uncontrolled build up of vibrations in machinery, which could be very damaging. Relatively small anti-sound vibrations can be used to control what could be a catastrophic build up.

Musical sounds

Now I should like to turn to musical sounds. We have already seen that the simplest kind of musical sound is that known, both by musicians and by scientists, as a pure tone, and we have seen that the waveform associated with it is that of a sine wave. Electronic generators are the best means of producing such tones. They can be imagined to go on for ever, never changing in amplitude or frequency, and having a well-defined musical pitch. They are, of course, incredibly dull unless varied in some way. The simplest mechanical approximation to a pure tone is the sound produced by instruments such as the recorder or flute. These sounds are being produced by 'edge tones'. Air is directed from the mouth against an edge, or wedge, and passes alternately first on one side and then on the other. If the frequency of alternation matches the natural frequency of the pipe then a continuous sound can be produced. The natural frequency is set by the time it takes for a compression wave to travel from one end of the tube to the other and back again.

Resonance

The interaction between the edge tone and the air in the pipe is an example of the phenomenon of resonance that plays an extremely important part in most musical instruments. It is most easily introduced by thinking about a child's swing. If the person pushing the swing times the impulses exactly at the right moment during the oscillation, a very large amplitude can be built up with very little effort. However, if an attempt is made, for example, to push the swing forward when it is moving backwards the result can be disastrous. A large amplitude of oscillation can also be built up if an impulse is applied every alternate swing, or every third or fourth swing. This effect leads to what are called privileged frequencies and we shall return to discuss them later. If the impulses are fed in at twice, three times, or any whole multiple of the natural frequency of the swing the oscillation will still be maintained. These higher frequencies are called harmonics and they too will be discussed later.

One of the most famous demonstrations of resonance was done by John Tyndall at the Royal Institution in London in the mid nineteenth century. Figure 8 shows the apparatus. A small gas flame on the end of a metal pipe is enclosed in a glass tube some 30 cm long. By carefully adjusting its height within the tube the flame can be made to 'sing'. If the tube is then raised slightly and the sound is stopped by momentarily placing a hand over the end, the sound can be restored if the experimenter sings exactly the right note near the tube. Resonance is excited and the disturbance is enough to restart the sound.

Reed excitation

A short-lived note can be produced from a 50 cm length of 2 cm diameter plastic tubing by merely hitting one end with the flat of a hand. A compression wave travels up and down but rapidly dies away. A small microphone inserted through a hole in the side of the tube will pick up the oscillations and display the exponential decay on an oscillograph. To turn such a tube into a useful musical instrument the first requirement is to feed in more energy to keep the note going. The demonstrator's lips can be used to do this in the same manner as the playing of a brass instrument. If the lips open and shut at exactly the natural frequency of the tube then resonance will occur and the note can be maintained.

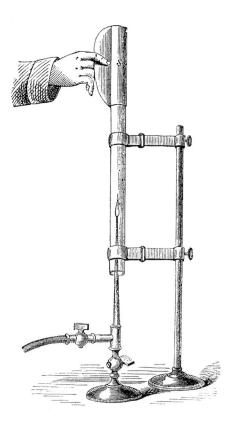

FIGURE 8. Tyndall's 'singing flame' apparatus to demonstrate resonance.

Another basic example of reed excitation can be demonstrated with a plastic drinking straw. The straw is flattened at one end by drawing the back edge of a knife over it. The flattened end is then placed wholly inside the mouth, with the lips closed round the tube below the flattened portion. Blowing hard will then excite the reed and produce a sustained note.

Strings

A vibrating string will produce a musical note but normally it will be too quiet to be heard. The reason for this is that the string is so small in cross-section that the air rushes round it as it vibrates and only very small compression waves can be produced. If, however, the string is mounted on some kind of box or board, the vibrations are transmitted to the board and it is able to excite substantial pressure changes in the air. A tuning fork illustrates this principle quite well. The vibrating prongs, like the string, are too small to produce large pressure changes, but when the fork is stood on a table the whole table vibrates and produces a large sound.

Plucking a string produces a very short-lived note because the vibration soon dies away. In order to produce a sustained note a bow is needed. The bow uses the principle of 'stick-slip' motion.

Stick-slip motion

A good example of stick-slip motion may be demonstrated using a 50 cm length of 5 mm diameter solid brass rod. The rod is held at its mid point in the left hand and is stroked with the right hand, which is wearing a cotton glove that is covered with powdered resin. Resin has rather strange frictional properties. Its static friction is very high so that when the rod is gripped with the right hand the glove sticks to the rod and it is possible to stretch the rod very slightly. Immediately the restoring forces in the rod overcome the friction and dynamic friction, which is very low, takes over and the glove slips over the rod. It then grips again and the cycle is repeated. Each time the glove slips, a compression wave travels to the end of the rod and back again and this in turn sends out compression waves into the air. Once the vibrations have started the sound can be maintained with very little effort.

The mechanism of bowing is very similar. The resin on the bow causes it to stick to the string; the string is pulled to one side; the bow then slips and the string moves back to its other extreme position and the cycle repeats.

The musical saw

Many of the principles of stringed instruments can be displayed by a musical saw. The saw I use is an ordinary cross-cut saw about 60 cm long. To play it the wooden handle is gripped between the knees and the saw is bent into an 'S' shape (see Figure 9). Striking the saw with a knuckle produces a short-lived musical sound but bowing produces long notes. The saw has such a large

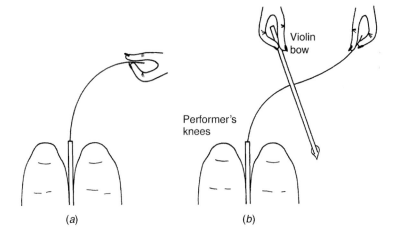

FIGURE 9. The musical saw. (*a*) In this position it is 'dead'. (*b*) In this 'S' shape it is very lively and the bow can produce sustained notes whose pitch can be varied by altering the bend nearest the knees of the player.

surface area that it produces a very loud sound, without the need for amplification. The pitch of the note can be varied by altering the degree of bending at the handle end, while maintaining the 'S' shape. The bow excites the vibrations using stick-slip motion.

Modes of vibration

If the saw is kept at a fixed degree of bending, the pitch of the note can still be altered. Three or four significantly different notes can be produced if bowing takes place at different places along the edge of the saw. What is happening then is a change of mode. Perhaps the most useful model of mode changing is a length of rubber cord. Take, for example, a 5 mm diameter soft rubber cord about 5 m long. One end is held by an assistant and the demonstrator holds the other end so that the cord is under slight tension. The cord is then plucked and a transverse wave can be seen travelling back and forth along the cord. Even after it is no longer clearly visible, the arrival of the wave at each end can easily be felt. This part of the experiment not only demonstrates the wave but also indicates to the demonstrator the fundamental frequency of vibration. If the end of the rope is then raised up and down at this frequency, a single mode can be shown with a node (fixed point) at each end and an antinode (point of maximum displacement) at the middle. If the end is now raised and lowered at twice the frequency of the fundamental, the second mode with a node at each end and one in the middle and with two antinodes at a quarter and three-quarters along the length can be produced. Vibration at three times the frequency produces nodes at each end, and at a third and two-thirds of the length, and three antinodes at a quarter, half and three-quarters of the length. With care, up to five modes can be demonstrated.

Harmonics

If the frequencies of the modes were exactly in the proportions $1 : 2 : 3 : 4 : 5$ etc. they could be called harmonic modes – so-called because mathematicians describe the sequence 1, 2, 3, 4, 5, etc., as a harmonic series. In practice the ratios are not quite whole numbers. In fact no mechanical system is capable of producing precisely harmonic modes. In theory a cord could produce precise harmonics only if it had no mass, no stiffness and the end points were totally immovable. In practice the only way of producing precise harmonics is by means of an electronic generator. For example, a Yamaha DX7 synthesiser may be programmed to produce the first 15 harmonics of a particular fundamental. Table 3 shows the frequencies and corresponding notes for the first ten harmonics on a note of frequency 220 Hz. The seventh harmonic does not correspond to a recognisable note on the Western musical scale.

Overtones and partials

Many musical systems produce multiple modes of vibration but only in long thin vibrators, such as pipes and strings, do the modes approximate to a harmonic sequence. They are sometimes described as 'overtones' and are numbered in sequence from the first one higher than the fundamental. Most vibrating systems are capable of vibrating in several modes at once and the modes are then described as 'partials' or 'partial vibrations'. Confusion can easily arise in numbering these various modes unless a rigorous application of the rules occurs. As an example, a pipe stopped at one end will give modes that have only odd harmonic numbers. Thus the fundamental will be the first harmonic (one

Table 3. *Frequencies and notes for the first ten harmonics on a note of 220 Hz*

Harmonic number	Frequency	Nearest note	
1	220	A_3	
2	440	A_4	
3	660	E_5	
4	880	A_5	
5	1100	$C\#_6$	
6	1320	E_6	
7	1540	?	
8	1760	A_6	
9	1980	B_6	
10	2200	$C\#_7$	

times the fundamental), the first partial, but will not be an overtone. The next mode up will be the first overtone, but it will be the second partial and the third harmonic (because its frequency is three times that of the fundamental).

In systems such as plates, bells, gongs, etc., none of the partials is likely to be harmonic.

Origins of quality differences

In the 1930s physicists studying musical instruments began to think that the principal origin of quality difference, as for example between a clarinet and an oboe, lay in the mixture of modes of vibration being produced simultaneously. The idea of frequency analysis was thus born. The mathematical theorem known as Fourier synthesis was invoked. It says that any periodic wave can be

(a)

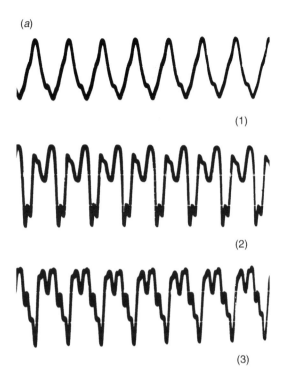

(1)

(2)

(3)

FIGURE 10(a). Oscillograph traces for (1) a flute, (2) a clarinet, and (3) a guitar, lasting 1/100th second.

represented as the sum of a large number of harmonically related waves of given amplitude. Consequently it appeared to be possible to synthesise the tone of any musical instrument by adding together electronically generated harmonics with the appropriate amplitudes and phases. The results of this idea were two electronic organs both developed in 1932, the Hammond and the Compton Electrone. Examples of these still exist and, although interesting instruments in their own right, they do not begin to imitate the tones of real organ pipes.

The reason why they fail lies in the correct interpretation of Fourier's theorem. For some reason that is not clear, the physicists of the day examined only very short lengths of the waveforms. In Figure 10 we see waveforms lasting 1/100th second for the clarinet, flute and guitar. These appear to be periodic as

(b)

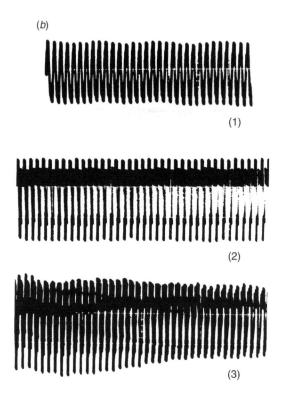

(1)

(2)

(3)

FIGURE 10(b). Oscillograph traces for (1) a flute, (2) a clarinet, and (3) a guitar, lasting 1/10th second.

required by the theorem. But wave traces lasting 1/10th second and 1 second soon show that they are nowhere near precisely periodic and consequently Fourier's theorem cannot be applied. The deviations from exact periodicity are factors that give real instruments their characteristic differences from electronic sounds. (It should perhaps be mentioned in passing that since the 1980s it has been possible to imitate these deviations electronically.)

Sources of aperiodicity

We now need to consider what gives rise to irregularities in the waveform. There are four principal sources. The first is irregularity in the driving mechanism of the vibration. For example, if we are dealing with a wind instrument, the

(c)

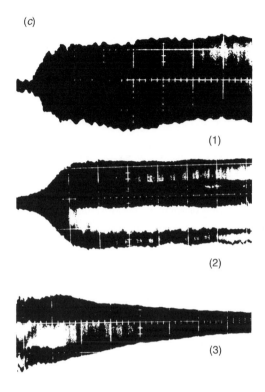

(1)

(2)

(3)

FIGURE 10(c). Oscillograph traces for (1) a flute, (2) a clarinet, and (3) a guitar, lasting 1 second.

inability of the player to maintain absolute constancy in the volume and pressure of the air produces characteristic 'wobbles'. These can be seen, for example in the waveforms of Figure 10 for the clarinet and for the flute. Similar variations occur in instruments of the string family, where slight variations of speed or pressure in bowing creates small changes. The second source of variations is the deliberate use of 'vibrato' in both strings and wind instruments. It is usually accepted that variations of frequency round about 6 or 7 Hz provide a pleasant sound and it has been suggested that this fact may be related to the natural 'hunting' frequency of the servo pitch control mechanism of the human hearing system. When a note is sung or played, the pitch is maintained steady by continuous comparison with the sound being produced. It takes approximately 1/7th second for a sample of a sound to be heard and compared with the sound about to be produced and so the system 'hunts' or wavers at a frequency of about 7 Hz. The third basic source of variation is the overall 'envelope' of the wave; that is, the way the whole waveform changes with time. Examples would be the sudden rise and exponential decay of the note of a piano or guitar. Finally there is the important effect known as the starting transient (which musicians sometimes call the 'attack').

Variations in the driving mechanism and vibrato

Slight variations in breath control or bow control make an extraordinary difference to the quality of musical sounds. If one hears a high note that is completely unvarying, the ear–brain system immediately recognises it as of non-human origin. This is one of the reasons why we recognise electronic sounds very quickly. The remarkable thing is that, even if an electronic simulation of the variations is included, the variations are frequently recognised by the ear–brain system as being artificial. The same is true of electronically produced vibrato; the vibrato is too regular and is recognised as artificial by the ear–brain system.

The envelope shape

One of the classic demonstrations of the powerful influence of the envelope shape on sound quality is the playing backwards of a recording of a piano. The notes that originally start with a sudden rise in amplitude and then decay exponentially are of course reversed, and so start with a slow rise, and then end quite suddenly. The demonstration can be made more striking by playing and recording the piece back from the last note to the first so that when the recording is played backwards the tune comes out the right way round but each note is reversed. The effect is reminiscent of a harmonium. But a very revealing feature is that, although that is the first impression, after a very short time the brain of the listener realises that something slightly odd is happening. This suggests that the initial part of the note is more important in determining the quality than the remainder. This suggestion is confirmed when the significance of the starting transient is considered.

The starting transient for strings

It is well known that a tuning fork produces a very quiet sound unless its stem is placed on a table or box. As was mentioned earlier the prongs are too small to produce large changes in air pressure because the air rushes past them. When the tuning fork is placed on a table the vibrations are communicated to the table and because of the size of the table the air is unable to rush past and so quite large pressure variations are produced. The question of the apparent source of extra energy is often raised. There is, in fact, no problem with energy conservation, the louder sound lasts for a very much shorter time. The matching of the tuning fork to the air through the table improves the radiation of the sound. But it takes a little while for the table to begin vibrating. One can imagine a very complex series of waves in the wood of the table spreading out and back over a period of perhaps a tenth of a second or so before a steady state is reached. The initial complicated interactions form the starting transient, so called because it occurs when the note starts and is very short lived. If a struck tuning fork is lowered carefully onto a table the starting transient can be heard as a slight rattle just as the fork touches the table.

It emerges that for all musical instruments this initial fraction of a second is all important. In effect it triggers the perception mechanism in the brain and the nature of the instrument is already recognised long before the steady-state portion serves to confirm the identification.

In the string family, where improvement of radiation by means of a sound box is important, the transient is further complicated. If two notes are played in succession, the response of the sound box to the first note must be overcome at the same time as the response to the second is initiated.

The starting transient for wind instruments

In wind instruments the origin of the transient is somewhat different. Let us consider as an example the initiation of a note on a double reed instrument such as a bagpipe practice chanter, or an oboe. The reed of such an instrument operates like a tap, allowing successive puffs of air to pass through. The first puff to travel along the tube travels as a compression until it finds an open side hole. It then expands out of the side hole and the air immediately behind it

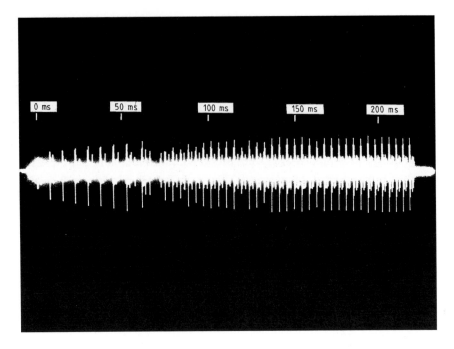

FIGURE 11. Oscillograph trace for the first 1/5th second of a note on a bagpipe chanter, showing the starting transient.

expands and so on, so that what set off down the tube as a compression travels back up the tube as an expansion. If it arrives back at the reed just as it is about to deliver another puff of air then the oscillation can continue. The effect is like that of resonance with a child's swing discussed earlier. But, if the puff arrives back at the wrong part of the reed's cycle the oscillation dies out. If the player is moderately skilled the reed is allowed to adapt itself to the rate at which the puffs return and so a steady note is built up. If the player is new to the instrument some quite disastrous squeaks and squawks can result as the player tries to force the reed to vibrate unnaturally. With a very skilled player there is complete cooperation between player, reed and tube and beautiful sounds can result. But even with the most skilled player it takes 10 to 12 transits of the tube before a steady note is established, and the sound produced in this period is the very characteristic starting transient (Figure 11). As was mentioned in connection with the beginning of the envelope shape, the transient provides the ear–brain system with very rapid recognition of the instrument.

Factors affecting the steady-state sound produced by an instrument

There are many factors that affect the steady-state sound produced by an instrument and I shall describe just two as typical examples. The first involves the body of a violin or guitar and is the factor that differentiates between a cheap violin and one by Antonio Stradivari. The second involves the operation of the clarinet, with particular reference to the finger holes.

Chladni's plate

The immensely complicated operation of the body of a violin as an amplifier is best introduced by considering one of the classic Victorian experiments on sound. The apparatus is known as Chladni's plate and consists of a thin plate of cast brass mounted on a pillar at its mid point. The one I use in my demonstrations is about 20 cm square. The plate can be used to amplify the sound of a tuning fork and the quality of the resultant sound depends very much on the point of the plate at which the fork is placed. The reason is that resonance occurs between the fork and one or other of the many possible modes of vibration of the plate. These can be displayed by scattering sand on the plate. When the edge of the plate is bowed in different ways different modes are produced and the sand collects along the nodal lines. Figure 12 shows some examples. It is quite difficult to imagine the vibrations that will give rise to these patterns but computer simulations make it easier to understand their origins. Figure 13 shows two examples. The back and front plates of a violin or guitar vibrate in different modes in much the same way and the maker must arrange the shape and thickness of the plates so that the most useful modes are involved. Chladni patterns were used at one time but in recent times holograms of the vibrating plates are produced and these show the patterns of the modes more readily. Figure 14 shows an example for a relatively high frequency mode on a guitar.

The clarinet

Many people imagine that the finger holes and keys on a clarinet perform merely the function of changing the pitch of the note produced. In fact they

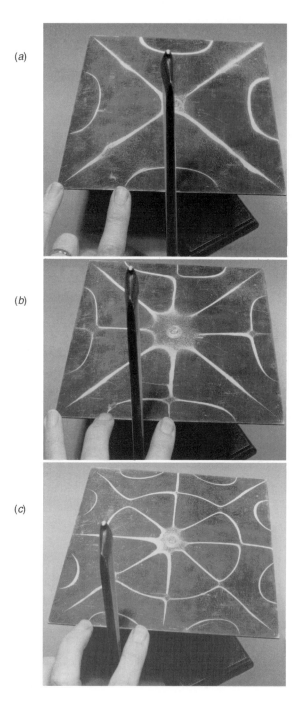

FIGURE 12. Three sand patterns produced on a Chladni's plate.

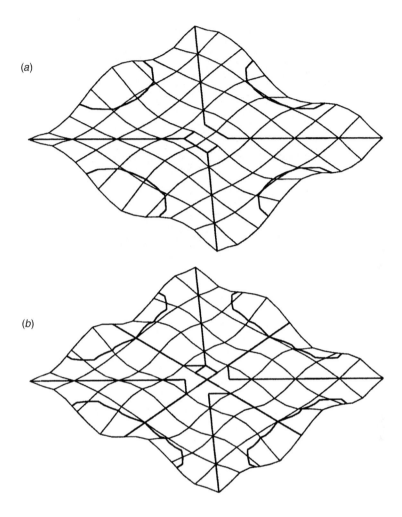

FIGURE 13. Computer simulations of the vibration of a Chladni's plate: (a) corresponds to Figure 12a and (b) to Figure 12b.

perform two other important functions as well. Because, therefore, there are three functions to be considered, three variable features of the holes are required and the clarinet maker has the difficult job of optimising all three features. The three variables are (a) their position, (b) their diameter, and (c) the degree to which the edges of the holes are raised or lowered relative to the outer surface of the tube. The first function is to enable the oscillation to be

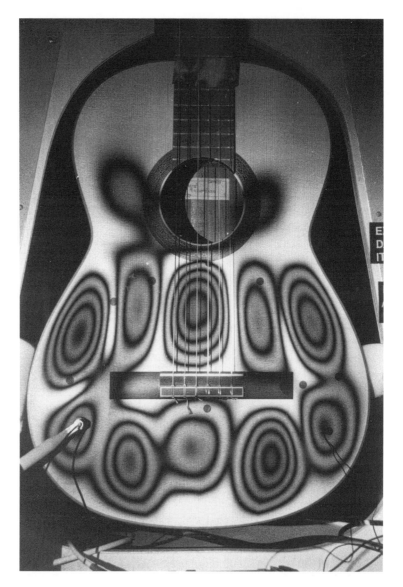

FIGURE 14. Holographic interferogram for the front plate of a complete guitar in a fairly high frequency mode.

maintained in the tube. In order that this should happen, part of the vibrational energy must be reflected back up the tube and part must be radiated out. The second function is to control the way in which the sound is radiated from the side hole (not as is sometimes supposed, from the bell at the end). A dramatic demonstration of this can be performed by playing a note with the bell removed and with the flat of a hand blocking the lower end of the tube. Apart from the lower two or three notes, this has little effect on the quality of the sound.

The maintenance of the oscillation by reflection back from the side holes can control the relative proportions of the harmonic components within the pipe (sometimes called the 'recipe') and hence can have a substantial effect on the quality of the steady-state sound. The radiation from the side holes is very directional and different frequency components travel in different directions. The proportions of the various harmonic components radiated is also controlled by the finger holes.

The brass family

In the brass family the basic method of pitch changing is to change the mode of vibration by altering the frequency of excitation by the lips. The notes produced are members of the harmonic series and (as seen in Table 3) the lower notes are widely separated. In order to play tunes it is therefore necessary to fill in the gaps between these notes and this is done by changing the effective length of the tube either using valves or a trombone slide.

Simple physics would suggest that a tube closed at one end (by the player's lips) and open at the other end (the bell) would produce only the odd members of the harmonic series. In fact brass instruments are much more complicated and the mouth piece and the bell play a very significant part in modifying the behaviour in order to produce a full series of harmonics. Earlier in this chapter, while discussing resonance, the idea of 'privileged frequencies' was introduced and these can play a very important part in the behaviour of brass instruments. Table 4 shows the sequence of notes that it is possible to produce from a simple tube.

A skilled trombone player can use these additional frequencies to perform some paradoxical feats. It is possible to produce a continuous glide down and up without moving the slide; it is possible to maintain a note absolutely

Table 4. *Some privileged frequencies for a pipe open at both ends*

240	480	720	960	1200	1440	1680	1920	2160
120	240	360	480	600	720	840	960	1080
80	160	240	320	400	480	560	640	720
60	120	180	240	300	360	420	480	540
48	96	144	192	240	288	336	384	432
40	80	120	160	200	240	280	320	360

constant in pitch whilst moving the slide in and out over its full range. It is possible to play a full scale starting on the lowest normal note and ending a full octave lower than the normally accepted lowest note.

Conclusions

The last few sections have been dealt with in a very sketchy manner but should serve to illustrate the point that the physics of sound, and of musical instruments in particular, can be extremely complicated. It is also important to make the point that most of the errors that have been made by physicists in the past have resulted because they tried to examine musical instruments as laboratory equipment. The behaviour of a violin or clarinet playing a single note under laboratory conditions bears little resemblance to that of the same instrument played under concert conditions. It is good to report that during the last 10 to 20 years great strides have been made in studying the behaviour of players and instruments under concert conditions.

FURTHER READING

Johnston, I., *Measured Tones*, Bristol: Institute of Physics, 1989.

Miller, D. C., *Anecdotal History of the Science of Sound*, New York: Macmillan, 1935.

Pierce, J. R., *The Science of Musical Sound*, New York: Freeman, 1992.

Pippard, A. B., *The Physics of Vibration*, Cambridge: Cambridge University Press, 1978.

Taylor, C., *Sounds of Music*, London: BBC Publications, 1976.

Taylor, C., *Exploring Music*, Bristol: Institute of Physics, 1994.

3 Hearing

JONATHAN ASHMORE

Unlike the eye, about which Charles Darwin had much to say, the *Origin of Species* is silent about the ear. Darwin used the eye as a example of the evolution of a specialised organ because, at that time, the physiology of the eye – its optics and adaptations – were relatively well understood. Only the vestigial ear of the bird is mentioned in the *Origin*. Even to many professional biologists, the ear is represented by its exposed outer portion. Although the outer ear has several functions, particularly in helping us to locate the source of a sound, the main organ of hearing is the cochlea of the inner ear. Our cochlea is buried within the temporal bone on either side of the head. The cochlea is a coiled cavity – and hence its name, from the Latin for 'snail-shell' – which contains a great richness of structure. The role of the cochlea is to feed information about sound as a physical stimulus into the auditory nerve, which relays an encoded form of the sound on to the brain as a pattern of activity in its separate fibres. It has been the hidden nature of the cochlea, its small size and its fragility, that has slowed progress and understanding of how the ear functions. The structures of the inner ear and their operation are the main topics of this chapter.

Within Europe, loss of hearing represents a serious health issue for more than 15 million people. As we age, hearing may become progressively worse. By middle age all of us can expect to have a noticeable loss of hearing, with the top octave of the hearing range of our youth beginning to be eroded. By old age, increasing deafness begins to interfere seriously with communication. The image of the stone deaf relative is pervasive and the source of numerous jokes. Going deaf means not only the progressive reduction in sensitivity to sound (and particularly to high frequency sounds), but also the loss of ability to discriminate the pitch of a sound and to distinguish intelligible speech in noisy environments. Along with these problems go difficulties with social interaction. There are often also 'phantom' noises in the head (tinnitus), which can be disturbing and, for some, seriously so. For young children who lose hearing either through illness or as a result of one of the many congenital forms of hearing loss, the effect on learning and development can be catastrophic unless early signs of deafness are detected and steps taken to assist for their special needs. To make rational decisions about how best to detect and even possibly to prevent deafness we need to understand how the hearing system functions. Physiology is about how animals (including ourselves) work. To understand how the ear can go wrong we must start by understanding the physiology of hearing and how it works when it is functioning normally.

The physiology of hearing: what needs to be explained?

The range of hearing in man extends from 40 Hz to about 20 000 Hz or over approximately nine octaves. Since middle C on a piano corresponds to a frequency of 256 Hz, this means that the hearing range extends approximately 2.5 octaves below and about 6 octaves above middle C (see Chapter 2, Table 1). This range is most simply specified when the sounds are pure tones, sounds consisting of a single frequency. In the real world, rather than in the laboratory, sounds contain a superposition of many component tones. In practice most musical instruments have many harmonics associated with each note so that at the bass end of the range the detection of sound may be helped by hearing harmonics rather than the fundamental itself. As musicians know, the particular qualities of the instrument are determined by the individual pattern of harmonics and the temporal structure of the sounds, by the attack and fall of a note when it is played. To provide information to the brain about the complex sounds, which include speech, entering the ear, the cochlea must be able to extract and relay information about the amplitude and timing of individual frequency components.

At the upper end of the auditory range, we can detect sounds that are not strictly 'musical', as it is difficult to assign a pitch. However, speech sounds contain frequencies above 4 kHz, and the detection of these frequencies is critical to ensure that speech is reliably understood. About 50% of the length of the cochlea is devoted to the analysis of frequencies below about 1000 Hz and the remaining half to frequencies above 1000 Hz. Intelligibility of speech demands a sound-analysing mechanism that is accurate in its timing. How then are different distinct frequencies in a complex sound – a piece of music, a speech from a Shakespeare play or the sounds heard in a (quiet) country walk – selected and how do they give rise to a recognisable percept?

The physiological description of hearing must also address the question of how different sound intensities are discriminated. Speech sounds contain a wide range of component intensities and the auditory system has to disentangle them. Loosely, we prefer to talk about 'loudness' rather than the physically measurable quantity 'sound intensity'. There is a connection in that the perception of 'loudness' does in general increase with the intensity of a sound but it is easier and more appropriate to define the properties of the ear in terms of strict physics of the input signal. Sound intensity is measured using the decibel scale. This scale is such that each step of 20 decibels (dB) corresponds to the intensity of sound increasing 10-fold (Figure 1). The scale starts at auditory threshold at 0 dB SPL (*sound pressure level*), and the intensity of a sound that is just audible under optimal conditions. Normal speech contains components with intensities of 40–70 dB SPL, or about 100- to 3000-fold higher than threshold. Because of the physics of the way in which sound is transmitted through the middle ear into the fluid-filled cavities of the inner ear, we are most sensitive to sounds with a frequency of about 2000 Hz. At any other frequency, our sensitivity to sound normally falls off. When we become deaf, the sensitivity falls still further.

The kind of hearing losses that occur with age affect the high frequency end of the hearing range especially. Typically, hearing sensitivity falls by at least 100-fold. As we shall see, this change in sensitivity is thought to arise as a result of the loss of a particular subclass of cells in the cochlea. But even in normally hearing individuals, quite why the absolute threshold corresponds to 0 dB SPL or how a disturbance of 2/10 000 000 000 of atmospheric pressure can be detected, is a question that physiology seeks to address. The answer lies in the structure of the inner ear.

The structure of the inner ear

The machinery of the inner ear is composed of very small parts. Over the past 140 years it has been advances in seeing the detail in the cochlea that have unlocked an understanding of the mechanism. We find that, by the mid eighteenth century in the works of naturalists of the Enlightenment, there were

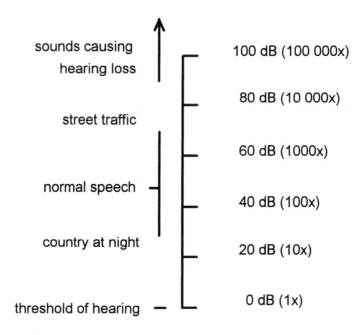

FIGURE 1. The range of intensities in everyday sounds. The scale is given in the decibel (dB) scale and also as multiples of the intensity at the auditory threshold.

rudimentary views about how the inner ear worked. It was appreciated that the auditory nerve had to be stimulated, but quite how was a mystery. The first significant contributor to the modern physiology of the ear was Herman von Helmholtz. (It is interesting to see that the career progression of Helmholtz was the reverse of many biomedical scientists today: he started as physiologist and having made major contributions to our understanding of the workings of the eye and the ear eventually proceeded to the Chair of Physics in Berlin.) The key to Helmholtz's progress was the arrival in the mid nineteenth century of light microscopes and tissue-staining techniques effective enough to provide information about the fine structure of the cochlea. Eight years before the publication of Darwin's *Origin of Species*, Marquis Alfonso Corti working in Würzburg published a description of the cochlear structure that bears his name – the organ of Corti. This structure is the key to understanding how the inner ear works and how it sends information to the brain.

Figure 2 shows the general relation between the structures of the ear. The external ear shapes the spectral content of the sound and funnels sound to the eardrum, from where it is transmitted through the chain of ossicles of the middle ear to the inner ear. The inner ear is located 3–4 cm from the surface of the temporal bone and contains not only the cochlea but also the organs of balance. The inner ear is in reality a set of complex cavities within the bone, which are filled with fluid. All the components involved in detecting and analysing sound are in the cochlea. The cochlea is by design a tube, but it is coiled through three turns. The coiling is there solely for packing purposes and has virtually no functional consequences for the propagation of sound. Were the cochlea to be uncoiled it would be about 3.4 cm long, but it packs up into a much smaller volume.

It is worth considering the small size of the cochlea. The surprise for physiologists is that cochlear length does not vary as much between mammalian species as one would expect from the size of the animal. Although the cochlea of a mouse is about 10 mm long when uncoiled, in humans it is 34 mm long, but in an elephant it is only 50% longer. The underlying reason for this absence of scaling is that mammals have relatively comparable hearing ranges. While this may be three to four octaves for the smallest animals, the total hearing range for most animals does not significantly exceed the eight to nine octaves that human beings possess. Although there are some exceptions, the machinery for detecting such sounds seems to be very similar in design between species, and hence the cochlear size depends on the range rather than the animal itself. On anatomical grounds alone, there could be no justification for suddenly switching to a whale as an experimental animal in which to study basic hearing mechanisms.

The cochlear duct is further subdivided into three compartments arranged in parallel along the length of the tube. One of the dividing partitions between two of these compartments has a particular significance and is known as the basilar membrane. It is a membrane made of fibres of collagen and is associated with the cells of the organ of Corti, about which we shall hear more below. The basilar membrane is a relatively large-scale structure in cochlear terms, between 0.1 and 0.5 mm wide, and extending along the entire length of the cochlea. The basilar membrane is the primary structure, which allows distinct incoming sound frequencies to be separated.

How sound frequency separation occurs in the cochlea was first suggested by

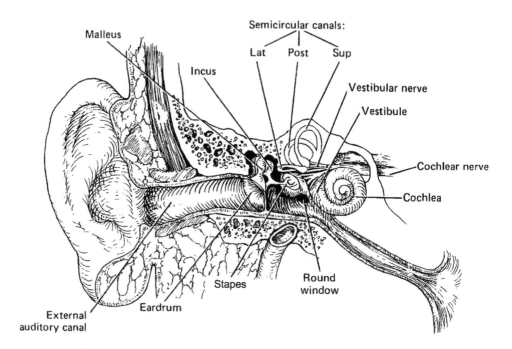

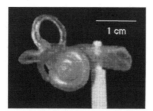

FIGURE 2. (Top) A schematic cross-section of the human ear, showing the relation between the outer, middle and inner ear (Bottom). A cast of the cochlea and vestibular system canals.

Helmholtz, using the analogy of a piano. The idea was reformulated by a Dutchman, E. ter Kuile, in the early 1900s, but was elaborated in its more modern form in the 1930s and 1940s by a Hungarian telephone engineer-turned-physiologist, Georg von Békésy. By a series of careful experiments carried out on the cochleas of both mammals and human cadavers, von Békésy laid the foundations of what we now understand as cochlear mechanics. There were, in addition, important contributions made by many others, including E. D. Adrian at Cambridge, and E. G. Wever and H. Davis in the USA. In 1961 von Békésy was awarded the Nobel prize for Physiology for 'his discoveries of the physical mechanism of stimulation within the cochlea'.

How the cochlea separates sounds

The central idea is that the basilar membrane acts like a sound spectrum analyser. Spectrum analysers are used by electrical engineers to analyse the contributions of different sound frequencies in a complex sound. Spectrum analysers are now usually implemented in software, as the mathematical computations are eminently suited to a computer. The cochlear spectrum analyser is not only considerably smaller than its engineering equivalent but uses hardware that depends upon an interaction between electrical and mechanical properties of the inner ear. Figure 3 shows a schematic view of the uncoiled cochlea incorporating the basilar membrane.

The mechanical properties of the basilar membrane vary along the basilar membrane length: it is stiffer at the basal end and most flexible at the end furthest from the middle ear. When sound is injected into the fluids of the cochlea by the stapes of the middle ear, the basilar membrane vibrates but it does so in a manner that depends on the input frequency. As von Békésy realised, the consequence of the stiffness gradient is to separate frequencies. The gradient of stiffness allows each part of the membrane to resonate at one frequency only and as a result each sound frequency produces a unique basilar membrane vibration pattern, with each frequency 'mapping' onto one place along the membrane. The same idea occurs in a piano, where the shortest and most tensioned strings resonate at the highest frequencies and the longest strings resonate at the lowest frequencies. Like the piano, the mechanics of the cochlea is organised so that each octave occupies a constant fraction of the length of the

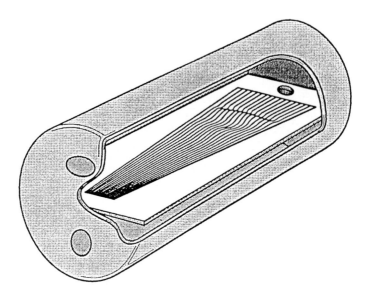

FIGURE 3. A schematic view of the cochlea, showing the uncoiled cochlea as a tube, with the travelling wave produced by a sound propagating along the basilar membrane within.

duct. This analogy with a piano is not perfect, for in a piano individual strings are struck before they resonate, whereas in the cochlea the whole basilar membrane is shaken as sound enters the duct from the middle ear and stimulates the fluid. This arrangement is like a piano immersed in a fluid, which can be played only by sounding a note at the treble end and letting the wave propagate over the frame to resonate the appropriate strings.

It has become apparent that this simple model of the cochlea, where the basilar membrane is deflected only passively by sound entering the cochlea, is not adequate to explain how we hear. Instead it is now thought that cells within the cochlea actively enhance the motion of the basilar membrane. We can distinguish pure tones that differ in frequency by about 3 parts per 1000, or equivalently better than one-tenth of a musical tone. For such spectacular tone discriminations to be made, it is clear that a single tone must be able to excite only a very limited number of nerve fibres in the auditory nerve. However, the basilar membrane mechanics proposed by von Békésy does not produce a vibration pattern that is sufficiently precisely localised to excite only the requisite few

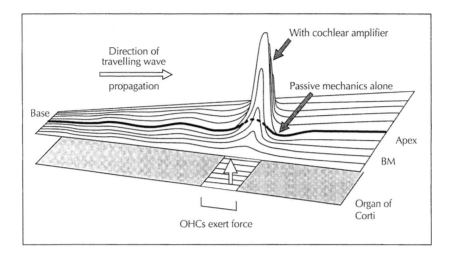

FIGURE 4. Cochlear amplification: the basilar membrane is drawn schematically and the travelling wave causes a disturbance along it. The outer hair cells (OHCs) act to boost the peak movement of the basilar membrane (BM). The vertical scale is considerably exaggerated.

nerve fibres. A related piece of physics applies to the pianist playing under water – the resonant strings would be damped out far too quickly and the excitation would spread to neighbouring strings. Von Békésy recognised this problem when he developed the travelling wave description of cochlear mechanics and thought that the central nervous system could somehow 'sharpen up' the detection of fine frequency differences.

The solution to this problem was recognised only at the beginning of the 1980s. The answer is that the living ear contains a biological amplifier, termed the 'cochlear amplifier'. The action of the amplifier is two-fold: it increases the motion of the basilar membrane and it makes the vibration pattern much more localised. It achieves both of these results by opposing the fluid damping that exists in the cochlea. Without this amplifier the cochlea is effectively deaf, losing about 100-fold of sensitivity or equivalently allowing the threshold to rise by 40 dB. It is the loss with age of such sensitivity that makes us progressively harder of hearing.

Figure 4 shows how the basilar membrane pattern of motion is altered by the cochlear amplifier. Such figures are somewhat misleading as they suggest that the movements of the basilar membrane induced by sound are large

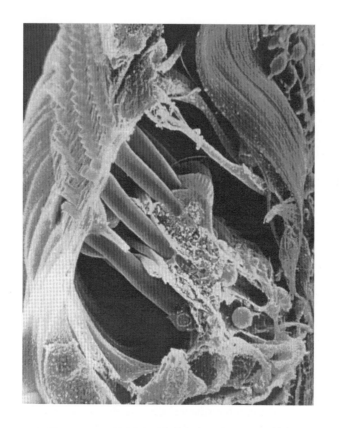

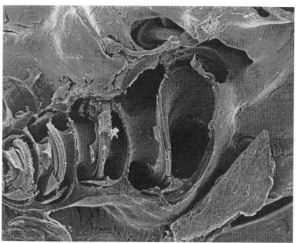

FIGURE 5. *Structure of the organ of Corti when observed through an electron microscope. Top left: the cochlear spiral shown inside the bone. Bottom left: surface view of the organ of Corti, the structures appearing as white represent the stereocilia of the hair cells. Top right: side-view of the organ of Corti now showing stereocilia projecting from hair cell bodies. Bottom right: high magnification of a bundle of stereocilia from one outer hair cell. The scale represents 1 μm.*

enough to be visible. At auditory threshold, when the weakest sound can just be heard, the peak amplitude of the vibration of the basilar membrane is about 0.3 nm, or about three atom diameters. To give some idea of these scales, imagine that the basilar membrane was expanded so that it stretched between Cambridge and my laboratory at University College London, a distance of about 100 km. The movement of this oversized membrane at its 'auditory threshold' would be a ripple of only about 1 mm. These very small scales found in cochlear mechanics, although now measurable with refined modern interferometers, have been notoriously difficult to measure reliably and have contributed to the relatively slow development of our ideas about cochlear mechanics.

Cochlear amplification, a term implying that the basilar membrane interacts with an energy source to augment its motion, has been explained by turning to the cellular physiology of the organ of Corti. Understanding the cochlea was seen as an engineering problem up until the 1970s and has been increasingly opened up in the 1980s by an emphasis on cellular physiology. The period we are now entering is one where the techniques of molecular biology are becoming essential to explore the mechanisms further.

The inner spiral of the cochlea reveals the complex system of cells and suggests many interactions between cells that could underlie the amplification step. The most important cells in the cochlea are the sensory cells, the hair cells. The cells derive their name from the fine processes or stereocilia that project from one end of the cell's upper surface. The set of stereocilia on each cell can barely be resolved by a light microscope at the highest magnification and appeared to the early microscopists to look like fine hairs. The term hair has remained in the description of the cochlea to the mutual confusion of physiology and trichology. Even with the tissue staining techniques introduced in the mid nineteenth century, these stereocilia were not large enough to be resolved individually and the true organisation and composition of the stereocilia have required the higher resolution of the electron microscope for its elucidation. Figure 5 shows a set of stereocilia from one cell when seen by the scanning electron microscope. The 100 stereocilia on each cell are stiff, rod-like structures, each about 0.2 micrometres (µm) in diameter and between 2 and 5 µm long. They are arranged in a distinct set of rows, with the tallest stereocilium facing away from the inner spiral of the cochlea. Hair cells are also found in other parts of the inner ear, such as in the organs of balance, and are found ubiquitously where mechanosensing organs have evolved for completely different purposes, as in the lateral lines in fish. In all these organs, however, hair cells respond to physical movement by changing the electrical potential across their membranes and this is the first step in sending signals along the appropriate sensory nerve fibre to the brain. I want to digress briefly into how displacement of the stereocilia is converted into an electrical signal.

How hair cells of the cochlea detect sound

Sounds entering the ear produce disturbances that are measured in molecular scales because the energy in a sound wave is so small. The process of converting the mechanical vibrations delivered to the hair cells into an electrical signal is called 'mechanotransduction'. The site in the cochlea where key events occur is in the organ of Corti, a collection of cells that includes the hair cells and the surrounding supporting cells. The organ of Corti runs the full length of the basilar membrane and in cross-section has a very stereotyped profile, with cells arranged in an orderly manner (Figure 5). The main feature of the organ of Corti, however, is that it has a geometry that converts the small motions of the basilar membrane into displacements of the hair cell stereocilia. The principle is that as the organ of Corti rides up and down on the basilar membrane it allows the bundles of stereocilia to be brushed backwards and forwards against a secondary gelatinous membrane of the cochlea overlying the hair cells. Thus the motion of the basilar membrane generated by sound entering the cochlea will deflect the stereocilia at the same frequency as in the original sound. In effect the stereocilia are tightly coupled to the basilar membrane movements. This suggests that the mechanotransduction mechanism that converts mechanical displacements into electrical signals has evolved to be both sensitive enough to respond to molecular scale displacements and fast enough to respond within microseconds to keep up with an auditory stimulus.

How mechanotransduction works in molecular terms is still not completely understood, but the favoured hypothesis is the following. This description is the outcome of both structural information about hair cells and a series of elegant physiological studies carried out on single hair cells particularly by Jim Hudspeth, now in New York, and his co-workers since the late 1970s. The stereocilia are held together partly by protein links and partly by a specialised linkage protein that runs between the very tips of the stereocilia. The importance of this

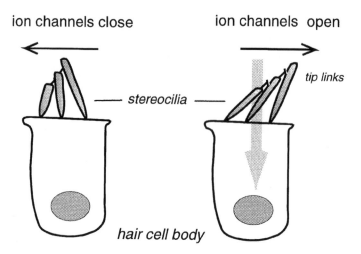

ion channels close   ion channels open

tip links

—— stereocilia ——

hair cell body

FIGURE 6. The mechanotransducing machine of a hair cell. The stereocilia are shown on the surface of the hair cell. As the bundle of stereocilia is deflected, ion channels open up to allow ions into the cell and to produce an electrical signal in the cell.

so-called 'tip-link' was developed by Jim Pickles in Birmingham in the mid 1980s, although with the advantage of hindsight the tip-link is apparent in many electron microscope pictures from 1962 onwards. The tip-link itself is probably a cluster of a very few proteins. What is surprising even to most cell biologists is that it is a connection made between two distinct and external parts of the cell and its formation appears to require very precise assembly. Following the observation of this structure, it is a relatively simple step to realise that when the stereocilia move together, there will be a relative slippage between them and this could cause the tension in the link either to increase or to decrease, depending which way the stereocilia have been pushed. It is thought that this link is coupled to ion channels at either end of the tip-link protein in the way that a rope is attached to pull open a trapdoor. Thus, when the stereocilia move, some of these ion channels in the hair cell membrane would be open and allow ions to enter the cell from the outside and change the electrical potential of the cell (Figure 6).

Baroque though this system seems at first sight, it has the advantage of relative simplicity. It would certainly meet the demands of speed and responsiveness to movements of molecular dimensions. This type of motion sensor achieves its sensitivity by directly coupling movement of a macroscopic structure (the basilar membrane) to a molecular structure (the ion channels in the stereocilia). The price that the cochlea pays for such a mechanism is that it can be easily damaged, since the tip-link is likely to be one of the first structures to be affected when excessively loud (indeed deafening) sound enters the ear.

The second consequence, although not irreversible, is that the coupling of the tip-link can produce an apparent distortion of sounds. The mechanotransduction scheme also has one peculiarity: pulling and pushing the stereocilia give rise to different types of response, as pulling on the link would open channels whereas pushing on the link would tend to close them. Indeed, if the bundle were to be pushed so far over that the link buckled, it is easy to see that pushing and pulling may not be equivalent stimuli. If this were the case, the system would be non-linear, producing an output signal (here, electrical potential in the hair cell) that is not linearly related to the input signal (the input sound pressure). The price of using a fast mechanotransduction mechanism may therefore be to introduce distortion into the cochlea before a signal is sent up the pathways to the brain.

This non-linear distortion can be appreciated as a perceptual phenomenon. Guiseppe Tartini, a virtuoso violinist in the early part of the eighteenth century, pointed out that under certain circumstances we can hear sounds that are apparently not there. These are the so-called combination or Tartini tones. If you play two notes separated by an interval of no more than a third, you can often hear a third lower note. The explanation escaped Tartini but Helmholtz seems to have been the first to provide an adequate physical explanation. His explanation was precisely that the auditory system must be non-linear so that two tones can mix together and produce a tone not present in the original stimulus. The physiological mechanism that underlies this physical mixing of tones escaped Helmholtz and has had to wait another 130 years for its explanation.

One simple way of demonstrating Tartini tones is to present two pure tones to the ear, one at a frequency $f_0 = 1000$ Hz, and a second at a frequency $f_1 = 1200$ Hz, for example. The combination tone is one with a frequency $2f_0 - f_1 = 800$ Hz and would be present at the output of any non-linear mixing device. Poor amplifiers also distort sounds, as anyone listening to a loud orchestral piece on a small radio will agree. However, it is curious to find that the ear itself is intrinsically distorting. In fact, in the kind of non-linear device represented in hair cells $2f_1 - f_0$ is one of the many tones that are generated. Luckily for us, the level of distortion is very weak and probably less than 0.5% of the two presented tones. The cellular explanation based around the non-linear coupling between stereocilial displacement and hair cell signal is certainly the simplest and seems to point to transduction itself being the main source of cochlear non-linearity.

How hair cells amplify sounds

Hair cells are devices that detect sounds. Although suspected by the more thoughtful physiologists since the 1940s, it has become clear that hair cells can also act in reverse and can reconvert electrical signals into displacements. As is apparent in Figure 5, the organ of Corti of the mammalian cochlea contains two types of hair cell, inner hair cells and outer hair cells. Both hair cell types are equipped with the mechanotransduction machinery to detect the displacements of the basilar membrane. This had for a long time been confusing, as other non-mammalian species contain in their hearing organs only one form of hair cell, not two as in the mammal. In the mammalian cochlea, there is now overwhelming evidence that the inner hair cells are the sensory cells that connect directly to the auditory nerve to relay information to the brain. The role of the outer hair cells has been much more obscure. Outer hair cells have a number of unusual features. Most importantly they do not appear to be sending substantial amounts of information to the central nervous system but seem instead to be the target of a neural pathway that descends *from* midbrain nuclei and terminates on them.

In 1985 it was found that outer hair cells can generate small but measurable forces when they are electrically stimulated. This observation was made when cells were experimentally separated from the tissues of the cochlea. The disadvantage of this type of reductionist approach is that the physiological significance of any discovered property of an individual cell becomes less certain but at the same time the experiments are much easier to conduct.

Figure 7 shows a picture of an outer hair cell. When observed by light microscopy, many features of a conventional hair cell can be seen. The cell shown here has a length of about 70 μm, the diameter of a fine hair. The critical

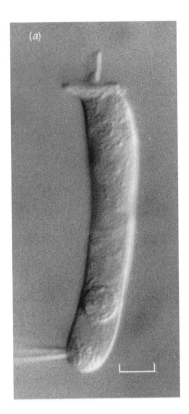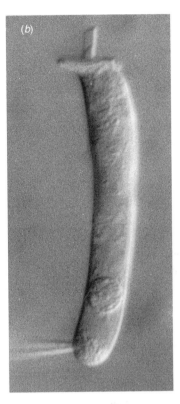

FIGURE 7. Picture of an outer cell from the guinea pig cochlea, taken with a light microscope, when its membrane potential is made (*a*) more positive and (*b*) more negative. A stimulating pipette is seen at the base. Stereocilia are evident at the apical surface. Scale bar represents 10 μm.

experiment carried out by Bill Brownell and his colleagues in Geneva and elaborated in my laboratory was to show that, when the cell's membrane potential changed, the cell also changed length. A change in membrane potential would come about normally when the cell stereocilia are deflected, although in this experiment the potential was changed by sealing onto the cell a fine glass micropipette which could conduct electricity into the cell. The change in length was so large (at least on the scale of the cochlea) that it could easily be seen down the microscope. Extrapolating from the anticipated membrane potential change expected in the normal cochlea (a few thousandths of a volt) the length change of an outer hair cell would be several tens of nanometres, quite enough to alter the mechanics of the basilar membrane. The polarity of the effect is such that when the cell potential was made negative the cell lengthened, and when the cell potential was made positive the cell shortened. It is worth adding that there is a more entertaining way of producing these length changes and this is to connect up the glass micropipette to a music source. I have found that *Rock around the Clock* with a good bass beat does a very satisfactory job of ensuring that outer hair cells, experimentally isolated, dance to the rhythm.

In our bodies there are many other types of cell that change length and shape. To give two examples, muscle cells contract and produce forces, and this contraction is known to depend on the interaction between actin and myosin; during development, cells move around and reorganise their shape and these changes are known to use structural scaffolds made of rapidly polymerising and depolymerising actin. The mechanism in outer hair cells seems not to depend on any of the 'conventional' motors of cell biology and this has been something of a surprise. The mechanism of outer hair cell shortening and lengthening has to run very fast to ensure that it can operate at acoustic frequencies (i.e. above 20 000 Hz). This is at least 10 to 100 times faster than even the fastest muscles. No other motor mechanisms in cells work quite as fast.

The clue as to how outer hair cells generate fast forces is in the shape of the cell. To a first approximation an outer hair cell is a cylinder. If water could move in and out, then an outer hair cell would change shape and tend to round up as more water entered. However, there is experimental evidence to suggest that water cannot cross biological membranes at the necessary rates: it would have to produce a shape change within 1/10 000th of a second. It seems reasonable to assume, therefore, that the volume of the cell remains constant. However, were the area of a cylindrical cell to change, maintaining the volume constant, then the cell would have to change length. The easiest way to see this is to realise that, for a given volume, a sphere has a smaller area than an ellipsoid of equal volume. Thus, if the outer hair cell membrane area were to shrink, the cell would get shorter and were the membrane area to expand the cell would get longer. This appears to be the best explanation for what happens in outer hair cells.

To look for special features of the cell membrane responsible, it is necessary to turn to electron microscopy. Andrew Forge working in London and Bechara Kachar at the National Institutes of Health in Washington, DC, found that the lateral membrane of the outer hair cell contains a very high density of particles. These particles are undoubtedly proteins and are about 10 nm across. This is

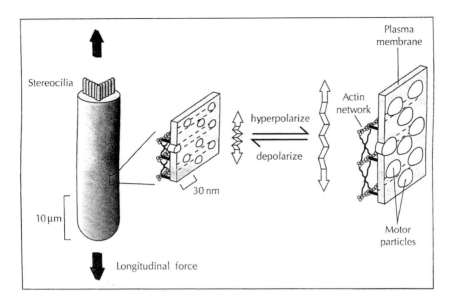

FIGURE 8. A proposed mechanism for outer hair cell length change. Each motor particle on the lateral surface of the cell, probably composed of a cluster of molecules, senses potential and changes area in the plane of the membrane. This alters cell length.

about the size that we would expect for a reasonably sized globular protein embedded in the membrane, with a molecular mass about 200 000 times the mass of a hydrogen atom. To give some idea of scale relative to the cell, imagine the outer hair cell being the height of a four-storey house, then each particle would be about the size of a small pea.

The other surprising feature of the outer hair cell membrane is that the particles are also very densely packed. There are at least 5000 particles per square micrometre on the lateral membrane of an outer hair cell. This immediately suggests a model. Suppose that when the membrane potential changes in an outer hair cell, the motor – for that is what we presume these particles are – detects the change in electric field and changes conformation. This is not impossible as there are now many proteins that are known to change shape when electric potentials are placed across them. The tight packing of the motor proteins in the membrane would then ensure that a small change in area of the protein becomes a change in area of each local patch of membrane and in turn ensure that the cell changes length (see Figure 8). Like the model for mechanotransduction, the mechanical simplicity of this scheme allows the outer hair cell to change length with extreme rapidity.

We do not know the identity of the molecule, which is important information so that we can direct drugs towards this most critical molecular component of hearing. It seems quite plausible that this molecule, which changes area under the effect of an electric field, may not be a single molecule but a small cluster, say two or four, of a yet simpler protein. Many proteins that can be embedded in membranes consist of chains of helically folded polypeptides that have charged amino acid side-chains and are able to respond to electric field changes; many form into the dimer or tetramers that we are considering here. Any change in membrane potential could produce a small rearrangement of the helices and result in a change in area of the protein or protein cluster.

One recent piece of experimental evidence suggests that this motor may be able to change shape at the necessary speed but that there may be a limiting frequency beyond which the motor will not work. This limiting frequency is at about 25 000 Hz, above the upper limit of the human hearing range. It may be no coincidence that most mammals have an upper limit to hearing that is not far from this figure. There are of course animals such as bats and cetaceans who use ultrasound for echolocation at frequencies above 60 000 Hz. There is structural and physiological evidence to suggest that, in these animals, the cochlea is further specialised, perhaps not even using the outer hair cell mechanism, but at these frequencies it may have a more limited repertoire for the analysis of arbitrary complex sounds.

How is the cochlea put together?

The structure of the cochlea tells only a part of the story about how it functions. To explain properties of the whole cochlea, such as its absolute sensitivity to sound and its ability to separate sound frequencies, it is necessary to have detailed information about the properties of the components from which it is constructed. Work from many laboratories in recent years has emphasised how the cochlea should be thought of not merely as a passive device but as one that selectively amplifies sound frequencies. At the cellular level it employs the forces that outer hair cells can exert on the basilar membrane.

The simplest models incorporating hair cell motors are built with computer software. So far it has not proved possible to encourage cells of the organ of Corti to grow back together in tissue culture and to test what single cell studies predict. The results of computer simulations are intended to show how outer hair cells could alter the mechanics. The models usually suggest that outer hair cells apply forces to the basilar membrane at a particular point in its vibration cycle. Imagine that a sound enters the cochlea and consider the point where the basilar membrane moves up and down maximally. The stereocilia of the hair cells will be deflected back and forth in phase with the basilar membrane and, as a result, the outer hair cell membrane potential will change cyclically at the same frequency. The overall consequence is that an outer hair cell will generate a force directed along its length that will be synchronised with the original basilar membrane vibration. A more detailed investigation of the pattern of electrical flow in the hair cell indicates that the outer hair cell forces are phased exactly so as to cancel those forces arising from the fluid in the cochlear duct and tending to damp out basilar membrane vibration. As we saw above, the fluid damping of the basilar membrane was the problem confronting von Békésy's model of the cochlea as it leads to a cochlea that appears to have much reduced sensitivity and a reduced ability to separate frequencies. Outer hair cells therefore appear to be part of the biological feedback mechanism in the cochlea, which leads to increased sensitivity by boosting the basilar membrane vibration and to improved frequency selectivity by allowing the vibration pattern to be more localised. The 100-fold increase in sensitivity of a normal cochlea over one that is physiologically compromised can almost certainly be attributed to the outer cells.

Very much the same idea of positive feedback – where a portion of the output signal is fed back to enhance the input signal – has been used by electrical engineers to improve radio receiver reception. This analogy was proposed and applied to hearing in 1948 by Thomas Gold, then working in Cambridge, before the physiology had developed far enough to support the hypothesis. As engineers (and anyone listening to a badly adjusted power amplifier system) know, feedback circuits can easily become unstable and the circuit oscillates. If positive feedback and active amplification is indeed employed by the inner ear, it might be thought that sounds could come out of the ear. Gold recognised this and attempted to show that the ear emitted sound, but unfortunately he did not possess sufficiently sensitive microphones. The prediction had to wait another 30 years before it was shown by David Kemp working in London that sound is produced by the cochlea, almost certainly as a by-product of the amplification processes going on in the cochlea. The measurement of such otoacoustic emissions are now used regularly by audiologists testing the function of the ear and are proving particularly helpful in the objective diagnosis of hearing loss in very young children.

From ear to brain

What happens to the sound information once it has been processed by the cochlea? The cochlea itself separates complex sounds into a pattern of activity in about 30 000 auditory nerve fibres. The activity of an individual fibre carries information about intensity and timing at a particular sound frequency, so that a 'picture' of the initial sound is built up in the midbrain and higher centres. Although we know from neurophysiological experiments how these signals are transmitted through the brain nuclei, there is still relatively little known about the global signal-processing that occurs at different relay nuclei. One reason for this lack of information is that neurophysiology is a particularly effective way of studying the behaviour of one or, at most, a few neurones at a time. But in the processing of speech sounds we have an example of a sensory system where the activity of many neurones is essentially involved. We have some indication that the routing of information and the numbers of neurones devoted to a particular auditory task may depend on the species being studied. Unlike the visual system, where it is relatively clear that the surface of the retina is mapped onto the cortex and visual space is processed as a sequence of spatial projections, the auditory system processes information coded in time and in a space representing frequency. Each of the 30 000 nerve fibres, and their projection neurones, carry a temporal pattern of codes that is much harder to disentangle.

There has therefore been considerable excitement with the advent of the technology of functional magnetic resonance imaging (fMRI). This technique detects blood flow in areas of brain by looking at the perturbation of an imposed magnetic field. The technique produces maps of the brain indicating which areas of the brain are active during any physiological stimulus. The current spatial resolution of fMRI is about 1 mm. Although this is a technique very much in its infancy, the approach may provide some insights into which areas of brain are used during more complex auditory tasks. The difficulties with the current generation of fMRI machines is that they produce considerable noise in their own right and are therefore not completely suitable to study aspects of hearing such as discrimination and detection of weak sounds.

Conclusion

I have tried to present you with an overview of the cochlea as an exquisitely designed machine that provides the brain with an interface to sound. I should like to think that we have made some progress over the past two decades in understanding how the cochlea functions. Although I have emphasised the cellular aspects of hearing, we still know relatively little about the assembly sequence of the component parts and little about the molecular signals that coordinate its development. There are potentially enormous areas in the molecular biology of hearing that are just about to open up. There are now new techniques that no longer regard the very small quantities of tissue in the cochlea as limiting and considerable strides have been made in identifying the molecular defects responsible for a number of types of genetically caused hearing losses. The understanding of the genetics, it is hoped, may begin to give an insight about the basic mechanisms of the hearing processes. As we have seen, the cochlea is one of the few structures in the body where there is a very intimate connection between the properties of the molecules and the performance of the whole system. The field of hearing has only recently reached a point where the application of new molecular biological techniques and new computational approaches to modelling the cochlea offer real expectation of progress. The richness of the structure of the cochlea can be both a deterrent to its understanding and a source of surprise that such a structure could evolve at all. But this is what makes studying how we hear particularly exciting.

FURTHER READING AND LISTENING

Houtsma, A. J. M., Rossing, T. D. and Wagenaars, W. M., *Auditory Demonstrations*, Institute for Perception Research, Supported by the Acoustical Society of America. Philips Compact Disc 1126–061, 1987.

Hudspeth, A. J., 'How hearing happens', *Neuron* **19** (1997), 947–50.

Nobili, R., Mammano, F. and Ashmore, J. F., 'How well do we understand the cochlea?', *Trends in Neuroscience* **21** (1998), 159–67.

Pickles, J. O., *An Introduction to the Physiology of Hearing*, 2nd edition, London: Academic Press, 1988.

von Békésy, G., *Experiments in Hearing*, New York: McGraw-Hill, 1960.

Yost, W. A., *Fundamentals of Hearing*, San Diego, CA: Academic Press, 1994.

4   Sounds Natural: The Song of Birds

PETER SLATER

> 'On the whole, birds appear to be the most aesthetic of all animals, excepting of course man, and they have nearly the same taste for the beautiful as we have. This is shewn by our enjoyment of the singing of birds ...'

Darwin (1871) *The Descent of Man* ...

If the complexity and attractiveness of the sounds birds produce is anything to go by, Darwin was certainly right in the above quote. While dogs may bark, crickets may trill and frogs may croak, there are not many animals that rival birds in the realm of sound production. For this reason, tempted as I am to extol the virtues of whales, I shall stick with birds in this chapter and, in particular, discuss what light has been shed on their song by scientific research.

Studies of bird song have made a very substantial contribution to our understanding of many basic processes in animal behaviour. One reason for this is the existence of the sound spectrograph or sonagraph. This equipment provides a paper trace plotting frequency against time, with the image dark where there is energy at that particular point (examples of such 'sonagrams' are shown in Figures 1, 5, 6, 7 and 8). With these traces we can analyse and compare bird sounds in much more detail than we can most other aspects of behaviour. The technique was first applied to animal sounds by Professor William Thorpe in Cambridge in his studies of chaffinch song development in the early 1950s. Today sonagraphs have largely been replaced by a variety of computer packages, but these produce similar plots that also enable us to examine sounds in much more detail than we can by ear.

In this chapter I consider some of the key issues that have been addressed in the scientific study of bird song, starting first with the basic question of why birds use sounds to communicate with one another.

Table 1. *A comparison of the main sensory channels of communication*

	Acoustic	Visual	Chemical
Nocturnal use	Good	Poor	Good
Around objects	Good	Poor	Good
Range	Long	Medium	Long
Rate of change	Fast	Fast	Slow
Locatability	Medium	Good	Poor
Energetic cost	High	Low	Low

Why sound?

Animals communicating with each other from a distance can use several different sensory modalities, of which smell, sight and sound are the most common. Each of these three modalities has its advantages and disadvantages, as outlined in Table 1. While many animals, including birds, display to each other with visual signals, such signals are of use mainly in short-range and private communication. They are of little use at night, or where objects may intervene between the signaller and its target. Olfactory signals are excellent where persistence is required and, as with dogs marking lamp-posts, will operate even after the signaller has moved on. Like sounds they can also be detected at long range and will spread round obstacles. But their very persistence raises a disadvantage. Changing from one message to another takes time. It would be a long lecture that consisted of a sequence of smells!

Compared with sight and smell, sound combines a number of features that make it ideal for many forms of communication. It travels fast, by day and by night, it spreads round obstacles, it can be detected at long range, and it can encode complex and changing messages. An ideal medium for many purposes, it is not surprising that it is adopted in our own language and in the song of birds.

How birds produce their sounds

The sound-producing organ of birds, the syrinx, is quite unlike our own larynx. While the larynx is high in the throat, the syrinx is much lower down at the point where the ducts from the two lungs (the bronchi) join to form the trachea (Figure 1a). Most birds produce quite simple sounds and have a syrinx that is likewise uncomplicated. On the other hand, the majority of complex singers belong to a group known as the songbirds (Order Passeriformes, Sub-Order Oscines), which comprises nearly half the known bird species. In keeping with the sounds they produce, one of the defining features of this group is that their syrinx is operated by five or more pairs of muscles, unlike the three or fewer found in most other bird groups.

The major role of the muscles of the syrinx is to alter the tension on two membranes, one on either side. Air passes from the lungs over these membranes and, as with a musical instrument, the sound produced depends on the tension in them. If they are held very taut, they will vibrate rapidly and produce a high pitched sound, if they are less so their vibration will be slower and the sound correspondingly lower. This remarkable apparatus accounts for the extraordinary speed and precision with which birds can sing.

The syrinx also has a feature that gives birds an edge on us when it comes to sound complexity. Because there are two membranes, each with its own set of muscles, birds can produce two separate and harmonically unrelated sounds at the same time. In some cases this does indeed happen, but many of the notes in bird song are produced by the two membranes simultaneously or by one side while the other is silent. Figure 1 gives an example, taken from the work of Roderick Suthers on the brown thrasher, an American species with a particularly varied song. This shows how the stream of notes produced by the bird is generated as air is released from the lung past one or other of the two membranes either in sequence or simultaneously. Although not shown in this example, both membranes may also sometimes produce identical sounds at the same time.

A further complication is that resonances within the vocal tract, for long ignored, are also now realised to be important. Experiments by Stephen Nowicki have shown that the sounds produced can be altered by changes in the shape of the singer's vocal tract. However, it is the use of two separate membranes and their subtle integration with each other that seems to account for the extraordinary ability of songbirds to sing per second up to 30 elements, often of quite complex structure.

Sounds simple and complex: calls and songs

Birds make a variety of different sounds, not all of which we would call song. For example, most small birds have simple and distinctive calls that they

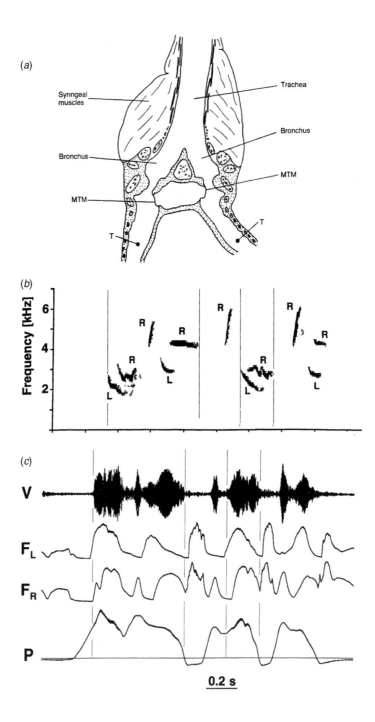

produce while moving around in their flocks, and these probably serve to keep individuals in contact with one another. Many birds also give alarm calls when they spot a predator. The best known of these is the 'seeep' call, originally studied by Peter Marler when he was in Cambridge, which many different European species produce when they spot a hawk, and which warns others of its presence. Making a sound when there is a predator about is a very dangerous thing to do, and there has been a good deal of speculation about the costs and benefits of such calls. The seeep call does sometimes occur in winter flocks, and many ingenious ideas have been suggested as to why this is the case. But it is commoner in the breeding season and at that time its most likely benefit is that it protects the bird's mate and offspring, as they seek cover and freeze when they hear it, so are less likely to be caught by the hawk.

All seeep calls are very similar and, unlike most bird sounds, it is impossible to identify the species producing one. One reason for this is doubtless that, in warning others that there is a hawk about, the identity of the caller is of no consequence. Another reason is thought to be that the seeep call is perfectly adapted to its function: its purity and high frequency make it extremely difficult to locate, and it has even been suggested that birds of prey may have difficulty hearing it at that frequency. So it seems that the costs of calling may not be as great as they might seem at first sight and might be made up for by a slight advantage, perhaps to the caller's relatives.

On the one hand, most calls are short and simple sounds, they are shown by both sexes, and many of them can be heard at any time of year. On the other hand, the word 'song' tends only to be applied to longer and more complex

FIGURE 1. (a) Frontal section through the syrinx of a brown thrasher, showing how the medial tympaniform membranes (MTM) are located at the point where the two bronchi converge to form the trachea. In experiments by Suthers and colleagues, airflow past the membranes was measured using two thermistors (T) implanted one on either side.

(b) A sonagram of the song of a brown thrasher, indicating which elements were generated on the left (L) and right (R) side of the syrinx. As can be seen from this, at several points left and right sides produce two harmonically unrelated sounds simultaneously.

(c) Plots of sound amplitude produced by the brown thrasher (V) and of air flow on the left (F_L) and right (F_R) sides of the syrinx. The final plot (P) shows pressure in one of the bird's air sacs, which builds up prior to sound production and then falls as air is released up one or both bronchi.

vocalisations. Most of these are produced only by males and only in the breeding season. But every rule has its exceptions. In Britain, female robins sing in the winter and in the tropics the females of many species sing, sometimes in the form of duets with their mates. The British male house sparrow has no song in the sense of a long and complex sequence of sounds, but the 'cheep cheep' he calls out from the roof top may well serve the same function. Some songs are certainly very simple. Nevertheless, most of them are easily distinguished as the longest and most complex sounds of a species, which are only produced by males in the breeding season.

Why do birds sing?

The fact that song is, in many species, a preserve of breeding males, provides a clue as to the role that it plays. There is now considerable evidence that this role is in part to attract and stimulate females and in part to repel rival males from the territory of a singing bird. A few examples will illustrate how such evidence has been obtained.

The respiratory system of birds is more complicated than ours, with a series of air sacs attached to the lungs. If one of these sacs is punctured the bird can still breathe adequately, but this has the effect of muting it until the wound heals. The bird goes through all the motions of singing but no sound emerges. Such an experiment, carried out by Douglas Smith on male red-winged blackbirds in America, showed that song was important in territorial defence. While the muted birds did not lose their territories, they suffered more intrusions from other males and had to engage in more aggressive displays as a result.

A neater and less invasive approach was taken by John Krebs (Figure 2). He removed all the male great tits from a wood outside Oxford. In some of the empty territories he set up loudspeakers playing great tit song, in some he placed speakers playing a control sound (a tune on a tin whistle), and in some he played no sound at all. He then watched to see how quickly new males moved in to occupy the different areas. Two replications of the experiment gave very similar results: in each case the area where tit song was being broadcast was the slowest to become recolonised.

These experiments indicate that song acts as a 'keep out' signal. What then of its part in attracting females? The neatest experiment here has been by Dag

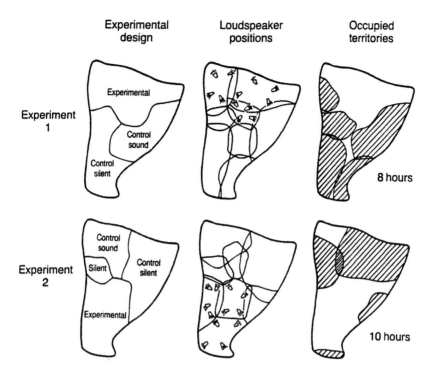

FIGURE 2. Maps of the wood near Oxford from which John Krebs removed all male great tits in two separate experiments to study the effects of song. In these different areas of the wood there were either no loudspeakers (control silent), loudspeakers playing a tune on a tin whistle (control sound), or loudspeakers playing great tit song (experimental). The final pair of maps show which territories had become occupied 8–10 daylight hours after the experiment started. It is clear that males took up territories in the control areas more rapidly than in the experimental ones.

Eriksson and Lars Wallin on pied and collared flycatchers in Sweden. They set up a number of nesting boxes in areas of woodland, each box attended by a stuffed model of a male flycatcher. They were also equipped with a spring-loaded trap so that any bird inspecting the box was trapped. From some boxes the appropriate species' song was played, while an equal number of others were silent. The results were clear: of ten females caught in the traps, nine were at the boxes where song was being played.

As well as attracting females, song stimulates them. Female birds that are

Table 2. *Some bird song repertoire sizes*

Number of phrases per bird	Species
1	European redwing
	White-crowned sparrow
	Splendid sunbird
1–10	Chaffinch
	Great tit
	Corn bunting
10–100	Blackbird
	Coal tit
	Rose-breasted grosbeak
100–1000	Nightingale
	Song thrush
	Mockingbird
2000+	Brown thrasher

ready to mate show a particular display to the male, referred to as soliciting, during which they adopt a horizontal posture, spread their wings and flutter their tail up and down. Perhaps not surprisingly, females do not normally show this display when played song from a loudspeaker. However, females of a number of species have been found to do so if made highly receptive by treatment with the female sex hormone oestrogen. Not only does song stimulate females to display, but it has also been found in canaries to increase their nest-building behaviour and boost the growth of the eggs in their ovaries.

Experiments such as these show that the two main functions of song are in holding territories and attracting females to males. But there is an added complication we must consider, and this is that the males of most bird species do not merely have one short and stereotyped song. Indeed, many of them have several hundred (see Table 2).

Repertoires of songs

In a small number of bird species there is clear evidence that different songs have different meanings. American and European warblers provide the best examples here. In many American warblers there are two types of song that occur in rather different circumstances. The so-called 'accented' song has a distinctive stress on the last note in each song and is produced largely in the pres-

(a)

```
..........A   A   S   S   S   C   C   C   C   C   C
   L   L   L   L   A   A   A   S   S   S   S   S
   C   C   C   C   L   L   L   L   L   L   A   A
   A   A   S   S   S   S   C   C   L   L   A..........

..........L   L   L   L   L   A   A   S   S   S   S
   S   C   C   C   C   C   C   C   L   L   L   L
   A   A   A   S   S   S   C   C   C   C   C   C
   L   L   L   L   L   A   A   A   A   S   S..........
```

(b)

```
..........L   L   L   S   S   S   S   S   S   S   A
   C   C   C   C   C   C   C   C   C   C   L   L
   L   L   L..........

..........S   S   A   A   A   A   C   C   C   C   C
   C   C   C   C   L   L   L   L   S   S   S   S
   S   S   S   S   A   A   A   C   C   C   C   C
   L   L   L   L   L   L   L   S   S   S   S   A
   A   A   C   C..........
```

FIGURE 3. Sequences of songs produced by the same male chaffinch on two mornings three days apart. The bird possessed four song types, each labelled by a different letter.

ence of females, while the unaccented song occurs mostly in male–male encounters. In the great reed warbler in Europe there is a short and simple song, used mainly in territorial contexts, and a longer much more elaborate one that is produced only by unpaired males and seems to be adapted to attract mates.

Such species are the exception. In most of those that have repertoires, all the songs are equivalent to each other in context and in function. In the chaffinch, males may have three or four different song types and sing with a series of one followed by a series of another. They tend to cycle round their repertoire, not returning to the first until each of the others has been sung (Figure 3). But there is also a tendency in many such species for a bird that has it in his repertoire to

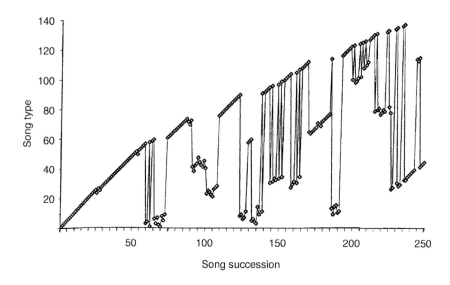

FIGURE 4. The sequence of song types in a succession of 250 songs produced by a singing nightingale as described by Dietmar Todt and Henrike Hultsch. Each song in the sequence is represented by a diamond-shaped symbol and successive songs are connected by a line. Songs of the same type occur at the same level on the vertical axis. During the sequence, 136 different song types were produced. The same song seldom occurs twice in close proximity, but particular groups of songs tend to be associated with each other, a phenomenon known as 'packaging'.

reply to another male with the same song as he is producing. These small song repertoires may help males to match the songs of their neighbours during this countersinging. Repertoires certainly seem to enhance the effectiveness of song as a territorial signal: in another experiment where he removed male great tits from a wood, John Krebs showed that speakers excluded newcomers for longer if they were playing a repertoire of songs rather than just a single type.

Male–male interaction is much less likely to account for repertoires where these are very large. In the nightingale, males usually have over 100 song types. Again a bird tends to cycle through its repertoire, but in this case without repeating the same song several times before moving on (Figure 4). Indeed, after a particular song is produced it is very unlikely to occur again for a long period. In a noisy world, repeating a song type several times may make sure that the message it conveys is received. On the other hand, what nightingales appear to be doing is maximising the contrast between their successive songs. The message here is one of variety.

Why might a bird benefit from maximising the variety of its output in this way? The best evidence here comes from Clive Catchpole's work on sedge warblers in Britain. These birds have long and highly varied songs. They are made up of stereotyped elements but these are put together in many different sequences. Indeed, a single bird may never produce precisely the same song twice in its life! Each song starts with a pair of elements alternating with each other, there is then a middle section where many new elements are introduced, and the song ends with a sequence in which two out of these ones alternate once more. These are the two elements selected to start the next song.

That sedge warbler song functions primarily in attracting females is suggested by the fact that it ceases entirely once a bird is mated. The males arrive back in Britain from their winter quarters in Africa before the females do, set up their territories and sing at a rate of several hundred songs a day. One by one they become mated as the females return. Catchpole examined the sequence in which males obtained their mates, and found a remarkably good correlation with repertoire size: the larger the number of elements a male had at his disposal, the earlier he attracted a female (Figure 5). Females are also more stimulated by larger repertoires. Laboratory experiments showed that they gave more sexual displays in response to more elaborate songs.

Results such as these suggest that large song repertoires have evolved through sexual selection, because large repertoires are more effective than small ones in attracting and stimulating mates. As Darwin put it, somewhat less prosaically, 'the sweet strains poured forth by the males during the season of love are certainly admired by the females'.

Sedge warblers have a fixed number of stereotyped elements that they string together in various different ways. A male chaffinch has a certain number of song types, and the sequence of each of them is identical every time it is sung. While the nightingale may sing hundreds of song types, every one of these is identifiable as being the same type on each occasion that it appears. In other words, although the casual listener might think otherwise, birds do not perch atop their trees improvising but, once they are adult, each

Peter Slater

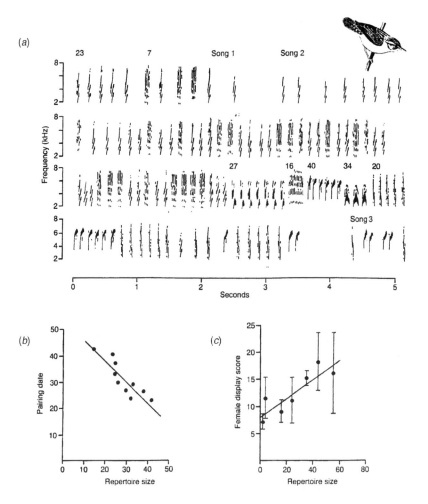

FIGURE 5. (*a*) Sonagram of sedge warbler song. The first song ends and the second begins by an alternating sequence of elements 23 and 7. Then, in the middle of the second song, several new elements are introduced (27, 16, 40, 34, 20) and, of these, two (40 and 20) are singled out to alternate at the end of this song and start of the next. (*b*) The date (1 = 20 April) on which 10 different male sedge warblers obtained mates plotted against the number of elements in their repertoires. (*c*) The number of sexual displays given by captive female sedge warblers to playback of varying different repertoire sizes.

100

one generally has a fixed repertoire of song types. How then do they obtain these?

Song learning

It has been known for a long time that learning plays a part in song development. Darwin himself referred to a house sparrow imitating a linnet, and Daines Barrington, writing in 1773, had already given a number of similar examples. But the scientific study of song development dates most clearly from the pioneering studies of the chaffinch by William Thorpe in Cambridge, published in 1956. Thorpe showed that young males reared out of earshot of others developed songs that were rudimentary. They were about the right length and frequency and, like the normal song, they also consisted of a series of distinct elements. But they lacked the clear phrasing and detailed structure of the song of wild birds, and often also the distinctive flourish with which the male chaffinch signs off at the end of his song (Figure 6a). By contrast with these isolated birds, young males that were played recordings of normal male song in the first year of their lives, would copy them with a high degree of accuracy (Figure 6b).

Since Thorpe's experiments, many other bird species have been examined. Learning of sounds has been found in three separate groups: the parrots, the hummingbirds and the songbirds. The last of these accounts for almost half the bird species that exist, and all of them that have been studied have been found to learn their songs. Interestingly, their closest relatives, the Sub-Oscines, a smaller group occurring primarily in the tropics, appear not to learn their songs. The simplest explanation for this is that song arose once amongst them, very soon after these two groups separated from each other.

Song learning provides one of the clearest examples of the intricate interplay between nature and nurture that occurs during the course of development. While it may be possible to teach a young male an alien song, and some bird species are noted mimics, in the great majority of cases wild males sing only the song of their own species. They learn their songs, but there are clearly constraints that effectively limit them to copying only those that are appropriate.

What are these constraints? An early theory of song development,

101

(a)

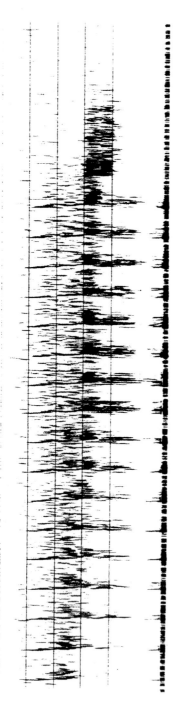

FIGURE 6. (a) The song of a young chaffinch reared in isolation. (b) (see below) Four songs played on tape-recordings to a young chaffinch and the copies that he produced. The young male failed to reproduce sections of the first and last of these, but in all other respects his copying was detailed and accurate.

(c) (see below) The auditory template model of song development. This model pictures young birds as hatching with a rough or crude 'template' defining the approximate characteristics of their own species' song. During a sensitive phase for memorisation, when they may hear songs of many other species, only those that match this template are memorised, at least in a form that will later be linked to their own singing. The crude template thus becomes an exact template: precise specifications for the song or songs they will sing. This may be achieved well before the bird starts to sing, or memorisation and production may overlap with each other, depending on the species. When song production commences, as it usually does once testosterone begins to circulate in their first spring, the young bird matches its output to the exact template it has formed. This does not happen instantaneously. As song begins to develop the young male goes through a period of subsong, which is quiet and highly variable, followed by plastic song, during which its output becomes louder and more normal in structure, but is still not as stereotyped as full song. At this stage, for example, successive syllables within a chaffinch phrase may not be identical, and the bird may produce songs that are a mixture of two types. Slowly the song 'crystallises' from this into the full song typical of adults of the species. It is during this period, which may last some weeks in birds singing for the first time, that the young bird is thought to perfect its output in relation to the template it has developed.

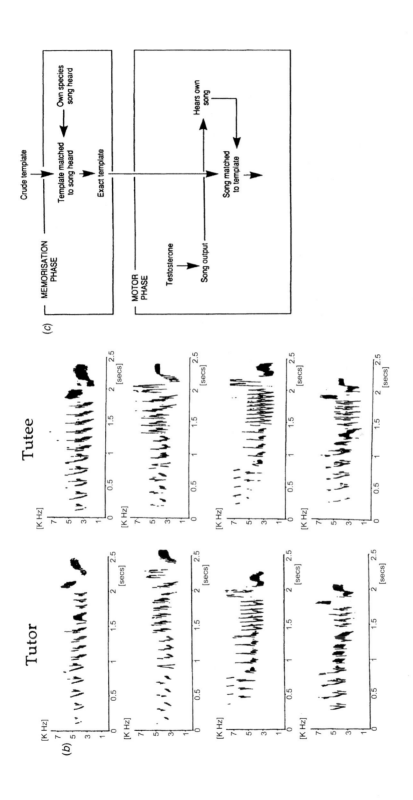

Tutor   Tutee

(b)

(c)

MEMORISATION
PHASE

Crude template → Template matched → Own species
                  to song heard   song heard

                  Exact template

MOTOR
PHASE

Testosterone   Song matched   Hears own
    ↓   to template   song
Song output

elaborated principally by Mark Konishi and Peter Marler, was referred to as the 'auditory template model' and is outlined in Figure 6c. This proposed that young birds hatched with a rough idea of what their own species' song sounded like and that this effectively excluded all songs that they heard other than those of their own species. This may indeed be true in some species, but a number of other factors may also be involved. One that has come to the fore particularly in recent years has been the importance of social interactions.

Unlike the chaffinch, some species will not learn from tape-recordings but must have a live tutor with which they can interact. In my own group we have worked for some years on one such species, the zebra finch from Australia. This is a common cagebird, which breeds easily in captivity and will do so all year round. It also has the great advantage for studies of this sort that young birds mature at around three months of age. Males usually learn their songs in the second month of life, shortly after becoming independent of their parents, and will produce a precise copy of the song of a male with which they are housed at that stage. They must, however, interact with him. They will not learn from a tape, nor from a live male from which they have an audio link, nor from one behind a hessian screen. If they are housed with several singing adults, they tend to latch onto one and copy his song rather than blending the characteristics of more than one. They do not necessarily choose the male that sings the most, but they do tend to copy the one that looks and sounds most like their father did, and this is probably simply because they had spent most time in association with him.

That interaction is a crucial factor here has been shown by some neat experiments carried out by Patrice Adret in St Andrews, Scotland (Figure 7). He trained young males to peck at a key that released 15 seconds worth of song from a loudspeaker. The birds would do this for no reward other than that of hearing the song. They would, as a result, hear that particular song many hundreds of times. Far from habituating to it, they came to prefer it: if given two keys offering a choice of songs, they would opt for that playing the song on which they had been trained. They also learnt that song, producing a faithful copy of it in adulthood. By contrast, other males in nearby cages, which had received exactly the same song experience, but without the key to control it, failed to learn. The critical factor was the measure of interaction between the bird and the song that the key provided.

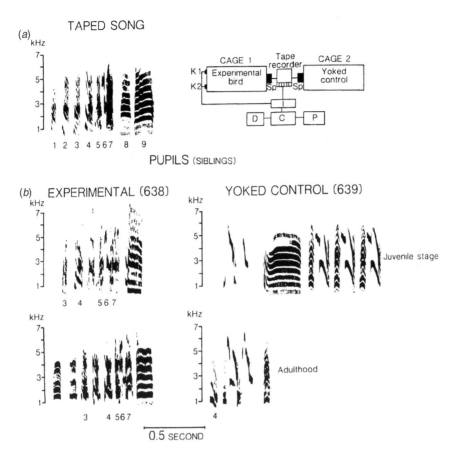

FIGURE 7. (a) Diagram of the apparatus used in song learning experiments by Patrice Adret. In this, two birds in adjacent cages are both played songs from a computer-controlled tape-recorder (D C P), but one of them has a key to control the tape whereas the other does not. Sp, speakers. (b) Sonagrams of the song on the tutor tape played to two young birds and of their own songs at two different ages. The experimental bird, which could switch the tape on, produced a good copy of the tutor song, whereas the song of the yoked control was highly abnormal.

In the wild, the interaction between territorial birds and their neighbours may be an important factor in song learning. When young birds first start to sing, they go through a period of subsong, during which they produce a much wider variety of sounds than they use subsequently. In species with simple songs it may even be the case that they produce every conceivable sound of their species at this stage, and that learning is more a matter of weeding out those that will not be used than of copying new ones. This process, referred to as 'action-based learning' by Peter Marler, takes place as the young bird countersings with its neighbours and may enable it to develop songs that it will share with them. A good example here is in the field sparrow, studied by Douglas Nelson in New York State. These birds sing two or more song types when first settling on territories, but usually drop all but one of these after a period of interaction with neighbours. The one they select for retention is that most like the song of a neighbour.

Another form of interaction that may be important in song development is with females. The most interesting case here is that of brown-headed cowbirds, studied by Meredith West and Andrew King in North Carolina. Cowbirds are brood parasites, so the young do not interact with adults of their own species early on, and do not therefore have an opportunity to copy their songs. They do, however, form into flocks within which young males and females interact. West and King found that the songs of young males were influenced by their female companions. If the females were of a subspecies different from that of the males, the males developed songs more like that of the alien subspecies than their own. As females do not sing, this was indeed a remarkable discovery. It turns out that the young females have a display, referred to as 'wing stroking', which is quite like the soliciting display of an adult female. The young female produces this when the song of a male attracts her. West and King found that the male is then more likely to repeat this song, and thus the songs he produces become progressively more matched to those that the females with him prefer. As a major function of song is to attract and stimulate mates, the fact that female preferences should channel its development would seem highly adaptive. We have evidence that something similar may be going on in zebra finches, but there has as yet been little work on female influences on song development in other species.

Why learn?

Song learning has many consequences. It leads males in a neighbourhood to share songs with each other. Because it is not always totally accurate it also often leads to new songs being created and these can sometimes spread through a population as one bird copies from another. Likewise songs that are not copied become extinct. These processes lead the songs in an area to change through time, and also to variation between the songs in different areas. Where these differences are strong, they have often been referred to as dialects, analogous to those that exist in human languages.

All the evidence we have, from studies of several species, is that changes of these sorts are random by-products of the learning process, rather than having any functional significance in themselves. What then are the benefits of song learning? There are really two questions here: first, why did song learning originate and, second, what maintains it in all those species that show it today?

As song learning is thought to have started amongst the passerines some 30 million years ago, it is not easy to examine why it originated. However, a number of theories have been put forward to explain why it persists today. One, which seemed most attractive when first proposed, was that song learning might have a role in mate choice. If males learn songs in the area where they hatched and females seek out mates like those with which they are familiar, then birds adapted to a particular area would tend to mate with each other. But the evidence does not support this idea. Most song learning seems to occur after birds disperse, not before, and there is little evidence that females preferentially mate with males having songs of a particular type. Indeed, in Darwin's finches, which are among the few species where males are known to copy songs from their fathers, females mate randomly with respect to song types.

Other ideas have gained more support, though none appears to apply across the whole range of species that have been studied. One suggestion, originally put forward by Poul Hansen, was that song learning might help to match the song to the bird's habitat. If young birds learn their songs from others who are singing some distance away, then those sounds that travel best through the habitat are those most likely to be copied. As a result, over the course of many cultural generations, songs will become more and more honed to that particular environment. Perhaps the best evidence in favour of this idea comes from studies on the chingolo sparrow in South America, most recently by Paul Handford and his colleagues (Figure 8). The song of the chingolo changes rather little over wide areas of the pampas in Argentina, but more rapidly in mountainous regions where the habitat is more varied. The border between different song forms is also often coincident with, or close to, habitat changes. The song ends

107

Peter Slater

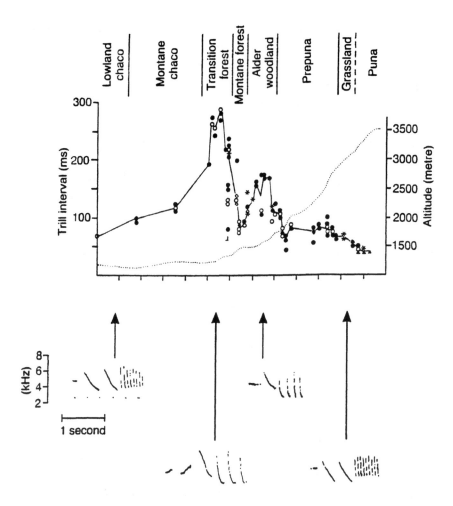

FIGURE 8. How trill rate changes in chingolo sparrows in South America along one transect across various original vegetation types and with increasing altitude. The sonagrams give examples of songs from four different vegetation types.

with a trill and it is this part of the song that shows the most striking link with habitat. In wooded areas, where echoes would be liable to distort it, the trill is much slower than in open areas where such effects are less of a problem.

A particularly interesting feature of chingolo song is that it varies quite considerably in agricultural areas, despite the fact that the environment there is

108

very uniform. Handford and his colleagues argue that such variations are matched to the habitats that existed in particular areas before agriculture was introduced a century or more ago. Chingolos are among the few species in such farmland, with territories densely packed together, so there may be less pressure than elsewhere for sounds to be adapted to the current environment if they are to carry well to neighbours. If this is the case, and if birds copy their songs very accurately, then perhaps the form of song in an area would indeed persist over a long period.

Another theory of song learning has been put forward by Eugene Morton, and this also relates to how song carries through the habitat. He argues that it benefits males to learn the songs of their neighbours so that, when they hear them, they can judge the distance away of the singer and so tell whether or not he is intruding. Morton then suggests it may benefit singers to be able to modify their songs through learning so that neighbours do not know them and cannot assess their distance away: a sort of arms race. While this idea remains speculative, Morton proposes that it may account for both song learning and the development of repertoires.

Amongst a number of other theories two seem most plausible, and these hark back to the functions of song discussed earlier. First, song learning may enable neighbours to match each other, and this may lead songs to be more effective in excluding intruders and in interactions with rivals. In line with this, Bob Payne has found that male indigo buntings that share songs with neighbours are more successful in various measures of reproduction. Second, song learning may be a good way of generating variety and may therefore be favoured where sexual selection confers advantages on males with the most complex and varied songs. It does seem that, for some reason, birds build up their repertoires through the precise copying of other individuals rather than by improvisation. Indeed, mimicry of other species, which is a striking aspect of song in some birds, appears to be simply another means to variety. Perhaps the most notable mimic described to date is the marsh warbler, which nests in Europe and migrates down to East Africa, and has been studied by Françoise Dowsett-Lemaire. The young males do not learn from other marsh warblers, as these have stopped singing before they hatch, but they copy the sounds of numerous European and African species that they hear during the winter, and end up with a song which is a medley of the notes they have heard. While they may copy 70 or 80 different species, and so achieve great variety, the way that they structure these means that the song is still recognisably that of a marsh warbler.

Conclusion

Although bird song has been studied extensively, there remains a great deal amongst its perplexing variety that we do not understand. Song learning is a key issue and, once it had evolved, probably led to a number of other changes. Occasional transcription errors would have led to individual differences between birds in their songs, and thus to changes in space and in time. While neighbours would tend to share songs through mutual copying, giving rise to dialect areas, repertoires may have been favoured to allow matching of as many individuals as possible. Sexual selection may then have taken this process of repertoire growth further, where females preferred males with more elaborate songs.

Many of the links in these chains of argument are speculative. While our understanding of bird song has advanced enormously in the past few decades, quite a few puzzles remain, and just why some birds learn their songs while others do not is a particularly perplexing one. It is an issue that is, of course, also of great interest for human evolution, as vocal learning is at the root of our own language and music. Here again, however, the reasons why it originated remain obscure. Among the mammals, three other groups are known to modify the form of their sounds through learning: seals, whales and dolphins, and bats. These are both evolutionarily distant from each other and from ourselves, suggesting four separate evolutions of vocal learning to add to the three among birds. Interestingly, there is no evidence for vocal learning among our closest relatives, the apes and monkeys. It seems to have arisen in our own lineage very recently in evolutionary terms, some two million years ago. Just why this occurred may remain a mystery, but there is no doubt of its dramatic consequences, such as those that concern many of the other chapters in this book.

FURTHER READING

Adret, P., 'Operant conditioning, song learning and imprinting to taped song in the zebra finch', *Animal Behaviour* **46** (1993), 149–59.

Catchpole, C. K., 'Bird song, sexual selection and female choice', *Trends in Ecology and Evolution* 2 (1987), 94–7.

Catchpole, C. K. and Slater, P. J. B., *Bird Song. Biological Themes and Variations*, Cambridge: Cambridge University Press, 1995.

Janik, V. M. and Slater, P. J. B., 'Vocal learning in mammals', *Advances in the Study of Behavior* 26 (1997), 59–99.

Kroodsma, D. E. and Miller, E. H. (eds.), *Ecology and Evolution of Acoustic Communication in Birds*, Ithaca and London: Comstock Publishing Associates, 1996.

Marler, P., 'Song-learning behavior: the interface with neuroethology', *Trends in Neuroscience* 14 (1991), 199–206.

Nowicki, S. and Marler, P., 'How do birds sing?' *Music Perception* 5 (1988), 391–426.

Slater, P. J. B., 'The cultural transmission of bird song', *Trends in Ecology and Evolution* 1 (1986), 94–7.

Slater, P. J. B. and Jones, A. E., 'Lessons from bird song', *Biologist* 44 (1997), 301–3.

West, M. J. and King, A. P., 'Female visual displays affect the development of male song in the cowbird', *Nature* 334 (1988), 244–6.

5 The Sounds of Speech

PETER LADEFOGED

Once upon a time the most important sounds were those of predators and prey, and possible sexual partners. As mammals evolved and signalling systems became more elaborate, new possibilities emerged. Now undoubtedly the most important sounds for humans are those of language. Spoken language, which always precedes written language, is our way of expressing awareness of what goes on around us. Because of this, language provides a storage system that represents our knowledge of the world. Our language and what we say and write in it bear the same relationship to our view of the world as a map does to the terrain it represents. Words and sentences are our way of forming maps that show what we think the world is like. Without language we cannot represent what we know.

As this series is named in honor of Darwin, it is appropriate to think about the origin of language. Unfortunately, nobody knows how vocal cries turned into language; but then Darwin did not know how life began. He was concerned not with the origin of life but with the origin of the various species he could observe. In the same spirit, we will not consider the origin of language, but we will note the various sounds of languages and discuss how they became what they are. We will think of each language as a system of sounds subject to various forces.

Languages are constrained, first, by what we can do with our tongues, lips and other vocal organs and, second, by our limited ability to hear small differences in sounds. These and other constraints have resulted in all languages evolving along similar lines. No language has sounds that are too difficult to produce within the stream of speech (although, as we will see, some languages have sounds that would twist English-speaking tongues in knots), and every language has sounds that are sufficiently different from one another to be readily distinguishable by native speakers (although, again, some distinctions may

112

seem much too subtle for ears that are unfamiliar with them). These two factors, articulatory ease and auditory distinctiveness, are the principal constraints on how languages develop.

There are some additional factors that have shaped the development of languages, notably how our brains organize and remember sounds. If a language had only one or two vowels and a couple of consonants it could still have an infinite number of words, but many of the words would be very long, difficult to remember, and sound much alike. If words are to be kept short and distinct so that they can be easily distinguished and remembered, the language must have a sufficient number of vowels and consonants to make many different syllables. But we do not want to have a large number of sounds that are all completely different from one another. It puts less strain on our cognitive capacities if the sounds of our languages can be organized into groups that are articulated in the same way. This is a principle that my colleague Ian Maddieson has called gestural economy. There is a pressure to select the sounds of a language so that they form a simple pattern within the vast set of possible speech sounds. Typically, if a language has one sound made by a gesture involving the two lips such as **p** as in *pie*, then it is likely to have others such as **b** and **m** as in *by* and *my*, made with similar lip gestures; if it has *pie*, *by*, *my*, and also a sound made with a gesture of the tongue tip such as **t** as in *tie*, then it is also likely to have other sounds made with the tongue tip, such as **d** and **n** as in *die* and *nigh*. The sounds that evolve in a language form a pattern, and there is a strong pressure to fill gaps in the pattern.

Societies weight the importance of the various constraints – articulatory ease, auditory distinctiveness, and gestural patterning – in different ways, producing roughly 7000 mutually unintelligible languages in the world. But despite the variations in sound that make each language distinct, there are common features that occur in all. For example, every language uses vowels (speech sounds that can be said on their own) and consonants (which generally can be sounded only with an accompanying vowel) to produce a variety of syllables, and all languages use the pitch of the voice in a meaningful way. In this chapter I consider the use of vowels, consonants and pitch changes in different languages.

Producing pitch changes in speech

When we listen to people talking we do not think of the sound as being that of a musical instrument. But the voice is an instrument that we all use to produce tunes when talking. Some people think that they cannot be producing tunes because they consider themselves to be tone deaf. But nobody is completely tone deaf, unless they are literally deaf in every respect. Everyone can hear and produce the tunes required in speech. We can make and distinguish statements and questions. We can use the pitch of the voice to make the subtle grammatical differences that are marked by punctuation in the written language such as 'When danger threatens – your children call the police' as compared with 'When danger threatens your children – call the police'. Some different tunes in sentences are not even marked by the punctuation; the reader (or listener) has to get them from the context. For example, we can tell the difference between sentences such as 'Jenny gave Peter *instructions* to follow' and 'Jenny gave Peter instructions to *follow*'. The first means that Peter was told what to do, and the second that he was told to come along after Jenny. The words are the same in the two sentences, but the meaning is different because of the differences in pitch and rhythm. Other pitch changes in speech can be used to convey other kinds of information. We can usually tell whether a speaker is angry or loving by listening to the tune without even hearing the words. Much of the emotional content of speech is carried by the pitch of the voice.

Being somewhat tone deaf does not mean that one cannot hear and produce different pitches accurately. It is just a matter of not being able to sing in tune. People for whom this is true probably did not have music in their background when they were young. Learning to sing is like learning a language, easier to pick up and do with perfection if you are a child, but more difficult when older. Singing differs from speaking in holding the pitch of the voice constant, usually for a syllable or two, and then jumping to the next note. In speech the pitch is always changing, never remaining the same, even within a single syllable. The pitch often goes down to mark the end of a sentence. It rises, at least in English, in questions that can be answered by yes or no. Statements such as 'I'm going home' typically have a falling pitch; only yes or no questions such as 'Are you going home?' usually rise at the end. However, it is almost impossible to generalize about the pitch changes that can occur in a language. The neutral way of asking the question 'Where are you going?' is to say it with a falling pitch.

Table 1. *Examples of words differentiated by tone in Standard Chinese and in Cantonese*

	Standard Chinese		ma		Cantonese	si
媽	˥	high level	'mother'	詩 ˧˩	high falling	'poem'
蔴	ˊ	high rising	'hemp'	試 ˧	mid level	'to try'
馬	˅	low falling rising	'horse'	事 ˨	low level	'matter'
罵	ˎ	high falling	'scold'	時 ˩	extra low	'time'
				使 ˊ	high rising	'to cause'
				市 ˏ	mid rising	'city'

But one can say 'Where are you going?' with a rising pitch, and 'Are you going home?' with a falling pitch, causing differences in emphasis and meaning. The tune of the voice in speech is one of the most difficult aspects of languages to describe, as it can be used to convey so many small nuances of meaning.

In English, and in most European languages, the meaning of a word remains the same irrespective of whether it is said on a rising pitch or a falling pitch. But this is not true in languages spoken in other parts of the world. In Standard Chinese the syllable **ma** has four different meanings, depending on the pitch on which it is spoken; and in Cantonese, another language spoken in China, a syllable with the same consonants and vowels can have up to six different meanings. Examples of words differing in pitch in each of these languages are given in Table 1. Differences of this type are called differences in tone. Standard Chinese is said to have four tones, and Cantonese has six tones on syllables of the type shown in Table 1. Although tonal differences are rare or non-existent in most languages spoken in Europe and India, well over half the languages spoken in the world use tones to differentiate the meanings of words.

Tones, and the pitch of the voice in general, depend mainly on the tension of the vocal folds, two small muscular flaps in the larynx. When the larynx is pulled forward the folds become longer and thinner so that they vibrate more quickly. The vibrations are the result of the air from the lungs sucking the folds together and then blowing them apart again. They behave in some ways like

Table 2. *Words illustrating the vowels* **a**, **e**, **i**, **o**, **u** *in Spanish, Hawaiian, Swahili and Japanese. (The qualities of the vowels are not exactly the same in each of these languages)*

Spanish		Hawaiian		Swahili		Japanese	
masa	'dough'	**kaka'**	'duck'	**pata**	'hinge'	**ka**	'mosquito'
mesa	'table'	**keke'**	'surly'	**peta**	'bend'	**ke**	'hair'
misa	'mass'	**kiki'**	'rapid'	**pita**	'pass'	**ki**	'tree'
mosca	'fly'	**koko**	'blood'	**pota**	'twist'	**ko**	'child'
musa	'muse'	**kuku'**	'thorn'	**puta**	'thrash'	**ku**	'suffering'

the lid of a boiling kettle. When the pressure of the steam below the lid becomes too great it is blown upward, releasing the pressure. When there is no pressure beneath it, it falls down; and then the pressure builds up again. In the case of the vocal folds there is a slight complication. The pressure of the air in the lungs will blow them apart, but, when the pressure is less, they do not simply collapse together. There is an additional mechanism drawing them towards one another by the air. The vocal folds are actively sucked together by the air passing between them. Air travelling at speed through a narrow gap drops in pressure (a fact that can be noticed by anyone in a vehicle when another vehicle travelling in the opposite direction passes it and the two vehicles are sucked towards one another). This suction causes the vocal folds to be sucked together faster than they were blown apart. The rapid, repetitive, closing of the vocal folds is what produces the sound of the voice. Each time the vocal folds close, the air in the throat and mouth is set into vibration so that a sound wave is produced.

Vowels

Many languages use just the five vowels that can be represented by the letters **a, e, i, o, u**, as exemplified by the words in Table 2. Languages as diverse as Spanish, Hawaiian, Swahili and Japanese manage with these five vowel sounds. English has a larger number; in southern British English there are 17 different vowels. We cannot find a single set of English words differing in only the vowels as we almost did for the languages in Table 3, but we can demonstrate the possibilities that can occur by considering syllables beginning with **b** and ending

Table 3. *English vowel sounds that can occur between **b** and **d** or **t** and **h** and **d** in one southern British style of speech, in which 'r' after a vowel is not pronounced*

b__d	b__t	h__d
bead	beat	heed
bid	bit	hid
bayed	bait	hayed
bed	bet	head
bad	bat	had
bard	(Bart)	hard
bod(y)	bot(tom)	hod
bawd	bought	hoard
bode	boat	hoed
bud(hist)		hood
booed	boot	who'd
bide	bite	hide
bowed	bout	howd(y)
bud	but	Hudd
bird	Bert	herd
beard		
bared		hared

with **d** or **t**, and those beginning with **h** and ending with **d**, as shown in Table 3. Many forms of English do not distinguish all these vowels – Californians, for example, have the same vowel in *hard*, *hod* and *hawed* (making *father* and *bother* rhyme, both having the same vowel as in *author*), and many Scottish speakers do not distinguish the vowels in *hood* and *who'd* (or *look* and *Luke*). Other forms of English have a slightly larger number of vowels. (We are, of course, concerned with the sounds that can occur as vowels in English syllables, and not the various ways vowels can be spelled in the written language; English spelling is notoriously odd.) Other languages such as German and Swedish have an even greater number of vowels. The record for the greatest number of vowels (excluding those with special voice qualities and tones which we will discuss later) is probably held by Austrian German dialects that can produce different syllables by choosing among 26 different vowel sounds, 13 long and 13 short.

Vowel sounds can be produced on any pitch within the range of a speaker's voice. I can say the vowels in *heed, hid, head, had* on a low pitch, when the vocal folds are vibrating about 80 times a second (a low E), and then I can say them again with vocal folds vibrating 160 times a second (the E an octave above). The pitch of my voice will have changed, but the vowels will still have the same quality. Different vowels are like different instruments. One can play concert pitch A on a piano, a clarinet, or a violin. In each case it will be the same note because the rate of repetition of the sound wave as a whole – the fundamental frequency – is the same. The quality will be different because the smaller variations within each repetition of the sound wave – the overtones – will be different. Similarly, vowels will retain their individual qualities irrespective of the pitch produced by the vocal folds.

When we listen to a musical note, or a vowel, we can tell which instrument produced it, or which vowel it is, by the overtones that occur. The reed of the clarinet or the vocal folds may be vibrating 120 times a second, but the sound that is produced at the mouth of the clarinet or the lips will contain characteristic groups of overtones at higher frequencies. For the vowel in *head* the most prominent overtones will be at about 550 and 1600 Hz, for the vowel in *had* they will be around 750 and 1200 Hz. These overtones will occur although the vocal folds may be vibrating at any rate from about 80 to around 250 Hz for a male speaker.

To see how these higher frequencies arise, we can liken the air in the mouth and throat to the air in a bottle. When you blow across the top of a bottle the air inside it will vibrate. The note that the bottle produces will depend on the size and shape of the body of air that it contains. If the bottle is empty it will produce a low pitched note. Pouring water into it so that the body of air becomes smaller makes the pitch go up, as smaller bodies of air vibrate more quickly.

The air in the vocal tract (the tube bounded by the vocal organs) is set in vibration by the pulses of air from the vocal folds. Every time they open and close the air in the vocal tract above them will vibrate. Because the vocal tract has a complex shape, the air within it will vibrate in more than one way. Often we can consider the body of air behind the raised tongue to be vibrating in one way and the body of air in front of it to be vibrating in another. In the vowel in *head* the air behind the tongue will vibrate at about 550 Hz, and the air in front of it at about 1600 Hz.

The resonances of the vocal tract are called formants. Trying to hear the separate formants in a vowel is difficult. We are so used to a vowel being a single meaningful entity that it is difficult to consider it as a sound with separable bits. But it is possible to say vowels so that their component parts are more obvious. One possibility is to whisper a series of vowels. When someone is whispering, the vocal folds do not vibrate; they are simply drawn together so that they produce a random noise like that of the wind blowing around a corner. Because this noise is in the pitch range of one of the resonances of the vocal tract, we can hear that resonance more plainly. If you whisper you will not hear a note with a specific pitch; but you will be able to hear the changes in the vowel resonances. Try whispering *heed, hid, head, had, hod, hawed*; there will be general impression of a descending pitch.

Another way of making one of the resonances more obvious is to say a series of words on a very low pitch. Say *ah* on as low a pitch as you can, and then try to go even lower so that you produce a kind of creaky voice. Say the words *hard, hoard, hood, who'd* in this kind of voice. You may be able to hear not only the constant low buzzing sort of pitch associated with the vocal folds, but also a changing pitch in one of the overtones. When saying the words *hard, hoard, hood, who'd* this pitch goes down. If you say the words *heed, hid, head, had* with the same kind of creaky voice, you may be able to hear an ascending pitch.

The sound that you hear when whispering is mainly that of the vibrations of the air in the front of the mouth. The pitch changes associated with saying *hard, hoard, hood, who'd* in a creaky voice are due to the vibrations of the air in the back of the vocal tract. This resonance is the lower in pitch of the two, and is called the first formant. The height of the bars in Figure 1 shows the mean pitch of this formant in the vowels in *who'd, hood, hawed, hod, had, head, hid, heed*. The words are listed from left to right mainly in order of increasing frequency of the overtone that is heard when whispering (the second formant). The highest first formants will be when the second formant is in the middle of its range. The lowest first formants will be when the second formant is very high (as you can hear it is when you whisper *heed*) or when it is very low (which does not occur in most dialects of English; there is no justification for placing the words *who'd, hood* on the left, other than the fact that they have low first formant frequencies). The solid curve in the figure shows the limits on the first and second formant frequencies that can occur, given an average size male vocal tract.

We can now see why so many languages have the five vowels **a, e, i, o, u**, pronounced as in the Spanish words *masa, mesa, misa, mosca, musa* (see Table 2).

119

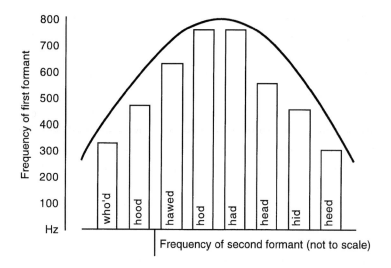

FIGURE 1. The values of the first formants in some English vowels. Except for the vowels in *who'd*, *hood* the vowels are shown in order of increasing values of the second formant (not to scale). The solid curve marks the limits of the possible vowel space.

Figure 2 shows the five Spanish vowels in relation to the boundaries of the formant space that can be produced by an average male speaker. These vowels are fairly evenly distributed near the perimeter of the vowel space. The vowels **i, a, u** are near the corners of this space, and thus as far apart from each other

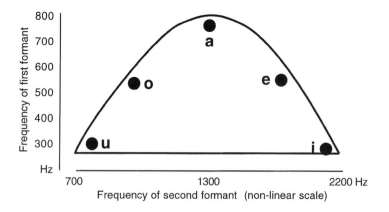

FIGURE 2. The possible vowel space, showing the five Spanish vowels.

as possible. If we want a set of three vowels that will be as auditorily distinct as possible, these are the vowels to use – which is why so many languages have evolved so that they include these vowels. Most languages use more than three vowels so as to have a sufficient number of distinct syllables. If a language has five vowels, like Spanish and many other languages, they will be easy to distinguish if they are distributed in the possible vowel space as shown in Figure 2. English uses a greater number of vowel qualities, making them distinct from one another by allowing them to vary in other ways such as length. The vowel in *heed* is different from that in *hid* not only by having a lower first formant, but also by being longer.

So far we have been considering vowel systems in terms of only the first of the pressures acting on the sounds of languages – the need to make the sounds within a group as auditorily distinct as possible. But the vowel systems of the world's languages also show evidence of another constraint – the pressure for forming patterns. Given that the auditory space for possible vowels is somewhat triangular, the selection of the three most distant vowels **i, a, u** is obviously beneficial. It would be possible for languages to add just one vowel to these basic three, and, indeed, some languages do. But it turns out that far more languages have three, five or seven vowels than have two, four or six vowels. There are plenty of exceptions to this generalization. Standard Italian is an example of a language that has seven vowels, including two types of **e** rather like the French *é* and *è*, and two types of **o**. But many dialects of Italian have lost one or other of these distinctions so that they now have six vowels. The pressures of gestural patterning will probably ensure that most forms of Italian will eventually end up with five or seven vowels.

We have been describing vowels as if they were distinguished by only two formants, but actually the situation is more complicated. There is a third formant that is important for distinguishing some sounds, notably the r-coloured vowel that occurs in American English pronunciations of words such as *bird*, and the French vowel that occurs in *tu* (you). There are also formants with even higher pitches that add to the overall vowel quality. We can see the more complete set of formants that occur by making a computer analysis of the sound waves in a set of words. The top part of Figure 3 shows the sound wave of the words *bead, bid, bed, bad*; below it is a computer analysis showing the component frequencies in the form of a sound spectrogram. Time runs from left to right, as for the sound wave. The frequency scale (shown on the left) goes up to

121

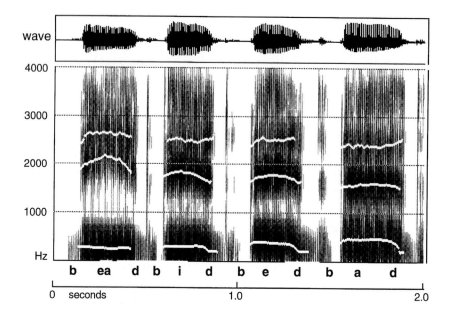

FIGURE 3. The upper part of the figure shows the sound waves produced when the author said the words *bead, bid, bed, bad*. The lower part is a spectrogram of these sound waves in which the complex sound waves are split into their component frequencies (overtone pitches), the amplitude (loudness) of each frequency being shown by the darkness. The three principal groups of overtones (the first three formants) are marked by white lines.

4000 Hz. The dark bands with white lines through them are the formants, with the degree of loudness (the amplitude) of each formant being shown by the darkness of the band.

In this spectrogram the formants are far from straight lines. But in general you can see that the first formant frequency in the first word is lower than it is in the second word, and becomes steadily higher in each succeeding word. You can hear this change in pitch when you say these words with a creaky voice. The second formant frequency goes steadily down, as it does when you whisper them. The third formant also moves slightly down.

We can start building up a list of the major acoustic characteristics of speech sounds by noting those that we need for describing vowels. Table 4 lists the technical acoustic terms and their more familar auditory counterparts. The

122

Table 4. *The major acoustic parameters of vowels and their auditory correlates*

Acoustic parameter	Auditory correlate
Frequency of first formant	Pitch of first group of overtones
Frequency of second formant	Pitch of second group of overtones
Frequency of third formant	Pitch of third group of overtones

vowels of English and most other languages can be characterized by stating the values of these variables.

Consonants

If I had said just the vowels in the words in Figure 3, the formants would have formed more or less steady black bars (with the white lines added in the centre of them). The extensive movements, particularly of the second formant, are due to the consonants. Many consonants can be described in terms of the changes of the formant frequencies of the adjacent vowels. Consonants such as **b**, **d**, **g** are really merely ways of beginning or ending vowels. When forming **b**, the lips are closed. As the lips open at the beginning of each of these words, the formants rapidly increase in frequency, as is particularly evident in the first three words. It is this movement that characterizes a **b** sound. At the end of each of these words the **d** is characterized by a downward movement of the first two formants, but an upward movement of the third formant, which is clearest in the third word.

The nasal sounds represented by **m**, **n** and **ng**, as at the ends of the words *ram*, *ran* and *rang*, can also be characterized largely in terms of their formant frequencies, but they differ from vowels in that the formants, the groups of overtones, are not all as loud as they are in vowels. The nasals are made by blocking the sound from coming out of the mouth while allowing it to come out through the nose, and this affects the relative amplitude (loudness) of the formants. We must add to the list of the acoustic characteristics of speech sounds given in Table 4, noting the possibility of varying the amplitude (loudness) as well as the frequency (pitch) of the three formants. Some other consonants, such as those represented by **w**, **r**, **l**, **y**, as in *what*, *rot*, *lot*, *yacht*, are also marked by these additional characteristics, which are listed in Table 5.

Table 5. *Some additional acoustic parameters of speech and their auditory corre-lates*

Acoustic parameter	Auditory correlate
Amplitude of first formant	Loudness of first group of overtones
Amplitude of second formant	Loudness of second group of overtones
Amplitude of third formant	Loudness of third group of overtones

There are several consonants that are produced without vibrations of the vocal folds. Figure 4 shows the waveform and spectrogram of the English words *sin, shin, thin, fin*, each of which begins with a so-called voiceless consonant. In these consonants the vocal folds are not vibrating and the sound is produced by air being forced through a narrow gap or striking an obstacle so that it becomes turbulent. The spectrogram of the hissing sound of **s** at the top left of the figure shows that it has random energy throughout a wide range of high frequencies.

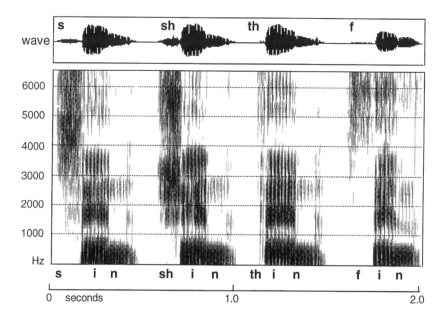

FIGURE 4. The upper part of the figure shows the sound waves produced when the author said the words *sin, shin, thin, fin*. The lower part is a spectrogram of these sound waves. Note that the frequency scale extends higher in this figure than in the previous figure.

Table 6. *The major acoustic parameters required for specifying sounds in which the vocal folds are not vibrating, together with their auditory correlates*

Acoustic parameter	Auditory correlate
Centre frequency of the semi-random noise	Pitch of the voiceless components
Amplitude of the semi-random noise	Loudness of the voiceless components

The **sh** sound has energy that is centred at a slightly lower frequency. If you make a long **s** you can hear that it sounds higher pitched than **sh**. The other two consonants, **f** and **th**, are less loud, and have less well-defined frequency characteristics. This spectrogram also shows a consonant that we have discussed but not illustrated previously, the nasal consonant **n**. At the end of each of these words there is an **n** in which the amplitudes of the formants (the darkness of the bars) are substantially different from those in the vowels.

Voiceless consonants can be characterized in acoustic terms by adding two more variables to the list that we have been building up. As we noted the major difference between **s** and **sh** is in the centre frequency of the band of semi-random frequencies that occur. The major difference between **s**, **sh** and **f**, **th** is that the former pair is louder – has a a greater amplitude – than the latter. With this in mind we will add the acoustic parameters shown in Table 6. A precise specification of voiceless consonants such as those in Figure 4 is beyond the scope of this chapter, and it should be noted that the parameters in Table 6 provide only a very rough characterization of these sounds.

In order to describe the sounds of speech we have to add one more variable, which we discussed at the beginning of this chapter, the pitch of the voice as controlled by the rate of vibration of the vocal folds. This parameter is not relevant in voiceless sounds such as those at the beginnings of the words in Figure 4. But in all other sounds the vocal folds are vibrating at some particular rate that has to be noted. The complete set of acoustic variables is therefore as shown in Table 7. This table summarizes the nine most important acoustic parameters of speech. We can characterize nearly all speech sounds in terms of the values of these parameters.

The parameters listed in Table 7 can be used to synthesize very natural sounding speech, as was demonstrated by the British communications engineer John Holmes over 30 years ago.

Table 7. *The major acoustic parameters of speech and their auditory correlates*

Acoustic parameter	Auditory correlate
Frequency of first formant	Pitch of first group of overtones
Frequency of second formant	Pitch of second group of overtones
Frequency of third formant	Pitch of third group of overtones
Amplitude of first formant	Loudness of first group of overtones
Amplitude of second formant	Loudness of second group of overtones
Amplitude of third formant	Loudness of third group of overtones
Centre frequency of the semi-random noise	Pitch of the voiceless components
Amplitude of the semi-random noise	Loudness of the voiceless components
Fundamental frequency of voiced sounds	Pitch of the voice

Some sounds of the world's languages

As we have seen, many languages have five vowels fairly evenly distributed in the possible vowel space. There are also some well-favoured consonants whose first merit is that they are as different as possible from vowels. Vowels are produced with very little obstruction of the vocal tract, and with vibrating vocal folds. In the best consonants the vocal tract is completely obstructed and the vocal folds are not vibrating. They are the sounds (or, more accurately, the silences) known as voiceless stops, the most common of them being **p, t, k.** About 98% of the world's languages have sounds that are something like these three sounds (although not necessarily exactly as the English versions), and the remaining 2% have sounds similar to two of the three.

The sounds **p, t, k** are very distinct from vowels, but they are less well distinguished from each other. If you say each of these sounds by itself, without a vowel after it, you will be able to hear slight differences in the pitch and loudness of the burst of noise that occurs (the two parameters listed in Table 6). The differences arise from each of these stops being made at a different place within the mouth. There are also small differences in the movements of the formants in the adjacent vowels, similar to those we discussed for **b, d, g.** It is possible to make consonants in which the airstream is blocked at several different places in the mouth. Some languages, such as Malayalam, a Dravidian language spoken in India, have voiceless stops made by stopping the air at six different places within the mouth. But the necessity for auditory distinctiveness without having too great an articulatory complexity forces restrictions on the

Table 8. *Some words contrasting in their nasal consonants in Malayalam, a Dravidian language spoken in India. The headings of the columns are the traditional phonetic terms that specify the place of articulation in the mouth*

Bilabial	Dental	Alveolar	Retroflex	Palatal	Velar
kʌmmi 'shortage'	pʌn̪n̪i 'pig'	kʌnni 'virgin'	kʌṇṇi 'link in chain'	kʌɲɲi 'boiled rice and water'	kuŋŋi 'crushed'

consonant space. Most languages find that it becomes too crowded when there are stops made at more than three or four places in the mouth. Our third constraint on the ways languages develop, the pressure for gestural patterning, is also very evident in the formation of consonant systems. Malayalam, for instance, has not only six voiceless stops but also six voiced stops and six nasal consonants, all made with very similar articulatory gestures. The nasal consonants are illustrated in Table 8 in a phonetic transcription using the symbols of the International Phonetic Alphabet (the IPA). The IPA is an internationally agreed set of symbols that can be used for transcribing all the contrastive sounds that occur in the world's languages. The headings of the columns in the table are the traditional phonetic terms that specify where in the mouth the sounds are made.

Sounds in which there is a turbulent airstream producing noise, such as the English **s**, **sh**, **f**, **th**, are less common than stop or nasal consonants. Some languages, such as Hawaiian, have no sounds of this type. But others, such as Polish and Standard Chinese, have additional possibilities. The best sounds of this type in evolutionary terms – those that produce the loudest and most distinctive sounds for the least effort – are the sibilants like English **s** and **sh**. Polish has not only two sounds rather like these English sounds, but also a third possibility, made with the tongue a little further back in the mouth. Table 9 shows words illustrating the six sibilants of Polish, three voiced and three voiceless. These words are given in the Polish orthography, and also in a phonetic transcription using IPA symbols.

The Polish sibilants shown in Table 9 cannot be adequately described in terms of the parameters in Table 6, which listed only the centre frequency and the amplitude (the pitch and the loudness) of the noise as characterizing voiceless sounds. To describe these sounds accurately we need to include more

Table 9. *Words illustrating the Polish sibilant sounds in between vowels. The columns on the left illustrate voiceless sibilants, those on the right illustrate voiced sibilants*

Orthography	IPA	English	Orthography	IPA	English
kosa	kosa	scythe	koza	koza	goat
kasza	kaṣa	kasha, groats	gaza	gaẓa	gauze
Basia	baca	Barbara (dim.)	bazia	baẓa	catkin

complex properties of the noise. This becomes even more apparent when we try to describe sounds in a language such as Toda, which is spoken in the Nilgiri Hills in the south of India by a few hundred people. Toda is remarkable in that it has four voiceless sibilants – one more than Polish – all of which can be used to distinguish words. The four sibilants that can occur at the ends of words in Toda are shown in Table 10 . Toda has never been written in the roman alphabet, so the words are given simply in IPA symbols.

There are hundreds more consonants in the world's languages than can be described in this chapter. I will conclude by commenting on a few of the more unusual sounds, and noting why they might be less common. So far we have considered sounds in which the vocal folds are either vibrating (as in voiced sounds) or not (as in voiceless sounds). There are, however, intermediate possibilities. The few hundred speakers of Mpi, a language spoken in northern Thailand, produce one set of vowels in which the vocal folds are vibrating somewhat laxly so that the voice is slightly breathy, and another set in which there is more tension in the back of the throat, so that the voice has a harsher, slightly

Table 10. *Words illustrating the sibilant sounds in final position in Toda, a Dravidian language spoken in the south of India*

IPA	English
koṣ	money
pɔs	milk
pɔʃ	language
pɔṣ	name of a clan

Table 11. *Words illustrating vowels with different voice qualities and different tones in Mpi, a Tibeto-Burman language spoken in Thailand*

Tone (pitch)	Lax voice	English	Tense voice	English
Low rising	si	'to be putrid'	si	'to be dried up'
Low level	si	'blood'	si	'seven'
Mid rising	si	'to roll rope'	si	'to smoke'
Mid level	si	(a colour)	si	(classifier)
High falling	si	'to die'	si	(name)
High level	si	'four'	si	(name)

tense, quality. As Mpi also distinguishes words by tones, on similar lines to Cantonese, which we discussed earlier, a single consonant and vowel combination such as **si** may have 12 different meanings as shown in Table 11.

The subtler adjustments of the vocal folds required for lax or breathy voice and tense or creaky voice need greater articulatory precision than that required for regular voiced sounds. They are also hard for listeners to distinguish, particularly as a breathy or creaky voice quality may be simply the person's normal way of speaking. Most of us can think of individuals who have a Marilyn Monroe breathy voice quality or a Louis Armstrong creaky voice quality. As a result these voice qualities are used by a comparatively small number of languages.

The vocal folds can be used to produce not only differences in pitch and voice quality, but also sounds of a very different type. If they are held tightly together and then moved upwards, the air above them will be pushed out of the mouth. But if the lips are closed, or the tongue is making a closure against the roof of the mouth, the air in the mouth will be compressed. When the closure is released there will be a popping sound as the compressed air rushes out. Sounds of this type, which are called ejectives, occur in about 20% of the world's languages, including many American Indian languages. Examples from Quechua, a native language spoken in several regions of Peru and Bolivia, are given in Table 12 in an anglicized orthography. An apostrophe after a letter indicates that the pressure for the sound was produced by the tightly closed vocal folds being raised upward to form an ejective. Although these sounds are auditorily very clear and distinct, the articulatory mechanism is more complex than simply using outgoing air from the lungs to produce pressure. The increased

Table 12. *Some Quechua words in a partially anglicized orthography. The apostrophe indicates that the preceding sound is an ejective, produced with air being pushed out by the closed glottis. The raised* h *indicates aspiration – an extra puff of air after the sound. The* **ch** *sound is similar to* ch *in English (but not exactly the same). The* **q** *corresponds to a sound made with a closure at the back of the mouth, near the uvular*

Plain		Aspirated		Ejective	
chaka	'bridge'	**ch^{h}aka**	'large ant'	**ch'aka**	'hoarse'
kuyui	'to move'	**k^{h}uyui**	'to whistle'	**k'uyui**	'to twist'
qalyu	'tongue'	**q^{h}alyu**	'shawl'	**q'alyu**	'tomato sauce'

complexity accounts for ejectives being comparatively rare. Note, however, that once a language has some ejectives, the principle of gestural patterning often results in there being ejective sounds made with the same articulatory gestures as those used in other sounds in the language.

Probably the most striking unusual sounds found in the world's languages are the clicks that occur in some of the languages spoken in Africa – and nowhere else (as part of a regular language). Click sounds are used by many speakers of English, but not as part of the regular language. The sound that novelists write as *tsk, tsk* is used to express disapproval. Linguists call this a dental click, as it is made with the blade of the tongue touching the upper front teeth. Some people use a clucking sound as a sign of approval or encouragement. This is a lateral click, as air comes in at the side of the mouth. Clicks can also be made with the tip of the tongue curled up so that it touches the roof of the mouth behind the upper front teeth (a so-called alveolar click), and with the body of the tongue raised up against the hard palate in the centre of the mouth (a palatal click). Note that in all clicks the air comes *into* the mouth, as opposed to going out of the mouth as in almost all other sounds. This ingressive airstream is the major characteristic of a click.

Table 13 illustrates the 20 clicks of Nama, arranged in four columns and five rows, labelled with the technical terms that linguists use for describing these sounds. We cannot here give detailed explanations of all these terms; many of them are fairly self-evident from what has been said earlier. The symbols are those of the International Phonetic Alphabet. The distinctions between the columns (the different types of clicks) are fairly easy to hear, but some of the dis-

Table 13. *Words illustrating contrasting clicks in Nama. All these words have a high tone*

	Dental	Alveolar	Palatal	Lateral
Voiceless unaspirated	kǀoa 'put into'	k!oas 'hollow'	kǂais 'calling'	kǁaros 'writing'
Voiceless aspirated	kǀʰo 'play music'	k!ʰoas 'belt'	kǂʰaris 'small one'	kǁʰaos 'strike'
Voiceless nasal	ŋ̊ǀʰo 'push into'	ŋ̊!ʰas 'narrating'	ŋ̊ǂʰais 'baboon's arse'	ŋ̊ǁʰaos 'special cooking place'
Voiced nasal	ŋǀo 'measure'	ŋ!oras 'pluck maize'	ŋǂais 'turtledove'	ŋǁaes 'pointing'
Glottal closure	kǀˀoa 'sound'	k!ˀoas 'meeting'	kǂˀais 'gold'	kǁˀaos 'reject a present'

tinctions between rows (the different click accompaniments, such as aspiration) are fairly subtle. As always in a table with completely filled in rows and columns as here, we can see the pressure of gestural patterning being exerted on the sound system of a language.

Clicks provide many puzzles for those interested in the development of language systems. Because they involve a sucking gesture, they seem difficult to integrate into the stream of speech. But this may not be true, as they have often been borrowed from one language into another. It seems likely that clicking sounds first developed among the ancestors of the people we now call the Bushmen. From there they spread to other tribes such as the Nama of Namibia. A few hundred years ago the Zulus, Xhosa and other Bantu tribes swept southward from central Africa and conquered the Nama and the Bushmen, taking them as wives and servants. They also took their click sounds into their languages. We know for certain that clicks are borrowed sounds in Zulu and other Bantu languages, as these languages did not have any clicks a few hundred years ago. But clicks are now very much part of their regular sound systems, appearing in print with the letter **c** for the dental click (as in the name of the warrior chief *Cetewayo*), the letter **x** for the lateral click (as in the name of the language *Xhosa*), and the letter **q** for a click in which the tongue tip curls up as it makes contact with the roof of the mouth. As a teacher of phonetics for many years, I have found it quite easy to teach people to say words with clicks in them. Students find it much easier than, for example, learning to produce a trilled **r** sound, or to produce some of the sequences of consonants that occur in Polish. Clicks are also auditorily very distinct from other sounds, and, although the different accompaniments (the rows in Table 13) are hard to distinguish, there seems no obvious reason why most languages should not have at least two or three different types of click. Perhaps eventually all languages will evolve so that they include some clicks among their consonants. The Bushmen arrived ahead of us and may have the most evolved languages in the world so far; perhaps in two or three thousand years time most languages will have a few clicks among their consonants.

FURTHER READING AND LISTENING

A book-length version of this chapter with a CD illustrating many sounds is:

Ladefoged, P. *Vowels and Consonants: an Introduction to the Sounds of Languages*. Oxford: Basil Blackwell, 2000.

The sounds of languages are described in most standard textbooks in phonetics, such as:

Borden, G. J. and Harris, K. S., *Speech Science Primer: Physiology, Acoustics and Perception of Speech*, 2nd edition, Baltimore, MD: Williams and Wilkins, 1984.

Clark, J. and Yallop, C., *An Introduction to Phonetics and Phonology*, Oxford: Basil Blackwell, 1990.

Ladefoged, P., *A Course in Phonetics*, 3rd edition, New York: Harcourt, Brace, Jovanovich, 1993.

Lieberman, P. and Blumstein, S. E., *Speech Physiology, Speech Perception, and Acoustic Phonetics*, Cambridge: Cambridge Univesity Press, 1988.

A more comprehensive, but more technical, book describing a very wide range of sounds is:

Ladefoged, P. and Maddieson, I., *Sounds of the World's Languages*, Oxford: Blackwells, 1996.

An introduction to the acoustics of speech and computer speech processing is:

Ladefoged, P., *Elements of Acoustic Phonetics*, 2nd edition, Chicago: University of Chicago Press, 1996.

The evolution of language is treated in:

Hauser, M., *The Development of Communication*, Cambridge, MA: MIT Press, 1996.

6 Ancestral Voices

CHRISTOPHER PAGE

As evening fell on 29 December 1170, four knights entered the north transept of Canterbury cathedral. History remembers their deed but has almost forgotten them, so their names sound faintly now under the wind of 800 years. They were Hugh de Morville, William de Tracy, Reginald Fitzurse and Richard le Breton. The archbishop, Thomas Becket, had insisted that the cloister door should be left open for them because 'God's house should be closed against no man'. The monks who had forced Becket into the cathedral for sanctuary were now hiding from the intruders in the darkest corners of the building, but Becket confronted his assailants; he knew their purpose well enough and rounded upon them in fury. 'So this is my reward for all my presents to you, Reginald Fitzurse, you pander', he cried. Becket, a man with nothing of the lean or hungry scholar about him, refused to make the concessions that they demanded and began to struggle with them. Eventually he fell, facing the altar of St Benedict. The knights left the cathedral and rode back to relative obscurity, but Thomas began a new life, joining the blessed a few days after the feast of Christmas.

The events of that Tuesday evening in 1170 inspired many poems. I would like to concentrate upon one which celebrates Thomas as 'a new soldier who follows the path of [Christ] the new king'. The verses refer to military action by Robert Beaumont, Earl of Leicester, in 1173, the year of Becket's canonisation; perhaps the musical setting dates from the same year. Figure 1 shows a three-voice version of the song that was probably copied in Paris around the year 1250, but there is a two-part version in a manuscript from Burgos in Spain; *Novus miles sequitur* was a truly European piece. The three parts are written in score, the text below the bottom voice, in accordance with medieval practice, but presumably to be sung by all three voices.

Can we hear the sounds of the past?

What did *Novus miles sequitur* sound like in 1173? The answer to that question will only be revealed when we see the face of Thomas Becket in paradise (however briefly). We are not in the fortunate position of those medieval monks who speculated about the sound of angelic singing; they believed that those voices might sometimes be heard on earth. If, by some such miracle, we could hear the voices of the monks, would we be as pleased as the monks were to hear the angels? Possibly not. It has been suggested that the Ancient Greeks would no longer be regarded as the fathers of Western rationalism if we could hear the music that they admired; might a twelfth century rendition of *Novus miles sequitur* be just as alien to our taste and experience? If so, we cannot hope to reconstruct any part of that performance except by making eccentric guesses, never knowing when we are coming close to the mark. Viewed in that light, modern interpretations of medieval music must be wrongheaded and perhaps even mischievous. As a friend of Thomas Becket once remarked, 'there are many frivolous people who use music to advance their own interests' (John of Salisbury, *Policraticus* i:6).

There are persuasive reasons for taking this sceptical position, albeit with a more generous view of the motives involved in modern performance. A liking for clean, clear and objective sounds, with little or no vibrato, seems to be as characteristic of twentieth century music in performance as it is of early-music sonority worldwide in the 1990s. Both kinds of music making have been affected by what is arguably the most important development ever to occur in the history of music, namely the invention of recording, which allows musicians to hear their own performances objectively and repeatedly. Recordings of the 'standard' repertoire show that the prevailing musical tastes of the twentieth century have evolved in ways directly comparable to the emergence of 'early-music' taste; in both, there has been a move towards greater clarity of texture and more even tempo, while portamenti and some other 'romantic' nuances have almost vanished. When set beside this luxurious and persuasive evidence, ready to be forged into a cultural history of our own times, the suggestion that modern performance *can* capture aspects of medieval practice may seem barely worth attention.

And yet the importance of early-music performance cannot be explained away so easily. Let me briefly mention two reasons. The first is broad: performances that are historical remind us that history is performative. To construct and imagine the past, then to express it in acts of writing with a complex and shifting rhetoric – part personal, part professional – is a performative art. The legitimacy of rendering medieval music in a historical manner today is therefore involved with the credentials of a much more comprehensive enterprise. My second reason is just as broad. No matter how emphatic we might wish to be about the impossibility of truly understanding the arts of the past, we can frame that sceptical argument only because we *do* understand something. As I shall argue, we do know a little about the interpretation of music in the twelfth century. Historical performance is so obviously bold, and so obviously a communicative act, that it magnifies some of the fundamental moves we make in approaching the past. When they are writ so large, the crudity of those moves, their daring and their inevitability become plain.

The complacent ear

The Roman dramatist Terence has a famous maxim: 'I am a man and I count nothing human foreign to me'. Let us adapt it: we are human and we regard no music as alien to us. High ideals are usually designed to restrain the strongest impulses of our nature and in this case the impulse is strong indeed; history shows that the sense of hearing may be the most complacent of the five with which we are endowed. Figure 2 shows Hans Holbein's portrait *The Ambassadors*, painted in 1533 and perhaps the best-known picture ever made in England. Behind the two nonchalent diplomats who give the painting its modern title, there are some astronomical instruments and two fine globes, precise tools for an Age of Exploration. In the words of John Donne, these two ambassadors wish to be seen as men who 'have found new sphears and of new lands can write' (*Holy Sonnets*, v, 6). Some of these instruments rest upon a magnificent Turkish rug whose association with a great and hostile Islamic power seems of no account to the ambassadors. They do not see it as an emblem of Othello's 'malignant and turban'd Turk' but as a sign of their broad horizons in every sense. How would they have reacted to Ottoman sounds? The answer probably lies with the first Westerner to record a response to Turkish music, the Flemish composer Johannes Tinctoris. In 1481 he encountered Turks in Naples and heard various melodies that they played upon the *tambura*. 'The extravagance

FIGURE 1. The beginning of *Novus miles sequitur*. Left, transcription; right facsimile.

and rusticity of these pieces', writes Tinctoris, 'were such as only to emphasise the barbarity of those who played them'. After Tinctoris, we shall meet this disdain for 'exotic' music repeatedly during the Age of Exploration. The singing of the Muscovites will be reported as 'dreadful howling' in 1662; the instruments

FIGURE 1. (*cont.*)

of the Congolese as 'wretched and ridiculous' in 1674; the bowed instruments of Siam as 'very ugly little rebecs or violins' in 1693. We may repudiate those judgements if we wish – and I believe we should – but the shade of Tinctoris cannot be dismissed so easily. The *tambura* he heard was a form of the *saz*, a long-necked lute that is still played in Turkey. For many Western listeners

137

FIGURE 2. Hans Holbein, *The Ambassadors*, 1533.

today, the sound of a fifteenth century masterpiece by a composer whom Tinctoris admired, followed by the sound of a *saz*, may be a peculiarly intimate way to sense that some faint, trace elements of Tinctoris's fifteenth century mind remain in our mind, however much we may wish to repudiate them.

Losing the tricks of past trades

This complacency of the ear takes another form which historical performance can combat. We are accustomed in the West to associate change with improvement, and it is a popular supposition that standards of musicianship have continuously improved during the centuries. Had I the style of Sir Thomas Browne I would describe that notion as 'a common and vulgar error'. None the less, early gramophone recordings may sometimes convey the impression that it is correct. There is a recording of Westminster Cathedral Choir that was made so long ago that some of the younger voices we hear were probably silenced on the Somme or at Passchendaele. Recorded in the summer of 1909, we hear a small ensemble selected from the choir singing part of Palestrina's Mass *Aeterna Christi Munera*, directed by their first Master of Music, Richard Runciman Terry. After 90 years, made sombre by events that the singers of 1909 could not have anticipated, the ensemble sounds like the chaos which Satan hears in Milton's *Paradise Lost*:

> a universal hubbub wild
>
> Of . . . voices all confused,
>
> Borne through the hollow dark

and yet how easily we forget that the singers are crowded around a horn and are probably making adjustments to their usual tone, phrasing and balance in order to overcome the limitations of the recording medium. Some of them have apparently been told to project and to hammer the notes to get them onto the wax cylinder. We also forget that nobody in England had much experience of Palestrina's music in 1909, and that the art of the male falsetto still had several decades to wait for the revival initiated in England by Alfred Deller. We do not hear the full choir of the cathedral on that recording so we may wonder whether that chamber ensemble was practised in singing one voice to a part. A good vocal consort cannot be created by extracting singers from a choir, giving them unfamiliar music and making them record with rudimentary equipment in a dry acoustic.

Stainer's 'cacophony'

Where does this leave us? Since we shall never know the truth about medieval sounds until Domesday, I cite John Donne a second time:

> when
>
> Things not yet knowne are coveted by men,
>
> Our desires give them fashion

If we attempt to reconstruct ancestral voices we must boldly fashion the music according to our desires, but our desires can be discreetly fashioned by our discoveries. To illustrate some of the ways in which progress can be made, I invite you to consider the case of John Stainer, composer, antiquarian and organist of St Paul's Cathedral. In 1901 Stainer published a thirteenth century motet with a texture akin to the song with which we began, *Novus miles sequitur*. For all the antiquarian care he lavished upon the piece, Stainer found the harmony 'barbarous' and emphasised the anonymous composer's 'toleration of cacophony'. In giving what is perhaps undue prominence to these remarks let me emphasise that I come to praise Sir John Stainer and not to bury him; he was a founding father of medieval musicology and on paper, at least, we may understand what he means by the 'cacophony' of the twelfth and thirteenth centuries. Let us take for example a transcription of *Novus miles sequitur* (see Figure 1). The part-writing creates many chords of a kind which, for the moment at least, we may classify as harsh dissonances. There are clashes of a major second ('mi-les') and minor second ('no-vi'). None of this is exceptional in music of the twelfth and thirteenth centuries, where melodies combine to make the perfect consonances of fifth and octave, but chafe together, sometimes severely, as they make their way to their destinations.

As a late Romantic, Stainer looked to music for the 'delineation of sentiment'; in common with some modern scholars and performers, he could discover little expressiveness of that kind in any music composed before 1500. That left him a little unsatisfied, but the dissonance of the music, where its most specific and challenging pastness is perhaps to be found, left him very unconvinced. In this respect, something has changed since 1901. Our sense of consonance and dissonance has been profoundly modified by the major composers of the century we are about to leave; when Stainer entered it, 'cacophony' meant sounds that were seriously at variance with the harmony and counterpoint taught in student textbooks, including Stainer's own, *A Theory of Harmony*, first published in 1871. To leaf through the pages of that high-Victorian manual is to appreciate how abruptly a piece like *Novus miles sequitur* violates what Stainer regarded as the treasured principles of counterpoint. In his textbook he proposes that the octave and fifth should be shorn of their 'unmeaning title', that is to say 'the perfect consonances', and he rules that 'the bare fifth is only used in barbarous music'; the third is the interval underwriting any music theory that is 'true to facts'. With polemical vigour, he champions equal temperament where the octave is divided into 12 semitones of equivalent size.

We are now in a position to say that none of this has the absolute authority that Stainer claims for it and all of it would have seemed barbarous to a musician of the 1170s. In *Novus miles sequitur*, and indeed in most polyphonic music before the later fifteenth century, the parts frequently combine to make bare octaves and fifths, sounds which are formed by the translucent ratios of 2:1 and 3:2. Because of this simplicity, medieval musicians were pleased to call them the 'perfect consonances' and they exposed them in their compositions to display precisely the elemental beauty that Stainer hears as a primeval naked-ness. In 1633 John Milton can still refer to the octave as the 'perfect diapason' while evoking its heavenly qualities in every sense of the word (*At a Solemn Music*). There are thirds in the texture of *Novus miles sequitur*, but they are for-tuitous, not tactical, and for the composer they were Pythagorean, quite unlike the corresponding intervals of equal temperament.

My critique of Stainer's position is, of course, just another position; it rests upon practical experiments supported by an international market for recordings of medieval music, and the emphasis I have placed upon Pythago-rean tuning reflects current interests that may soon fade to nothing. None the less, I would argue for a distinction between Stainer's views and the gloss here placed upon them; the gloss is based upon a thicker description of medieval music in both its technical and aesthetic aspects, including more medieval treatises on music than were available in Stainer's day and many more compo-sitions than he was able to study. That is fairly plain. More controversial, but just as important in my view, is the proposal that such information, brought together under artistic impact with the modernist aesthetic of clean, objective sound, allows us to imagine a timbre for a piece like *Novus miles sequitur*: a son-ority that may help us to explain why it is like it is. Stainer, I believe, could not do this; his taste in musical sound was set by Victorian instruments with sonor-ities that could be as lush as the fabrics in the Victorian parlour. By the second half of the nineteenth century the organ, Stainer's instrument, had undergone a minor technological revolution to meet a growing taste for thunderousness and for 'full harmony'; the sparse textures and the dissonances of medieval music cannot be reconciled with these late-Romantic appetites.

Reconstructing sonority: the psaltery

So I repeat the specific question: what did *Novus miles sequitur* sound like in 1173? There is only one way to frame an answer, and that is to reconstruct, as well as we may, the basic changes of sonority that have taken place in Western music. The technique of argument must be as sweeping as the question posed is specific. Musical instruments are a vital source of information for they have made visible, and sometimes measurable, responses to far-reaching changes. The markets of Jidda in Saudi Arabia are still selling lutes very similar to instruments shown on silver reliefs from Iran dating back to the time of the prophet Mohammed, and even earlier, but this conservatism is foreign to the European tradition; in Europe, instruments are the musical tools of a civilisation that long ago achieved a rate of technological advance unsurpassed until the rise of the Pacific Rim economies within our own lifetimes. If we review the last thousand years of musical history in Western Europe we can discern several periods when innovations in sound appear to have been particularly rapid and far reaching.

Let us look closely at the psaltery. Geoffrey Chaucer mentions this instrument in what is perhaps the most famous musical reference in all medieval literature. Describing the chamber of the Oxford scholar Nicholas (and, incidentally, providing the earliest known inventory of a student's room in the process) Chaucer relates that

> And al above ther lay a gay sautrie,
>
> On whiche he made a-nyghtes melodie
>
> So swetely that all the chambre rong;
>
> And *Angelus ad virginem* he song;

The Canterbury Tales, [1 (A)3213–3216].

For all the fame of this passage, the psaltery is an instrument that has never been studied attentively, even though it helps to identify certain nodal points in the history of Western sonorities. I would like to offer the brief outlines of a history here, incorporating some new material. No medieval psalteries survive, but the illustrated manuscripts of the Middle Ages contain hundreds of representations that establish the fundamental design (Figure 3). Sometimes it is played by humans and sometimes by angels; the modern craftsman must assess the size of the instrument from the physique of the player. This is an uncertain process because medieval musicians were generally smaller than their modern counterparts (as for the angels, I decline to comment). A famous medieval encyclopedia, the book entitled *On the Properties of Things* and completed

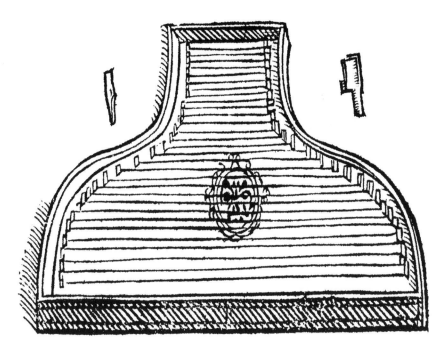

FIGURE 3. A psaltery, with plectrum (left top) and tuning key (right top).

around 1250 by Bartholomew the Englishman, reveals the vital information that 'the best strings of the psaltery are made from latten or silver'. They were plucked with quills, sometimes with the flights attached and cut into nibs similar to the quills used for writing. The resulting sounds must have depended upon many factors, not least the nature and position of the stroke, but some evidence suggests a medieval preference for the brilliance of a firm action near the bridges, rich in high harmonics. Chaucer describes the psaltery playing of Nicholas as so loud that all the chamber rang. Better still, the anonymous fourteenth century English poem *Cleanness* has a description of Belshazzar's feast where women cast metal goblets about to produce 'a ringing of rich metals which clattered as merrily as the music of a psaltery' (lines 1510–1515). The comparison has all the sharpness that we would expect of this particular poet; he associates the sound of the psaltery with a loud, metallic noise, no doubt because its metal strings were often plucked with a vigorous action.

In one illustration of a Paradise garden, dating from about 1410, a young woman holds a psaltery for the infant Jesus to play. From a musical point of view this unorthodox image is telling for it helps to reveal the imminent decline of the psaltery. The key for this interpretation is provided by a passage in Nicole Oresme's commentary upon the *Politics* of Aristotle, compiled around 1370. Oresme was puzzled by Aristotle's reference to a rattle, used to keep children happy 'so that they may not break any of the furniture'. His commentary reads:

> Peut estre que ce estoit un instrument de musique aussi comme est un psalterium, ou les enfans se esbatoient afin que il ne feissent aucun mal.
>
> [Perhaps it was a musical instrument like the psaltery that children amuse themselves with so that they do no harm.]

I will get into difficulties if I suggest that the infant Jesus would break the furniture in the Paradise garden if left unattended, but the practice described by Nicole Oresme surely does interpret that image of around 1410 and heralds the approaching end of the psaltery, regarded as a toy by that time and indeed before. By the sixteenth century it had virtually disappeared, and in 1618 Michael Praetorius illustrates one and labels it 'a very old Italian instrument'. We scarcely hear of the psaltery again until about 1900, when the father of the early-music revival in Britain, Arnold Dolmetsch of Haslemere, reconstructs one for the actress Florence Farr to play as she chants the poetry of W. B. Yeats under Yeats's direction.

Why did the psaltery decline? Since it was plucked with two quills, one in each hand, both hands were needed to play a melodic line of any complexity, alternating their strokes. No accompaniment was possible beyond the occasional striking of a drone course. This appears to have been a well-established technique, but the psaltery could not be pushed very far in the direction of true polyphonic playing. Towards 1400, a technology was found for solving this problem: the psaltery acquired a keyboard and became the harpsichord. By sacrificing the ability to vary both volume and tone colour, and by growing in size throughout the century to accommodate longer strings for deeper pitches, the psaltery might be said to have survived in a new form, its essential characteristics of metal strings plucked by quills finally being obliterated around 1800 with the triumph of the piano.

This miniature history of the psaltery and its sound exposes two vital periods: the generations before 1500, when the psaltery became the harpsichord, and the generations after 1800, when the harpsichord was eclipsed by the piano. These appear to be the two major periods of sound shift in Western music, and it will be helpful to examine them briefly with a wider reference.

Shifting sound forward: Early to Modern

Let us glance at *The Ambassadors* once more (see Figure 2). Below the Ottoman rug, on the lower part of the table, is a set of flutes. They form a set because they are of different sizes, the result of a process whereby makers around 1500 began to magnify the dimensions of certain medieval instruments to create lower-pitch versions, eventually producing whole families; the set of violin, viola, 'cello and double bass is the most familiar and coherent survivor from this revolution. The exploration of lower pitches is the essence of this Early–Modern shift and contemporaries knew that it was taking place. Tinctoris, for example, refers to a certain German invention whereby the lute was supplemented with brass strings 'tuned very deeply through an octave' making the sound 'not only stronger but also very much sweeter'. The theorist Adam of Fulda, active in the last decades of the fifteenth century, declares that Guillaume Dufay (d. 1474) had extended the usable pitches of music downwards for use in his polyphonic compositions. The transformation of the psaltery into the harpsichord resulted in something like a doubling of the string length at the lower end to produce the bass pitches now required. The last third of the fifteenth century brings real bass parts in the music of English and continental composers, both sacred and secular, and the names of singers celebrated for their bass voices; Ockeghem was one of them. The last quarter of the fifteenth century is also the period when the lute acquired a sixth, bass course and when the more advanced lutenists ceased to pluck their strings with a quill plectrum and began to use their fingers, producing a sound that is richer in low harmonics. We think we know the sound of the lute from a multitude of films and costume dramas, but what we know is the beguiling, intimate sound of the Renaissance lute; in the fifteenth century, a trio of lutes, plucked with quill plectra, may have sounded rather less sedate.

The Early–Modern shift owed something to the new printing press. After 1500, the presses sought to provide music for an international community of middle-class amateur instrumentalists, some originally composed a generation or so earlier as vocal music for choirs supported by ecclesiastical institutions.

Instrumental equivalents of alto, tenor and bass were needed to play such music, whence the necessity for magnifying the size of certain instruments so that they moved downwards in pitch. As late as 1538, music by Ockeghem was printed without words for the use of instrumentalists ('TENOR/TRIUM VOCUM CARMINA/ A DIVERSIS MUSICIS/ COMPOSITA', published by Hieronymus Formschneider). The two ambassadors of Holbein's portrait would certainly have needed their graded set of flutes to play the consort music available to them from French presses of the 1530s.

There was no shift of this magnitude in Western music until the decades after 1820: the Romantic shift. After a long period in which the harpsichord and the piano had existed side by side, the piano eclipsed its fellow as the desire for dynamic variation within the phrase and greater control over the balance of parts became ever more ardent. The last Kirckman harpsichord was apparently built in 1809. The piano acquired a cast-iron frame so that string tension could be carried much higher and volume increased; violins acquired higher bridges, tenser strings and a more angled fingerboard, again allowing greater volume. To make themselves audible over larger and louder orchestras, male singers began to cultivate the 'singer's formant', lowering the larynx to produce a vibration that varies between 2 kHz and 3.8 kHz. Since the sound output of an orchestra tends to decrease at frequencies above 1 kHz, this technique allows the singer to be heard clearly. This is perhaps the most important change which has ever taken place in the sound of Western art-singing.

This second shift is part of the passage from a quicksilver, Classical aesthetic to a fuller, more vibrant romantic sound, but it is also a reflex of technological change. An unexpected but vivid illustration is provided by the subplot of Thomas Hardy's *Under the Greenwood Tree*, a novel set during the period of the Romantic shift. An organ, the product of a quasi-industrial workshop, replaces the instruments of a gallery band in a country church. Hardy is evoking exactly the period when English organs underwent a change towards a Victorian ideal of 'smoothness and sonority, effect[s] suggestive of thunder ... gentle melodic movement and legato passages of full harmony'. The instruments of country musicians – essentially artefacts of the eighteenth century, and perhaps even of the seventeenth century in rural parishes – could not meet those ideals; they had to go.

Running sound back: 1800s to the Middle Ages

We have been working forwards. Now let us sprint backwards from the nine-teenth century to the Middle Ages, adding what information we can find on the way. As we pass back through the Romantic shift we lose the singer's formant; no medieval singer needed to adopt a vocal production ensuring a vibration mode around 2.5 kHz. As we pass back into the eighteenth century the sound of many instruments becomes lighter, less full and less penetrating. As we pass back through 1500 and the Early–Modern shift we lose the lowest pitches of voices and instruments, with the associated darker sonorities of bass voices and thick bass strings. By 1300 we are surrounded by the relatively small instru-ments of the Gothic era, especially those plucked with quill plectra, which pro-duce well-defined, distinct sounds rich in high harmonics. The quills used for psalteries were also employed for the lute, gittern and citole, while the harp was generally plucked with the fingernails, producing a sound quite unlike the romantic haze of the modern concert harp but probably akin to the sounds of harpists in Ecuador and Latin America, who derived their instruments, and no doubt some of their techniques, from the Spanish in the sixteenth century. The difference between our experience of the orchestral harp and the medieval experience of early harps is reflected in a passing comment by Paulus Paulir-inus of Prague, writing around 1460: '[the harp] projects its sounds to a great distance . . .'.

Sounds of medieval voices

The evidence for voices is less full, but is occasionally revealing. Around 1325 the musician and theorist Jacques de Liège declares that when a singer moves upwards in pitch the voice gradually mounts in intensity towards a 'greater and more perfect' grade, comparable to the intensification of a quality such as colour or whiteness:

> When the same man ascends from low pitches to high ones, he emits more breath when he sings the high notes than when he sings the low ones and he makes more and stronger impulses. A similar process to this intensification of the voice can be observed – it is a certain quality – when another quality is

> intensified, as for example colour or whiteness. There we find a movement from
> a lesser grade of such an essence to a greater and more perfect grade.

This account suggests a vocal production that remains in one register – either chest voice or head voice – the sound therefore becoming stronger and more brilliant as the pitch mounts. (The terms 'head voice' and 'chest voice' are found by the thirteenth century.) Elsewhere in his massive treatise, Jacques de Liège confirms the evidence of surviving compositions by remarking that a singer performing polyphonic music is expected to sing about 11 notes as a general maximum, which accords with the view that they were generally able to use a single register. (One author of similar date declares that sexual abstinence improves the voice, but we have no way of establishing whether singers generally took his advice.)

What of vibrato in voices and instruments? The vast majority of medieval instruments were incapable of producing it (the psaltery is an obvious example); singers, I believe, generally did not choose to. Important evidence is forthcoming once again from Jacques de Liège. He offers a passing remark, but one that is significant because a discriminating consciousness with regard to sound is uncommonly difficult to define, especially for an age long past, and he uses precise language. He declares that singers should not mistune a note 'by even as little as a comma'. The Pythagorean comma is an interval of 23.5 cents, spanning less than a quarter of the modern equally tempered semitone. A simpler way of expressing this is to say that the margin of error that Jacques de Liège allows a singer is small enough to be fitted eight and a half times into the gap between C and D (or any other tone step) on the modern piano. His comment makes sense only if the singers of 1325 were using a shallow vibrato or none at all. Many modern singers use a vibrato that is at least a half a semitone wide. (I am not suggesting that medieval singers were more skilled or exacting than their modern counterparts; we have no way of knowing that. I am suggesting, however, that they used a technique which made imperfections of tuning more apparent.)

Finally, we return to *Novus miles sequitur*, in honour of St Thomas Becket. How does the material we have reviewed – and anything we may add in passing – help to make sense of it? The three parts of *Novus miles sequitur* have the same compass, a range of nine notes, allowing the piece to be sung by three singers employing the same register, growing stronger and more brilliant as the pitch rises. Three singers performing in exactly the same tessitura and in the same register of their voices would provide the means for a blended sound, and Jacques de Liège in 1325 is emphatic that singers should have 'good and *concordant*' voices. The evidence that medieval singers used little vibrato, or none at all, helps to explain the contemporary preoccupation with tuning and temperament. Vibrato disguises the tuning by somewhat diffusing the ear's sense of where the centre of a note lies; etching their lines with little or no vibrato, medieval singers would have allowed the ear to savour the perfect consonances of octave and fifth in their purity. These intervals give shape to many of the chords in *Novus miles sequitur*. In such a performance, the dissonances of the piece are not softened, nor treated as exotic; the dissonances are the noise, so to speak, of the perfect consonances being prepared and are heard as beauty in the making. The abundant evidence of musical instruments suggests a Gothic preference for relatively bright sounds, rich in high harmonics, using the upper part of the voice, and moving cleanly from note to note (portamenti are impossible on virtually all medieval stringed instruments save the fiddle).

Fact and phantasy

At the beginning of this chapter I ventilated the idea that any modern performance of a medieval piece must be a phantasy. So it must be, but the quality is something akin to the 'high-raised phantasy' of John Milton. In his poem *At a Solemn Music*, Milton implies that we may have an experience of musical beauty where we sense a meaning in the sound – a truthfulness – that we cannot entirely explain in terms of present delight. Milton, whose feeling for musical sound must have been all the sharper for his blindness, believes that this sense of meaning is an intimation of the future: of heaven. Being perhaps blinder than Milton, I cannot sense that; I believe it is an intimation of the past: of ancestral voices.

FURTHER READING AND LISTENING
Brown, H. M. and Sadie, S., *Performance Practice: Music before 1600*, Basingstoke: Macmillan, 1989.
Boorman, S., *Studies in the Performance of Late Mediaeval Music*, Cambridge: Cambridge University Press, 1983.
Gothic Voices, *Music for the Lion-Hearted King*. Hyperion CDA 66336 (compact disc) [including *Novus miles sequitur*].

Knighton, T. and Fallows, D., *Companion to Medieval and Renaissance Music*, Oxford: Oxford University Press, 1992.

Munrow, D., *Instruments of the Middle Ages and Renaissance*, Oxford: Oxford University Press, 1976.

Page, C., *Voices and Instruments of the Middle Ages: Instrumental Practice and Song in France 1100–1300*, London: Dent, 1987.

7 Shaping Sound

BRIAN FERNEYHOUGH

The idea of shaping sound may well appear relatively unproblematic, even innocuous. After all, the shaping and ordering of sonic phenomena is presumably what composition is, and always has been, about, even though the means employed have differed widely over time, in keeping with constantly evolving social and aesthetic priorities. Even cursory reflection, however, reveals soon enough the deep fissures and ambiguities with which the concept is riven: the more we think about it, in fact, the more confusingly elusive it becomes. Put another way; though we frequently respond to perceived ordering of sound with extraordinary immediacy, we are not always able to render precise account to ourselves of the manifold paths over which this or that group of sounds has come to be invested with meaning, particularly when the sounds in question, as so often with unfamiliar, innovative or experimental constructs, are not immediately subsumable to already extant and, by implication, more conventionally evaluable categories of appreciation. While music is often discussed, in lay parlance, in terms of its elegance, it is not at all clear that it is the sort of elegance amenable to definition in terms of mathematical concision; indeed, it might legitimately be argued that ambiguity and indirect statement represent particularly powerful tools in the composer's arsenal of context-creating devices. Nevertheless, what we hear is, in large measure, dictated by what we are led to expect to hear. In the space available I will not be in a position to offer a generalized proposal concerning how and under what circumstances music might be a language. For my own part – that is, with respect to my own creative practice – it suffices to accept that musical discourse is somewhat amenable to being treated as if it were language; that is to say, exhibits, at least potentially, a sufficient number of structural analogies to the sort of hierarchic orderings typically encountered in verbal utterance to permit further procedural extrapolation. It is perhaps to be regarded as a melancholy but unavoidable fact that music, by and large, has remained resistant to the nurturing and development of a vocabulary exclusive to its own proper concerns; as a perpetual late developer among the fine arts it has remained obstinately promiscuous in its adoption of a veritable ragbag of terms from the fine arts, architecture or various scientific fields of study, often enough with little or no explicit recognition of the connotative baggage with which such terms are customarily burdened. In the unfolding of the various narrative strands making up what is loosely termed the history of twentieth century composition, it will thus be necessary to deal with a set of analytical tools less than perfectly adapted to issues of consistency and falsifiability than is usual in many other disciplines. While uncomfortably aware of this issue, I should emphasize that, for me, the harnessing and melding of the spiritual power of creative misunderstanding lies at the very heart of present-day aesthetic experience.

This question of language must be confronted even more directly, I think, when one is discussing some of the astoundingly diverse attempts made by contemporary musicians to achieve a working understanding of that most banal of media, sound. It is for this reason, I think, that the last 50 years have witnessed a number of wide-reaching attempts to re-articulate both the substance and mission of contemporary music in terms derived more or less directly from other intellectual fields, particularly those of the physical sciences and philosophy. In dissecting aspects of the composer's conceptual grasp with respect to these external scales of reference we will necessarily be questioning essential constitutive facets of our own world view – what, in other words, *count* as significant criteria for the adequate apperception, assimilation and assignment of meaning to discrete sonic entities.

That this is not merely academic hairsplitting will be evident from the very inclusive nature of the term 'shaping' itself. Nothing, at this stage, has been said regarding what might be termed the perspective of the task, i.e. the mental distance from which the nature of sound *as material* is customarily evaluated. It is certainly not insignificant that the very term 'material' has itself undergone radical mutation in the quite recent past. In contrast to a period of what has been seen by some as a naively aggressive expansion of instrumental and vocal sound-generating means characteristic of New Music during the 1950s and early 1960s, the last decade or so has witnessed an increased re-sensibilization to what might be termed the semantic dimension of composed sound, including, but not restricted to, the employment of intermodulation between the stylistic physiognomies of sometimes widely separated historical epochs. In his *Aesthetic Theory* the social philosopher and sometime composer Theodor Adorno cogently argued for a generous interpretation of 'material' which explicitly invokes culturally immanent dimensions inhering, as historically accreted 'sediment', in the naked physical phenomenon. We will have occasion to return to the productive tensions arising from the ideological opposition of objectively measurable sonic data and their culturally redolent artefactuality at a later point. Suffice it for the present to underline that, unlike many another art form, music conspicuously lacks any obvious referent external to itself and is thus largely constrained to enter into conversation with its own past – the active memory, as it were, of its own successivity and anteriority – if it wishes to advance beyond an overly restrictive assertion of unadorned and ultimately mute and inaccessible presence. Surely one of the core issues emerging from the tumultuous aesthetic travails of our century has been whether and, if so, how, the artificial shaping, rendering and conjoining of sounds can be said to be 'expressive', either in some unexplained manner recursively, in and of themselves or else by some form of manoeuvre of mimetic evocation.

In order to approach my topic as inclusively as possible, I propose to deal successively with four distinct but interrelated areas of concern. First, I will examine several of the historical precedents for the recent expansion and enrichment of the timbral dimension in instrumental composition; after that I propose to outline something of the rationale underlying the sudden expansion of sound-generating techniques for conventional instruments since 1945. My third topic will be the rapid expansion in strategies of formal disposition arising from the incorporation of certain aspects of non-musical, specifically socio-political discourses into our speculative understanding of how the mutual inter-dependence of temporal perception and musical architecture might be said to function, while my fourth and final topic will treat the creative consequences arising from the deepened appreciation of the internal structure of individual sounds and sound complexes made possible by recent developments in computer analysis. Unfortunately, even a summary outline of this latter field would necessitate several presentations for itself alone; I hope nevertheless to transmit to you some sense of which of its facets seem to me most important and how they have come to intensify the composer's understanding and appreciation of aspects of sound comportment, long accepted and pragmatically employed, which are now in principle available for more formally integrated and considered application.

In most occidental music up until the seventeenth century, specific instrumental timbre was not one of the most pressing concerns of the composer. This was certainly due, in part, to the vagaries of performance circumstance and the fact that, more often than not, the composer himself was actively involved in the realization of his works and was thus able to omit without further compunction precise indications as to the apportionment of instrumental sonorities to the musical voices at hand. Even so, this approach cannot but appear somewhat alien to our own sense of propriety, given our immersion in the relatively unchanging rituals of reproductive and museal musicmaking. For a considerable time now our major institutional formations at least have had their makeup graven in stone, and it has been the flourishing Early Music movement that has contributed much to our understanding of the flexibility of presentation which our own epoch has lost.

Percussion, the urban sound

What changed the sound world of Western concert music forever was the sudden increase in the importance of that hitherto most neglected of orchestral departments, percussion. In large measure this sea change is attributable to the powerful influence of vernacular musics, in particular jazz. It is not fortuitous that North America was at the forefront of this development, nor that the first indisputable masterpiece for percussion ensemble should be *Ionisation* (1934) by Edgard Varèse, an expatriot Frenchman working in the cosmopolitan frenzy of New York in the 1920s (Figure 1). When considering the *shaping* of sound, one might be forgiven for imagining that there is little leeway in the realm of struck, scratched or otherwise resonated bodies. In fact, this is far from being the case, as many innovative and sometimes virtuoso percussion works of later decades clearly demonstrate. The often explicitly industrial origins of many of these new sounds, their rootedness in a familiar urban environment, has frequently resulted in a revitalised approach to the mimetic and, with it, an intensified appreciation of the sheer physicality involved in making music.

With *Ionisation* we certainly find ourselves in uncharted waters, bereft of the

FIGURE 1. The final page of the score of *Ionisation* (1934) by Edgard Varèse.

structural support traditionally provided by pitch and interval and, in consequence, forced back upon the more intense reconfiguring of elements of musical discourse previously considered secondary or peripheral to a statement's core import. The path chosen by the composer to compensate for this potential deficiency was that of a radical rethinking of the function of the rhythmic motive – that is, the smallest unit of identifiable individual invariance (or, at least, consistency) amenable to being assembled into larger periods or phrases. What is particularly fascinating in this regard is the way the composer manipulates the many simultaneously unfolding layers of activity at his disposal. Although primarily concerned with highlighting those characteristics of a given instrument's line that distinguish it most readily from its neighbours, Varèse has also ingeniously created numerous momentary points of confluence, whereby a larger pulse structure, articulated by those fleeting moments of simultaneity occurring between two or more lines, becomes audible. It is perhaps the celebratory sense of iridescent unease emanating from the unstable intersection of each instrumental line's spirited assertion of untrammelled linear independence and its sly constraint within a larger matrix of communal order which is this extremely original work's most readily identifiable quality.

The newness of this vision resides less in the obvious innovatory élan that deploys the penetrating stridency of sirens to periodically rend its sonic fabric than in the altogether remarkable manner in which the composer contrives to subsume such brutal invasions on the part of the outside world to their musically assimilable component features: duration, volume, pitch-contour and the like. The final cross-referencing and summatory synthesis of these dimensions in the culminating entry of a piano, contributing violent clusters on groups of adjacent keys, serves once more to re-focus the listening ear and mind on the multitude of coherent musical relationships in the piece rather than allowing them to dwell merely on the surface texture, however varied and assertive it may be. It cannot be sufficiently emphasized, I believe, that to shape sound is simultaneously to enunciate (*pace* Arnold Schönberg) *idea*, the sense that material states, in aesthetic experience, are somehow transubstantiated, imbued with their own form of awareness or life force. *Ionisation* exemplifies almost absurdly precisely Arnold Schönberg's description of the musical idea as a form of unrest which, already animating the individual motive, is actively manifest in the unpredictable succession of transformations that the natural instability of the initial configuration sets in motion. In *Ionisation*, however, one senses that the dramatic curve of unrest–transformation–repose/resolution underlying Schönberg's largely tradition-oriented framework of aesthetic values has been decisively abandoned in favour of a more sharp-etched rejoicing in the positive nature of permanent transformation, set free from any need for ultimate resolution. The revolutionary nature of *Ionisation*'s sound world made possible an equally radical break with prior, all-too-comfortable reliance on received narrative convention.

After 1950, closely coinciding with the so-called 'parametric' deconstruction of the individual sonic event into its constituent basic qualities – primarily pitch and duration, although on occasion extending to intensity, timbre and even spatial distribution – the status of percussion had been elevated to equal that of the more traditional instrumental families, particularly in the field of chamber music–scale ensembles then much in vogue. The subtle gradations of nuance now made available by the pitched percussion, in particular, made these instruments invaluable allies in the search for ways of structually manipulating timbre. Just as 12 tone technique ordered pitch and, later, rhythm according to predetermined patterns, so now composers saw themselves in a position to extend this principle to more complex dimensions of colouristic synthesis. Although many composers availed themselves of these means, it was the Frenchman Pierre Boulez, in his chamber cantata *Le Marteau sans Maître* (1954), who provided the most widely admired model for emulation (Figure 2). The delicate intermingling of unpitched instruments such as maracas and claves with the wide range and scintillating colours of the exotic xylomarimba conspired to create a palette of textural nuance of unsurpassed variety, especially when combined with the manifold expressive possibilities of guitar, viola, flute and soprano voice. By selecting a group of instruments offering an unbroken transition from the most short-lived sound (claves, xylomarimba, plucked viola, guitar) to the most sustained (alto flute, bowed viola, voice), Boulez was able to weave a fabric of unprecedented pliancy and expressive authority.

At the same time as chamber music was welcoming the colourful palette offered by percussion, both mainstream orchestral composers and those more isolated, experimental figures such as the main American pupil of Schönberg, John Cage, were, in their divergent ways, instrumental in stretching the ear's capacity for the structural assimilation of unfamiliar timbres. Particularly in the latter instance, the spectrum was extended by the introduction of 'found

FIGURE 2. *Le Marteau sans Maître* (1954) by Pierre Boulez.

objects' such as brake drums or, in certain works by the Californian composer and theorist Harry Partch, the creation of totally new categories of resonating body such as his cloud chambers, fabricated from sawn-off glass carboys, which, when struck, produce delicate but long-sustaining sounds akin to those of some Balinese gamelan orchestras. Of even more long-term significance than newly invented sonorities was the intensified appreciation for the sheer scope of possible sound sources stimulated by Cage in many of those works in which the choice of specific instruments or objects is left to the performer, or else demands of the latter the exhaustive mining of sonic potential latent in a given situation, such as the ensemble of sounds to be drawn from dragging a large number of chairs from one place to another. The often more inherently erratic spectral characteristics of certain instruments, particularly gongs and tamtams, encouraged composers to seek ways in which this variability could be harnessed anew – either by more conscious definition of structural (rather than sonic) function or else – as in Stockhausen's *Mikrophonie* 1 – offering the performer an essentially actionistic map of permitted motions of a microphone across the stage, as it were, of the tamtam's surface. The amplified results of these actions, whatever their actual detailed content, are regarded as the legitimate sonic realisation of the work's engendering context.

All of these avenues, and more, opened up by percussion developments undoubtedly conspired to bring about a fundamental reimagining of more familiar instrumental resources. In particular, there occurred a transitory conjunction between Adorno's much-quoted pronouncements concerning the necessity to compose utilizing only the 'historically most advanced state of musical material' and the immensely compulsive drive by many composers towards the liberation, as they saw it, of sonic invention from the straitjacket of serially constrained principles of organization. This confluence illustrates, perhaps, how heavy with far-reaching consequences certain misinterpretations of theoretical or polemic positions have proved themselves during the course of the last half-century. Particularly in countries influenced by the German tradition of 'advanced' musical thinking, Adorno's strictures were interpreted in the context of that historically accreted (in his words 'sedimented') semantic connotation which any cultural artefact embodies as its most essential feature. In the eyes of a number of significant composers, on the other hand, 'most advanced' was already understood to mean the latest developments in the employment of instruments as concrete, quasi-abstract sound sources largely

divorced from the traditional reservoir of musical meaning that they had hitherto served to articulate, and within whose bounds the very lineaments of their
identity had been traced. The 'development of material' had thus curiously
come to mean precisely the opposite of that which Adorno had been advocat-
ing, and the transformation of the instrument by means of its sonic defor-
mation and alienation was to emerge as possibly the major defining innovative
attribute governing thinking on the shaping of instrumentally induced sound
in the 1960s.

Sonorism and sound mass

Typical of this way of mobilizing the hitherto inchoate, 'shadow' side of traditional instruments was a group of 'sonorist' composers, centred in Poland in
the 1960s and most readily identified with Krzysztof Penderecki, whose sound
world was graspable largely in terms of mass, volumes and contours. Indeed,
most of the scores of this school contain visual images more redolent of spatially disposed global figures or even biomorphic organisms than resembling
received conventions of musical notation. The ubiquitous presence of tightly
woven, impenetrable clusters of pitches succeeded in effectively de-
differentiating the various degrees of mutual interaction that had previously
served to convey structural moment, proposing in their place the impingement,
superimposition and interpenetration of planes of generalized motion, mobile
layers of translucent patina lending luminance and perspective to the aperiodic
convulsions animating the overall panorama. Whilst frequently impressive as
powerfully immediate and urgent expressive ploys, such strategies offered little
opportunity for more richly ramified internal working or the gradual accretion
of significance to which such elaboration frequently gives rise. It would nevertheless be unjust to underestimate the extent to which this drastic remapping
and recalibration of sonic rhetoric served to open the inner ears of another generation of composers to future opportunities for such elaboration at a later
time. Penderecki's *Anaklasis* (1959–60) is an early and ambivalent example of
this tendency – ambivalent in the sense that the composer is seeking first the
stark opposition and then progressive synthesis of massed cluster materials
and more punctual, rhythmically precise percussive textures (Figure 3). Balan-
cing the diversity of attack and timbre of the percussion we encounter many

160

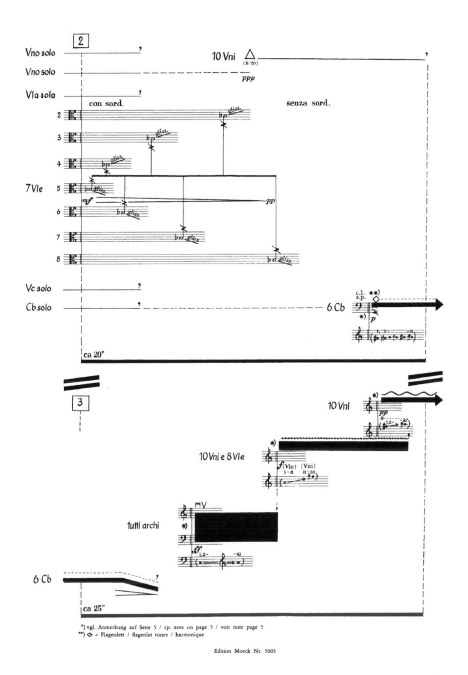

FIGURE 3. *Anaklasis* (1959–60) by Krzysztof Penderecki.

innovative string techniques such as striking the string with the wood of the bow, tapping the body of the instrument with the fingers and bowing behind the tailpiece at a point giving rise to complex sustained noises of indefinite pitch. This work is further quite instructive in suggesting to us to what extent our visual faculties, mediated by various alternative notational conventions, are instrumental in subtly prescribing to our imaginative faculties appropriate grammars of contextually licit discourse.

Sonic innovation, critical theory and social Utopia

The third of my initial subcategories comprises that group of composers whose thinking reflects tendencies towards increased differentiation of playing technique and instrumental usage while distancing itself decisively from what might be construed as its adoption of a typically unreflected stance with respect to the uncritical espousal of long-discredited ideologies of expression. Composers belonging to this category have consistently sought to expand still further the sound-producing means of their chosen instruments, but with very different aims in mind. The German composer Helmut Lachenmann has made abundantly clear on numerous occasions that his primary concern is with proposing a certain view of the Central European tradition via its dialectical undermining, dismemberment and reconstitution through a rigorously critical mirror. Far from seeking out the most conventionally effective or attractive extensions of instrumental capability, he obstinately sets out to create an instrument reduced to its bare physical bones, from which may emerge new sonic contexts, new paratraditions, based on the exhaustive definition and exploitation of playing techniques evolved exclusively from the permutated recombination of possible actions involving any part of the instrument's anatomy, thus thrusting into the foreground the mode of generation – the shaping – of each sound as an inalienable component of its aesthetic import. By these means Lachenmann aims at re-mobilizing tradition, *den schönen Schein* [the beautiful illusion of art], in its own negative image, as an integral part of the resonating body itself and, incidentally, paying homage to Adorno's vision of historically sedimented material mentioned earlier. The extreme reductionism exacted by this approach is especially evident in *Pression* (1969). This piece for solo cellist represents a frontal attack on practically the entirety of our assumptions concerning formal

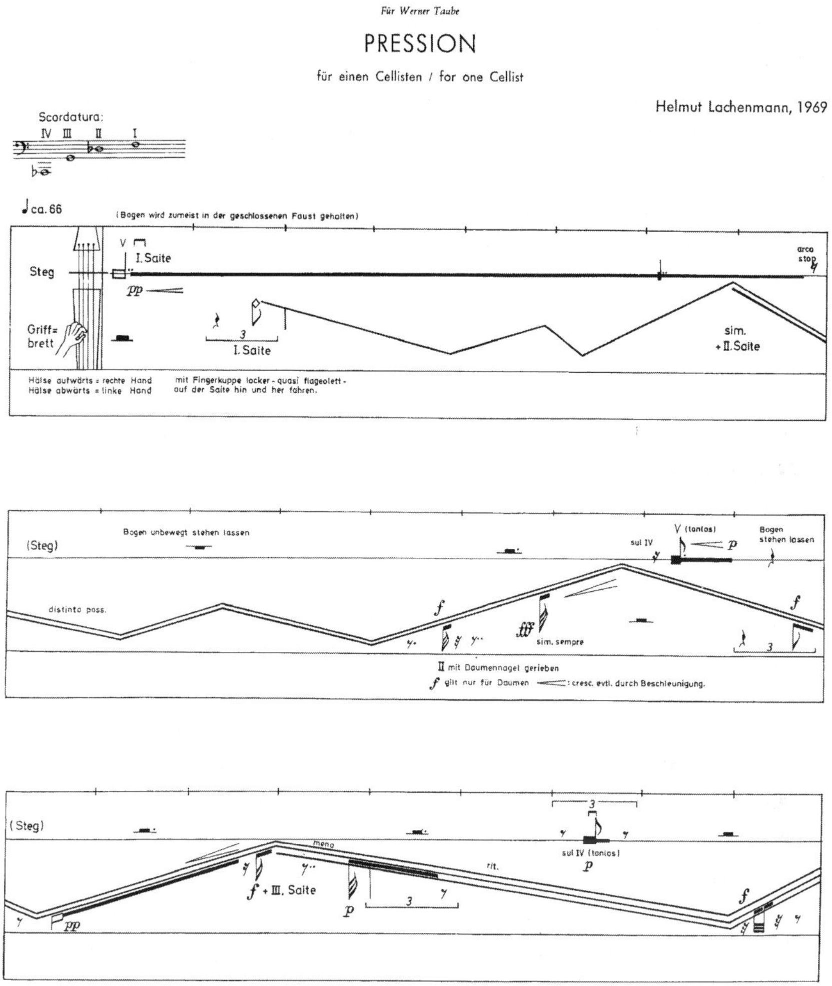

FIGURE 4. *Pression* for solo cellist (1969) by Helmut Lachenmann.

cogency, mediatory expression and categories of appropriate performer comportment (Figure 4). An examination of the score reveals very little in the way of standard notational practice; instead, the eye encounters representations of the body of the cello itself, diagrams of unconventional ways of holding the bow, some involving both left and right hands, as well as many more techniques calculated to disorient the unwary. The opening page of the score gives immediate warning of things to come: since there is very little to be heard by way of articulate sound, the visual dimension assumes a much greater responsibility for marking the structural subdivisions than is customary, thereby setting up a further obstacle to unreflected listening. Primary, for Lachenmann, is the desire to see each successive event provide a further stepping-stone towards the creation of adequate subjective criteria for the conscious positing of speculative listening categories on the part of the auditor: at the same time we continue to be made uncomfortably aware of the extent to which the fracturedly pro-visional discourse of this composition resists and subverts just such an all-too-comfortable reconstruction of any self-consistent aesthetic habitus, the pre-sumption of which, as historical instance, is nevertheless an essential if paradoxical prerequisite for the adequate reception of this many-layered musi-cal experience.

Dieter Schnebel is a composer who, for many years, collaborated with a highly specialized group of vocal soloists, the Schola Cantorum Stuttgart, in the elaboration of a series of works that might best be described as spiritual exer-cises harnessed in the service of social and spiritual liberation. In and through the very extremity of demands, both intellectual and physical, imposed on the performers during the learning process, the composer aims, ultimately, at empowering the performer's psyche by expanding the individual awareness of the freedom of choice inherent in specific compositional situations. The extens-ive utilization of material insights won from the study of the science of pho-netics enabled Schnebel to decompose the body of (generally intuitively employed) techniques used in acts of human speech into its smallest component units; that is, the many nuances available in the positioning of the vocal organs (tongue, teeth, lips and palate). By recombining these into hitherto unheard-of constellations he demanded of his performers both a high degree of intellectual application and an intoxicating sense of enhanced physicality, not to speak of a sharply honed awareness of group collaboration. Although it is possible to argue that Schnebel's work in this field would not have been possible without the relentless quantification of sonic characteristics brought about by integral serial thinking, his aims could not have been further from those of the immedi-ate postwar idealists gathered at the Darmstadt Summer Courses around 1950, in that, whereas the Darmstadt composers were aiming primarily at the super-cession of discredited stylistic and ideological stances, Schnebel wields his ana-lytical tools with a view to creating the social conditions for the expression of a much more egalitarian and, ultimately, more obviously irrational musical discourse.

Schnebel's *Atemzüge* (1968), from a larger group of compositions entitled *Maulwerke* [*Mouthpieces*] moves even further away from the treatment of sound as objective material amenable to manipulation (Figure 5). Instead it aims at the realization of an ideal of musical substance no longer seeking to *represent* material by means of a mediating instrumental or vocal vehicle, but itself to annul any clear distinction between the making audible of the body's own neural mechanisms and musical communication. The score in its entirety consists of visual representations of degrees of tension induced by detailed differentiation of the act of breathing. As with Lachenmann's *Pression*, but far more radically, this score vehemently insists on its direct rapport with the instantiation of physically immediate states, the while conspiring with equal tenacity to subvert the very foundations of the natural history of our listening assumptions. In this project, Schnebel was less concerned with new aspects of material than with the circumstances of its production, in particular the psychological, cerebral and physiological transformations accompanying the act of realization.

Parameter to spectrum: a natural history of sonic legitimation

Moving on from the local shaping of sound and its attendant socio-cultural priorities to a brief examination of how the shaping process has been projected onto the larger screen of specifically formal concerns, we nevertheless are brought full circle back to the nature of, and rationale for, the individual sound, since it is in this arena that the major issues of large-scale meaning have been primarily engaged. One of the most significant artistic figures in this struggle was, and still is, Karlheinz Stockhausen. The reason for this is to be sought not only in the innate qualities of individual works, as considerable as they may be, but also in his constant speculative engagement with these issues. In articles such as *Wie die Zeit Vergeht* [*How Time Passes*] Stockhausen attempts to outline a global theory addressing the necessary interrelatedness of temporal and pitch perception via examination of psycho-acoustic threshold values of frequency at which discrete pulses are transformed into the perception of continuous pitch. Regardless, in the final analysis, of the degree to which his theories can be

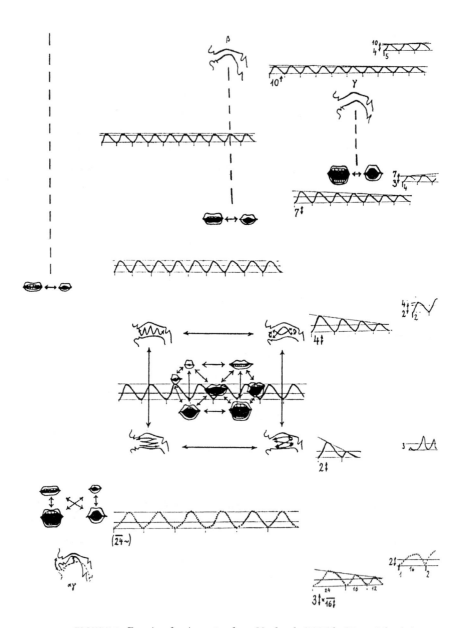

FIGURE 5. Exercises for *Atemzüge*, from *Maulwerke* (1968) by Dieter Schnebel.

successfully defended *as* theories, their consistency of internal structure played a vital role in assuring the sort of support system necessary to any large creative enterprise.

At an early stage of postwar renewal, both Stockhausen and Boulez were committed to the shaping of individual sounds on the basis of their assemblage from series of abstract values defining individual aspects of each sound – what might be termed its salient parameters. Even at the time the severe limitations imposed by this practice on any form of connected discourse were apparent. In particular, it was clear that series of values applied to only one musical dimension were not real in any musically palpable sense until brought together with those other characteristics necessary for the creation of an audible event. No matter how artfully such values were theoretically interrelated, however, in practice the resultant isolated sound proved obstinately resistant to being assimilated into a larger continuity. The translation from intellectually satisfying matrix to aurally plausible discourse remained, for the most part, obstinately beyond composers' reach. Although numerous strategies were tested, including frequent recourse to symmetrical patterns, it was quickly accepted by the leading figures of the day that there was no way of deducing large-scale discourse from isolated local events that was both intellectually and intuitively convincing. Confonted with this impasse, Stockhausen conceived in quick succession the principles of Group Form and Moment Form, the former no longer applying serially derived sonic characteristics to single events but to larger (and hence more aurally coherent) constellations or swarms of sound, the latter countering the enfeeblement of overarching narrative structure by the decisive rejection of linear conventions of discourse. It is important, I think, to bear in mind that the young Stockhausen maintained an almost mystical attachment to the communicative inner life of individual sounds. His private correspondence with Karel Goeyvaerts, a colleague from the early Darmstadt years, is replete with indications of the weight assigned, *pars pro toto*, to such local, briefly flourishing life forms.

The gradual, disorderly and perhaps slightly unwilling relinquishment of the sovereign Cartesian order manifest, if only as seductive mirage, by total serial techniques led to a proliferation of individually tailored solutions to the problem of achieving conceptual consistency on both the large and small scale, the most important of which was possibly the systematic espousal of statistical operations carried out on randomly derived source materials by the Greek composer Iannis Xenakis. Rather than pursue these radically diverging paths in more detail on this occasion, I would like to examine the increasingly significant contribution made by electronic sound synthesis and analysis to provisional resolution of this dilemma.

Very early essays in the electronic medium adhered to many of the serial principles already current in instrumental contexts. The *Elektronische Studie II* (1954) by Stockhausen adhered rigidly to the employment of the number five in the definition of nearly all its aspects; not only were the frequencies of individual component pure sine waves determined, albeit somewhat abstrusely, by the use of this value but each individual sound complex (consisting of five component pitches) was assigned to one of five categories according to whether the relations between its pitches were calculated as constant ratios of 1, 2, 3, 4 or 5 times 25 to the fifth root. The number of chords present at any one moment could likewise vary between 1 and 5. Listening to this piece today one is struck by the high level of homogeneity with respect to timbre, but also by the non-natural nature of attack and decay characteristics applied to individual sound complexes, this latter being a consequence of the tape cutting and splicing required in order to assemble the final result.

This issue of irritating artificiality, which dogged the medium for many years, was not present to any notable degree in the other main track followed, that of Musique Concrète, in which natural sounds (coins spinning, distorted voices etc.) were recorded close up and subsequently played back at different tape speeds, reversed and edited into other sounds. A remarkable range of works was produced in the space of a few years, and later works of Stockhausen, among others, integrated residual serial techniques with recorded and manipulated source sounds to remarkable effect. Nevertheless, it was not until the advent of digital editing and transformation that means began to become available for the wholesale moulding and reshaping of our sonic environment. Early essays in computer-generated sonic structures were frequently directed, as in the case of Stockhausen's *Studie*, towards the definition of totally synthesized sound complexes; in recent years the tendency has been towards a new fusion of natural sources and digital editing, spectral filtering and temporal dilation. One of the most striking examples of this trend is to be found in *Vivos Voco Mortuos Plango* (1980) by Jonathan Harvey, realized at the Parisian research institution Institut de Recherche et de Coordination Acoustique/ Musique (IRCAM). This work is a prime example of felicitous interaction of sound analysis and sound synthesis, being the projection of a boy soprano's voice onto the main partials of a tolling bell as analysed by computer. The advantage of reshaping the vocal material so as to conform to an already-familiar model are obvious; on another level, the aura of secondary associations arising from this particular conjunction is, I feel, particularly powerful. While the human voice has been often employed as a way of ensuring a degree of naturalness in the rhetorical structure, it has only been quite recently that technical means have enabled us to conjoin two so richly suggestive natural sound sources in this particular fashion.

The detailed digital analysis of complex spectra in recent decades has led in two directions: first, towards the creation of models for artificial synthesis of natural sources, for instance musical instruments, which are notoriously recalcitrant owing to their propensity for discrepancy and irregularity, sometimes from pitch to pitch; second, and as yet perhaps more immediately fruitfully, the employment of insights gained from spectral research in recasting the interaction of timbre and harmonic function in instrumental composition. Particularly in France, again centred on IRCAM and the specialist new music ensemble Itinéraire, an important group of composers has sought to integrate spectral analysis into the very heart of its compositional thinking. The most publicly profiled proponents of this tendency, Tristan Murail and Gérard Grisey have, since the mid-1970s, utilized the natural overtone series as their point of departure in the exploration of, as it were, the microcosmic interstices of individual sounds, thus elevating tone colour to the status of a major conduit channelling the flow of musical information. Murail insists that there are no insuperable boundaries separating sound from noise, and that the same is true of other conventional distinctions such as those of frequency and rhythm or harmony and timbre. He argues that the overly rigid nature of older categories of ordering prevented efficiently organized intermediate states precisely because it forcibly imposed inflexible conceptual grids onto the fluid nature of sonic reality. For him, the natural structure of sound, rather than those aspects of sound most amenable to notational and procedural categorization, lies at the core of musical experience. Listening to the opening measures of *Partiels* for 16 instruments by Gérard Grisey, we are able to distinguish with some clarity the natural overtone series being schematically outlined over the emphatic iteration of the low E fundamental, rather in the nature of some programmatic enunciation of intent. Later parts of the composition set out to demonstrate how the detailed analysis of the natural source material makes possible a multitude of smooth transitions between chaotic noise and new, synthetically generated group sonorities.

Given the journalistically induced and alimented animosity between the 'spectralists' and 'neoserialists' that has continued to smoulder fitfully in France, it is interesting to observe the extent to which residual facets of supposedly superceded serial thinking have found a place in the works of these composers. Grisey, in particular, has set himself the task of projecting the shadow of his vertical ordering, as unfolding process, onto the temporal axis, thus assuming not only the plausibility of procedural equivalence between different musical dimensions but also – much more problematically – the consequent mutual permeability of inherently different types of sonic experience such as are represented by timbre and time. The composer himself speaks of projecting an inner, microphonic space onto an artificial, imaginary screen. The paradox, that this revelation of the inner nature of sound has been made possible by the most technological of means, is by no means lost on the composer; nor, more importantly still, is he unaware that the natural overtone spectrum offers us few obvious clues as to how its inner structure might be compositionally elaborated. *Partiels* (1975) by Grisey inhabits what may best be seen as a rather loosely defined zone separating the didactic parsing of insights won from the electronic analysis of sonic phenomena and the subsequent launching of those parsed elements into expressive autonomy as part of the temporal and textural flux created by the impingement of competing 'clusters of forces' (as the composer terms them) on larger formal contours derived from other metaphors of natural states such as that of human breathing. In a lecture given at Darmstadt in 1978 Grisey says:

> One might even go as far as to say that the material has now no existence as an independent quantity, for it is sublimated into a state of pure flux, of mutating sonority . . . There are no fixed, stationary sounds, any more than the rock-formations of mountains are fixed. Sound is by definition transitory.

It is of course not necessary that all seeming contradictions be resolved before a work of art can succeed in its own terms. Indeed, I believe that, in large measure, it is precisely the continuing destabilizing power of these residual unbalanced equations that lends an artistic utterance much of its unique flavour. At the same time one cannot help but remain disturbingly aware, I think, of the massive conceptual problems weighing down what amounts to the utopian enterprise of unifying all dimensions of a sonic material by means of processes explicitly appealing to the structure of the natural phenomenon itself. In artistic terms, mimesis is not confined to an exact mirroring of natural states, and it would be ingenuous to maintain that aesthetic authenticity be primarily conferred by the closeness and thoroughness with which such a mirroring is accomplished. In attempting to arrive at a particular envisaged goal, the artist frequently succeeds in arriving somewhere else – in a place whose qualities he had not been able to imagine before undertaking his journey, whose qualities, in a certain sense, might be said not to have existed at all. Are they then, for that reason, any the less 'natural' in terms of the creative environment of which they form an integral part? The ultimate test of the validity of spectral analysis as a compositional tool must rest on subjective judgement: from my personal point of view as a practising composer, there is absolutely nothing in principle preventing musicians of many stylistic persuasions from coming to creative terms with the insights into the basic laws of sound thus revealed, while remaining true to their individual structural or processual means. The superficially attractive similarities between scientific and aesthetic models of cognition frequently evoked during the last hundred years will scarcely, I venture to predict, lead any time soon to the creation of some unified field of discourse in which both may be comfortably lodged, if only because the arts only loosely conform to paradigms of linear progress. If for this reason alone, it will be fascinating to see how the shaping of sound keeps pace with and assimilates technological developments in coming decades.

FURTHER READING AND LISTENING

Boulez, P., *Le Marteau sans Maître* on *Adès* 14,073–2, Paris (compact disc).

Erickson, R., *Sound Structures in Music*, Berkeley: University of California Press, 1975.

Griffiths, P., *Modern Music and After*, Oxford: Oxford University Press, 1995.

Grisey, G., *Partiels* on *Musique française d'aujourd'hui*, RCA STU 71157 (long playing record).

Harvey, J., *The Music of Stockhausen*, London: Faber and Faber, 1974.

Harvey, J., *Mortuos Plango Vivos Voco* on *Erato* STU 71544 (long playing record).

Lachenmann, H., *Pression* on *Accord-Una Corda* 202082 MU 750, Paris 1993 (compact disc).

Stockhausen, K., *Studie no. 2* on *Stockhausen 3*, Stockhausen-Verlag, Kürten, Germany (compact disc).

Varèse, E., *Ionisation* on *Elektra/Nonesuch* 1987 (compact disc).

Whittal, A., *Music Since the First World War*, London: Dent, 1977.

8 Sound Worlds

STEVEN FELD

Of the materials forwarded to me in advance of the Darwin Lectures, I was quite taken by the poster announcing the entire series (Figure 1). On it one sees the titles and local details of the lectures and associated sound events, superimposed over a striking background profile of Mr Darwin. 'Silence' floats above his scalp. Then 'Physics of Sound' and 'Ear to Brain' rest at his head. 'Birdsong' falls to the neck, and 'Speech' is poised at his throat. Finally, 'Ancestral Voices', 'Shaping Sound', and 'Sound Worlds' descend in order through his formidable chest, ribs, and belly.

While hardly wishing to impute an evolutionary message (or some devolutionary mischief) to the lecture committee, I was nonetheless struck by an anthropological implication in the poster's iconography. I read it to suggest that sound maps the body. This suggestion excited me, because I wanted to devote my contribution on 'Sound worlds' to the spatial and temporal metaphors of sonic geography. In other words, I wanted to question just how sound locates abilities, histories, habits and practices, how sound figures in bodily ways of knowing and being in the world.

Such a project is located at a significant anthropological intersection, one where the phrase 'sound worlds' conjoins its dual possibilities, namely 'worlds of sound', and 'sounds of the world'. The idea of the former, of 'worlds of sound', instantly denotes the multiplicity of distinctively local environmental soundscapes mapping the globe, and the complex ways their distinctiveness blurs as they change through space and time. Likewise, 'sounds of the world' equally denotes the diversity of human musical practices both in their most distinct and their most amalgamated forms. Together the two ideas imply that sound worlds are entities both distinct and cumulative, built up from the interaction of diverse communities, diverse acoustic environments, diverse languages and

173

THE TWELFTH DARWIN COLLEGE LECTURE SERIES 1997

SOUND

17 January **Silence** **Philip Peek**
(Drew University)

* Fri. 24 & Sat. 25 Jan. *Stories from the Pre-World*
COMPANY OF STORYTELLERS
8pm. Cambridge Drama Centre

24 January **Physics of Sound** **Charles Taylor**
(University of Wales)

* Wed. 29 Jan. *Sound Connections*
FRANK PERRY
10pm. Old Library, Darwin College

31 January **Ear to Brain** **Jonathan Ashmore**
(University College, London)

* Sat. 1 Feb. Film: Le Pays des sourds (t.b.c)
Arts Cinema

7 February **Birdsong** **Peter Slater**
(University of St Andrews)

* Sat. 8 Feb. *Birdsong and Music*
JEREMY THURLOW and PETER SLATER
8.30pm. Dining Hall, Darwin College

14 February **Speech** **Peter Ladefoged**
(University of California, Los Angeles)

* Wed. 19 Feb. *Poetry of Many Tongues*
6pm. Old Library, Darwin College

21 February **Ancestral Voices** **Christopher Page**
(Cambridge University)

* Sat 22 Feb. Concert: Drake's Progress
SIRINU
7.30pm. Emmanuel United Reformed Church

28 February **Shaping Sound** **Brian Ferneyhough**
(University of California, San Diego)

* Sat. 1 Mar. *Time and Motion*
ENSEMBLE ACCROCHE NOTE (Strasbourg)
7.30pm. Kettle's Yard

7 March **Sound Worlds** **Steven Feld**
(University of California, Santa Cruz)

* Sun. 9 March *International Music Feast*
by Darwin members & friends
7.30pm. Dining Hall, Darwin College

FRIDAYS AT 5.30 p.m.
The Lady Mitchell Hall, Sidgwick Avenue, Cambridge
ALL WELCOME

FIGURE 1. Series poster announcing the 1997 Darwin Lectures on Sound.

musics. In short, the idea of sound worlds is that social formations are indexed in sonic histories and sonic geographies.

Sound worlds and 'world music'

But that, of course, only goes so far, for surely we now all live in vastly more complex and potentially confusing circumstances, where all 'sound worlds' are simultaneously local and translocal, specific yet blurred, particular but general, in place and in motion. This is because our present is one where virtually all sound worlds are actually or potentially transportable and hearable in all others. It has taken only 100 or so years of sound recording technologies to amplify sonic exchange to this extraordinary degree of circulation. This circulation encompasses ways sound recording has intersected histories of travel, migration, contact and isolation, conflict, colonization, missionization, domination, diaspora and displacement, and of course, reclaimed, renewed and reinvented traditions. In the current moment this history has created a rapid traffic in global sounds, one where cultural separation and social exchange are mutually constituted, one where musical identities and styles are more transient, more in states of constant fission and fusion than ever before. The cumulative effect is an uneven global soundscape, a contentious sound world, where we can see and hear equally omnipresent signs of struggle over augmented and diminished acoustic diversity.

An indication of this complicated and uneven plurality is found in the now ubiquitous label 'world music'. Until a decade ago this label was considerably more obscure. How did it become naturalized in the public sphere? How has it participated in the ways we have come to imagine, interpret, or contest the very notion of 'globalization'? In his classic work *The Archaeology of Knowledge*, Michel Foucault argues that the modern world is one productive of categorizations experienced as normalizing routines that render both concepts and ideologies invisible but known. If this is so, how might a genealogy of 'world music' help make more critically visible the ways a modernity is mirrored in its sound world?

Circulated first by academics in the early 1960s to celebrate and promote the study of musical diversity, the phrase 'world music' began largely as a benign and hopeful term. In the simplest sense it was a populist idea, a friendly and

175

less cumbersome alternative to the more strikingly academic label 'ethnomu-sicology' that emerged in the mid 1950s to refer to the study of non-Western musics, or, in some national contexts, musics of ethnic minorities. 'World music' was meant to oppose the dominant tendency of music conservatories, critics, and publics in the West to assume the synonymy of 'music' with Western Euro-pean Art Music. Likewise 'world music' was meant to have a practical effect on Western conservatories, namely to recognize and hire virtuosi musicians from non-Western societies, and to promote the study of non-Western performance practices and repertories.

Whatever its success in promoting a universal and unified world of music(ology) in the 1960s and 1970s, the terminological dualism of 'world music' versus 'music' also exacerbated a clear division in the academy. 'World music' helped keep those imagined as non-Western or ethnically other distinct from Westerners and their 'music'. And this reinforced and promoted the sep-aration of musicology, the historical and analytic study of Western European Art Musics, from ethnomusicology, the rather more cultural and contextual study of non-European musics. The relationship of the colonizing and the colonized thus remained intact in 'music' and 'world music', magnifying the divide between unmarked, prime-ologies for the West, and ethno-fields for its ethnic others.

Enter the world of popular commerce

In some ways, the situation would have been little different had 'world music' been more bluntly termed 'Third World music'. And outside of the academy, in the world of commerce, that was perhaps more the mood. For even though commercial recordings were increasingly made in every world location from the early days of this century, in the years immediately following the invention of the phonograph, the development of a highly visible commercial documen-tary music recording industry solidified considerably later, in the 1950s and 1960s. This took place around a diverse set of categories indicating a conjunc-tion of academic and commercial enterprise, namely recordings variously lab-eled and marketed as 'primitive', 'exotic', 'tribal', 'ethnic', 'folk', 'traditional', or 'international'.

If these recordings had much in common it was often in their politics of representation. Namely, they were frequently depictions of a rather sanitized world, one where missionaries, colonials, state policies or for that matter almost any intercultural influences were largely presumed absent, rendered epiphenomenal, or edited out of audibility. As ethnomusicology developed academic credibility in the 1960s, increasing prestige accrued to recordings produced by knowledgeable academics who could speak as to the originality and uniqueness of what was recorded. Academics thus became guarantors of musical 'authenticity'.

Ironically it was the turbulence of independence movements, anticolonial demonstrations, and the powerful nationalist struggles of the late 1950s and early 1960s in Africa, Asia and Latin America that fueled this marketplace creation of, and commercial desire for, 'authentic' (thus often nostalgic) musical elsewheres. Soundprints of the political struggles of that era would not be widely hearable on popular recordings, or celebrated for their own stunningly powerful authenticity, for another decade in the commercial music marketplace.

The 1960s and 1970s witnessed the rise and academic proliferation of ethnomusicology and its shadow version in 'world music' programs. But this proliferation was in many ways overwhelmed in the 1980s by the rise of popular music studies, whose international prominence was quickly marked by the emergence of professional journals (notably, *Popular Music* in 1981), professional societies (notably, the International Association for the Study of Popular Music, also 1981), and a succession of influential theoretical texts, from Simon Frith's *Sound Effects*, in 1983, and Ian Chambers' *Urban Rhythms*, in 1985, to Richard Middleton's *Studying Popular Music*, in 1990, and John Shepherd's *Music as Social Text*, in 1991. Even though much of the early emphasis was on studying Western popular musical forms, particularly rock music, popular music studies' concern to theorize the global dominance of mediated musics in the twentieth century signalled to ethnomusicology that its uncritical naturalization of 'authentic traditions' was in trouble. Simon Frith summarized this moment succinctly in the introduction to *World Music, Politics, and Social Change*, his 1989 anthology of papers from early and mid 1980s conferences of the International Association for the Study of Popular Music. 'Perhaps it is not a coincidence that IASPM has grown as an academic organization just as "world music", the sounds of countries other than North America or Western Europe, has begun to be recorded, packaged, and sold as a successful new pop genre'.

Alongside academic changes in the 1980s, the commercial potential of world music began developing rapidly. Reprising an earlier trend, one evident in the relationship of the Beatles to Ravi Shankar, new signs of pop star collaboration, curation and promotion became the key marketplace signifiers of world music from the mid 1980s through the mid 1990s. The ability of Western pop music élites to mobilize both fans and record companies fueled their forays into a simultaneously larger and smaller world. The best known examples were: Paul Simon's *Graceland* with South African musicians, and *Rhythm of the Saints* with Brazilians; Peter Gabriel's WOMAD promotions, the development of his Real World label, and his collaboration with artists as diverse as Youssou N'Dour and Nusrat Fateh Ali Khan; Mickey Hart's World Series on the Rykodisc label, his projects with Tibetan Monks and African and Indian percussionists, and his Endangered Musics series in collaboration with the US Library of Congress; David Byrne's Brazilian, Cuban and Puerto Rican music projects and his cultivation of groups such as Zap Mama for his Luaka Bop label; Ry Cooder's collaborations with Hawaiian, Mexican American, African and Indian guitarists and his promotion of Cuban music and musicians.

The marketplace successes of world music recording projects developed in synergy with industry, commercial and popular culture journalism. *Billboard* magazine reinvented 'world music' as a sales tracking category in 1990 and began charting its commercial impact. *Rolling Stone* and many other music magazines worldwide began reviewing 'world music' as an extension of pop and rock. In 1991, the American National Academy of Recording Arts and Sciences invented a 'world music' Grammy award category out of its former 'ethnic and traditional' one. *The Virgin Directory of World Music* appeared at about the same moment, as did the monthly magazine *Rhythm Music: Global Sounds and Ideas*. The next few years brought *World Music: The Rough Guide*, as well as the beginnings of commercial mail order catalogs exclusively merchandising world music, a proliferation of new recording companies devoted to the genre, and tremendously increased airplay, from exclusive radio programs to exclusive airline channels. Consumer recording, entertainment and audio technology magazines across class and stylistic lines, from Tower Records' consumerist *Pulse* to Britain's upscale *Gramophone*, developed world music news and review sections.

If, then, a world of consumers was, by the mid 1990s, increasingly familiar with groups as diverse in background and style as Ladysmith Black Mambazo,

The Mysterious Bulgarian Voices, Deep Forest, The Chieftans, Zap Mama, Carlos Nakai, Sheila Chandra, Zakir Hussain, Gipsy Kings, Apache Indian, Yothu Yindi, Ofra Haza, Gilberto Gil, or Manu Dibango, it was due to a complete refiguration of how the musical globe was being curated, recorded, marketed, advertised and promoted. No longer a matter of academic or commercial promotion of traditions, 'world music' became first and foremost a global industry focused on marketing, managing, promoting and circulating danceable ethnicity on the world pleasure and commodity map.

Anxiety and celebration: narrating world music's flow

What this industry, its products, and its commentators now indicate is that the 'sound world' of 'world music' is one where every style, every genre, every musical production narrates stories about uneven forms of global connection. At the same time each of these productions simultaneously narrates stories of local, regional, ethnic and social distinction. As the first book length studies of world music – Tony Mitchell's *Popular Music and Local Identity* (1996) and Timothy Taylor's *Global Pop: World Music, World Markets* (1997) – indicate, some of these stories explicitly embrace dominant hegemonic trends in the global popular music industry. Some explicitly resist those trends. And some simultaneously do both.

These trends participate in a new discourse on authenticity, a discourse forged out of narratives equally anxious and celebratory about the world, and the music, of 'world music'. It is anxious because a dominant public theme is the suspicion that capitalist concentration in the recording industry is always productive of a lesser artistry, a more commercial, diluted, and sellable version of a world once more pure. This suspicion fuels a kind of policing, both of the uses of 'tradition' and of the loss of musical diversity within 'world music', asking if such a loss is ever countered by the proliferation of new musics. Counter to this suspicion, celebratory perspectives tend to take ideas about a world blanketed by Western pop and turn them upside down, emphasizing fusion forms as rejections of bounded, fixed or essentialized identities. At the same time celebratory narratives counter anxious ones by stressing the transformed and reappropriated uses of Western pop forms.

To expand, celebratory narratives of world music applaud the production of hybrid subjects via hybrid musics. They place a positive emphasis on fluid, de-essentialized identities. Although in some ways like 'rainbow' musical politics from previous eras, today's celebratory narratives make larger assumptions about possibilities for cultural and financial equity in the entertainment industries. Here 'global' replaces the previous label 'international' as a positive valence term for modern practices and institutions. This has the effect of downplaying hegemonic managerial and capital relations in the music industry, and bringing to the foreground the ways in which somewhat larger segments of the world of music-making now get somewhat larger returns in financial and cultural capital to match their greater visibility.

Celebratory narratives of world music normalize and naturalize globalization, rather like the ways 'modernization' narratives once naturalized other grand and sweeping currents that transformed and refigured intercultural histories. As with these predecessors, to the questions of what has been brought, and what has been taken, celebratory narratives stress the costs to 'tradition' as rather surface ones, ones that will, in the larger sweep of things, be overcome by creativity, invention and resilience. Celebratory narratives then imagine a natural tenacity of the past resounding in possibilities for an amplified present, one of 'endlessly creative conversation' between 'local roots and international pop culture', as Sean Barlow and Banning Eyre put it in their highly celebratory 1995 book *AfroPop!*

In anxious narratives we see an insistence on the complicity of 'world music' in 'commoditizing' ethnicity, and a focus on understanding the hegemonic locations such commodifications occupy within globalization practices and institutions. In particular, it is the production and dissemination of 'world music' in cosmopolitan and metropolitan centers that clearly underscores the character of the exotic labor it imports and sells. As Ashwani Sharma writes, in *Dis-orienting Rhythms: The Politics of the New Asian Dance Music*, an exemplary 1996 collection of anxious essays, 'instances of "musical and cultural conversation" validated under the sign of World Music too easily mask the exploitative labour relationship of the very powerful transnational corporations with the "Third World" musicians, let alone with those of the Third World with only their photogenic poverty to sell.'

At the same time, anxious narratives also chronicle indigenization as a response to globalization, a response that is resistant, either to trends in cultural imperialism or increased cultural homogeneity. Likewise, anxious narratives also insist on world music's abilities to reassert place and locale against globalization. Indeed, in many anxious narratives, the very term 'global' comes to be synonymous with 'displaced'. In other words, displacement is a metaphor for globalization as a simultaneity of alienation and dispersal. But at the same time anxious narratives want to claim the potential and hope that every loss opens up for resistance, for reassertion, for reclamation, for response.

'World music', then, like 'globalization' more generally, is a discourse equally routed in the public sphere through overlapped tropes of anxiety and celebration. These narratives, these positions, are being asserted by complexly overlapping communities of musicians, fans, consumers, producers, critics and academics. Yet what everyone is responding to is an omnipresence of productions and consumables that has intensified exponentially in quantity, variety, imagery and speed of circulation. In a remarkably short time the diversity of 'world music', its promise, is always suspended in the spectre of 'one world music', its antithesis. The struggle to continually pluralize and rediversify is a dialectical necessity in a world where 'world music' increasingly consists of standardized and familiar sounds and commodities.

What this struggle tells us is that the sound world of world music is one that both stays at home and travels. It is a familial world, drawn close, intimate, local, intense to the point of a powerful essentialism. It is also a world in motion, open to fast movement and circulation, copy, blending, intense to the point of diffuse ephemerality. It is to the complexities of how one such very specific world is both at home and on the move, full of both celebratory difference and anxious contraction, that I now turn.

Localities within sound worlds, and sound worlds within localities

The Kaluli are one of four groups of 2000 Bosavi people who live in the tropical rainforest of the Great Papuan Plateau in the Southern Highlands Province of Papua New Guinea. On several hundred square kilometres of lowland and mid montane forest land, at an altitude of about 600 m, they hunt, fish, gather, and tend land-intensive swidden gardens. Their staple food is sago, processed from wild palms that grow in shallow swamps and creeks branching off larger river arteries that flow downward from Mt Bosavi, the collapsed cone of an extinct volcano reaching about 2400 m.

Bosavi was once relatively easy to describe as a classless and small-scale society, inasmuch as no traditionally fixed occupational specializations, stratifications, ranks, professions, ascribed or achieved statuses formed the basis for social differentiation. This was also a generally egalitarian society in matters economic and political. With no appointed or elected leaders, speakers, chiefs, bosses, or controllers, Kaluli people hunted, gathered, gardened, and worked to produce what they needed, taking care of themselves, their neighbors and kin through extensive cooperation in food sharing and labor assistance. The egalitarian dynamics here involved both a lack of centralized social institutions and a lack of deference to persons, roles, categories, or groups based on power, position, or material ownership.

Emergent hierarchy developed dramatically around the social changes that have more recently refigured Kaluli life, beginning with the advent of colonial government contact, particularly by the late 1950s. But it was evangelical missionization that brought sweeping changes to the Bosavi area, beginning in the mid 1960s with the building of an airstrip, and then developing from the early 1970s with the first resident fundamentalist missionaries. A new wave of national government impact followed after Papua New Guinea's independence in 1975. Into the 1980s and 1990s, the presence of a second airstrip, a hospital, schools, aid post stations, mission station, and government development personnel, and particularly local pastors in each village has introduced increasingly complex forms of deference based on differentiated wealth, particularly with a cash base.

Currently the Bosavi area is in the throes of a more complex set of changes that implicate cultural and ecological futures. Oil and gas projects are already transforming the surrounding region, and demands and debates about local logging, road access to the area, and large-scale development projects are current. With these have come the chaotic responses that occasional but large infusions of cash and material wealth bring following sporadic patterns of out-migration. The overall effect is the promotion of broader bases of conflict around real, perceived, and possible inequities, and the escalation of unequal access to power and resources along lines of gender, age, multilingualism and Christianization.

From sound as a symbolic system to acoustemology

My own engagement with the Bosavi region is complexly situated in this history. In 1976 I went to Bosavi because I had heard the first tape recordings from the area, made by Edward L. Schieffelin in 1966–8. I was taken by the musicality of Kaluli expression, but particularly by the relationship of that musicality to the sounds of the rainforest, initially described by Schieffelin in his 1976 book *The Sorrow of the Lonely and the Burning of the Dancers*. It was that relationship that I wanted to investigate.

The general hypothesis that people in some way echo their soundscape in language and music was first developed by R. Murray Schafer in his 1977 book *The Tuning of the World*, a synthesis of the ideas developed during his time as director of the World Soundscape Project and Simon Fraser University. In that book he develops the concepts of 'soundscape' and 'acoustic ecology', and analyzes trends in the transformations of sound environments through history. The work of Schafer and his colleagues was broad and stimulating, and invited anthropological and ethnomusicological scrutiny in grounded field studies.

With this in mind during my first Bosavi research in the 1970s, I developed the idea of an ethnography of sound, or study of sound as a cultural system, in order to relate the importance of acoustic ecology, particularly the avian rainforest soundscape, to the musicality and poetics of Bosavi laments and vocal song. The mediation between this rainforest ecology and Bosavi music turned out to be cosmological, for Kaluli consider birds to be not just singers but spirits of their dead. To one another birds appear and speak as people, and to the living their presence is a constant reminder of histories of human loss, an absence made present in sound and motion. The relationship between the construction and evocation of local expressive forms, and the bird world they 'metaphorized', was a deeply emotional one. From this, I found, came the great aesthetic force of Kaluli lament, poetics and song performance, the subjects of my 1982 book *Sound and Sentiment*.

In my subsequent Bosavi research in the 1980s and 1990s, a growing concern with place, poetic cartography, and everyday meanings of the Bosavi sound world has pushed the idea of sound as a cultural system somewhat farther, toward what I now call acoustemology. In one sense this step is a natural development in my concern to understand the place-name maps in Bosavi songs,

Steven Feld

and how vocal performance articulates their poetic and ecological relationship to the sounds and meanings of the rainforest. But I have also taken this step in critical response to research in acoustic ecology that artificially separates sonic environments from the pervasiveness of human invention. Soundscapes, no less than landscapes, are not just physical exteriors, spatially surrounding or apart from human activity. Soundscapes are perceived and interpreted by human actors who attend to them as a way of making their place in and through the world. Soundscapes are invested with significance by those whose bodies and lives resonate with them in social time and space.

By acoustemology I wish to suggest a union of acoustics and epistemology, and to investigate the primacy of sound as a modality of knowing and being in the world. Sound both emanates from and penetrates bodies; this reciprocity of reflection and absorption is a creative means of orientation, one that tunes bodies to places and times through their sounding potential. Hearing and producing sound are thus embodied competencies that situate actors and their agency in particular historical worlds. These competencies contribute to their distinct and shared ways of being human; they contribute to possibilities for, and realization of, authority, understanding, reflexivity, compassion and identity.

Following the lead established by Maurice Merleau-Ponty's *Phenomenology of Perception*, then echoed in Don Ihde's *Listening and Voice: a Phenomenology of Sound*, my notion of acoustemology means to explore the reflexive and historical relationships between hearing and speaking, listening and sounding. This reflexivity is embodied doubly: one hears oneself in the act of voicing, and one resonates the physicality of voicing in acts of hearing. Listening and voicing are in a deep reciprocity, an embodied dialogue of inner and outer sounding and resounding built from the historicization of experience. The ongoing dialogue of self and self, self and other, of their interplay in action and reaction, are thus constantly sited at the sense of sound, absorbed and reflected, given and taken in constant exchange. The soundingness of hearing and voicing constitute an embodied sense of presence and of memory. Voice then authorizes identities as identities authorize voice. Voice is evidence, embodied as experiential authority, performed to the exterior or interior as a subjectivity made public, mirrored in hearing as public made subjective.

184

Sound as a poetic cartography

How might an acoustemological perspective on voice and place help to reveal the connection between the powerful locality of the Bosavi sound world and its global emplacement? To begin, Bosavi songs are textually constituted as poetic cartographies of rainforest trails. This notion of 'poetic cartographies' is clearly delimited in local compositional and vocal practices around four concepts. These are *tok*, 'paths' of connected localities, whose *sa-salan*, 'inside speaking' or poetic revelation, consists of *bale to*, 'turned over words', metaphors, and *go:no: to*, 'sound words', mimetic phonesthemes. Making song 'paths' is how Kaluli people sing the forest as a poetic fusion of space and time where lives and events are conjoined as vocalized, embodied memories.

The importance of sound and voice to these memorial and performative practices cannot be overstated. That is because, while much of the forest is visually hidden, sound cannot be hidden. Acoustic revelatory presence is always in tension with visual hidden presence in everyday experiences of the forest. This sensory tension between the seen and heard, the hidden and revealed, is itself poeticized in two synesthetic metaphors Kaluli use to link forest emplacement to its aesthetic evocation. These are locally known as *dulugu ganalan*, 'lift-up-over-sounding', and *a:ba:lan*, 'flowing'.

'Lift-up-over-sounding' glosses the seamlessly staggered alternations and overlaps that comprise the sensual experience of the rainforest soundscape. One hears no unison in nature. In the tropical forest, height and depth are easily confused, and the lack of visual cues make depth often sensed as the diffuseness of height moving outward. 'Lift-up-over sounding' precisely yet suggestively codes that ambiguous sensation: upward feels like outward. This placing of sound is simultaneously a sounding of place. One knows the time of day, season of year and placement in relative physical space through the sensual wraparound of sound in the forest. This way of hearing and sensing the world is mirrored in the production of Kaluli song, where voices overlap and echo with surrounding forest sounds, with instruments, or with other voices to create a dense, multilayered, alternating and interlocking form of expression.

'Lift-up-over sounding' is as potentially omnipresent in the experiences and aesthetics of the Kaluli world as 'harmony' is in the experiences and aesthetics of the West. Like 'harmony', 'lift-up-over sounding' is a grand metaphor modeling sonic relations (the way tones combine together in space and time) as well as social relations (the ways people interact in concert). Whether it is the birds, insects, winds and watercourses of the forest, or the vocalizing of Kaluli, or the overlap and interplay of the two, 'lift-up-over sounding' always comes across as in synchrony but out-of-phase. By this I mean that, however cohesive, 'lift-up-over sounding' always seems to be composed of sound sources at different points of displacement from any momentary or hypothetical sense of unison.

Neither a clear-cut heterophony or polyphony, 'lift-up-over sounding' is more an echophony where one sound may stand out momentarily, then fade into the distance, overlapped or echoed by a new or repeated emergence in the auditory mosaic. The Kaluli concept of 'echo' helps reveal this idea of presence and diffusion. In the Bosavi language 'echo' is represented by the mimetic phonestheme *gugu-go:go:*. *Gu* denotes downward moving sound; reduplicated, *gugu* marks the action as continuous. *Go:* likewise denotes outward moving sound; reduplicated, *go:go:* also marks the action as continuous. So the auditorally ambiguous interplay of continuous downward and continuous outward moving sound is what is heard and felt as echo. In its constant play of immediacy and vagueness, *gugu-go:go:* is an everpresent soundmark of the up-is-over forest soundscape.

A similarity of convergences characterizes the metaphorical potency of *a:ba: lan*, 'flowing'. 'Flowing' first glosses the sensuous presence of water moving through and connecting rainforest lands. As it does so, water moves in and out of visual presence and immediacy, yet it always remains audible even when invisible. The local forests are multiply criss-crossed by creeks running off from the high mountain streams of Mt Bosavi. In the mid montane foothills, one cannot walk for more than a few minutes in any direction without crossing water of some variety. As one walks, these waterways constantly disappear and re-emerge through densities of forest shrubs, hills, and treelines. 'Flowing' is this ever-emerging and receding presence, this constancy of water moving and resounding through and figuring the ground.

'Flowing' equally characterizes the on and off, emerging and fading, circulatory motion of a song or songs. Whether within perceptual immediacy or long held in mind, 'flowing' is the lingering grip of a song's images, its progression of sounds and words which stay in mind. The Western metaphorical counterpart to Kaluli 'flowing' is the 'broken record', the sound that does not turn off but stays with a listener. These are both metaphors for an embodied repeating.

Kaluli notions of 'flow' converge in the vocal performance of songs whose texts are forest 'paths' of named places. Singing a sequence of named places is a way of taking listeners on a journey 'flowing' along local waterways and through contiguous lands. The flow of these poetic song 'paths' signals the connectedness of Bosavi places to people, experiences and memories. The 'flowing' nature of waters through lands, then, mirrors the 'flowing' nature of songs and places through local biographies and histories.

Song 'paths' derive experientially from everyday life, where people travel through the forest by foot to and from their home longhouse community, going to gardens, to sago places, or to other longhouse communities. Everyday experiences of the forest always involve the intermeshed experience of lands and waters. The most significant kinds of land formation come from the images of *fele*, 'thighs', attached to a *do:m*, 'body'. 'Thighs' are the relatively flatter, even and wide stretch of lands rolling off and downward to either side. These 'thighs' are reached from hilly segments of ascent, descent, and roll-off in the land that are its 'body' sides.

This sense of land as a grounded 'body' of sides and 'thighs' is closely related to the lay and motion of forest waterways. Walking a 'body' implies water below; once crossed there is another 'body' to climb on the other side. Likewise, 'thighs' usually have one or more *eleb*, 'heads' of waters lying off or below to either side. In other words, water reclines, moves along a body lying, typically flowing downstream along its 'thighs'.

These images construct a world where the body is imagined like the curves of land between, around and over which water flows. Moreover, as these primal land forms are connected like thighs to the body, so the passage of water through them flows like the motion of voice. Voice flows by resounding through the body, feelingly connecting its contiguous physical segments, sensually resonating throughout. This 'flowing' mirrors that of water through land, with its multiple presences across and along a variety of relatively contiguous but physically distinct forms. The 'flowing' of water and of voice moves through lands and bodies to link their segments and reveal their wholeness.

At their conjunction 'lift-up-over-sounding' and 'flowing' indicate the remarkable creativity with which Kaluli absorb and respond to the sensuousness of the rainforest environment. 'Lift-up-over sounding' naturalizes song form and performance by way of its resonance with the forest world. Likewise, 'flowing' naturalizes poetic cartography as the performance of biographical memory. Together these ideas fuse spatial and temporal experience, link

(a)

(b)

FIGURE 2. (a) and (b) Costumed ko:luba dancers turn into birds at forest waterfalls.

Steven Feld

everyday pasts and presents, join the powers of place and of journey. Most importantly, 'lift-up-over sounding' and 'flowing' directly emplace this world not just in texts, but in the reflexive relationship of voicing to hearing.

Singing in and out of place

My first example of song production within this sound world comes from a Kaluli genre called *ko:luba*. This one was composed by Bifo of the community of Suguniga, and it was one of 90 songs sung at an all night *ko:luba* ceremony when Suguniga visited the community of Sululeb on 5 July 1982 (heard on *Voices of the Rainforest*, track 10).

For *ko:luba* 12 costumed singer-dancers coupled in various pairs to sing from early evening until dawn (Figure 2); typically about 100 songs were sung in the course of the evening's performance. Each song was repeated in succession five times, first at the rear of the longhouse's main corridor, then in its center, then in the front, then back again in the center, and finally back to the rear. In between renditions the dancers moved with a skipping step from one house position to another.

Through each performance the pairs faced one another and moved up and down in place, rhythmically accompanying themselves through the pulse of their heels bouncing on the longhouse floor, the indexical sounds of costume leaves and feathers in motion, and the up and down flapping of a rattle of cray-fish claws (*degegado*, named for the clacking sound) arching out of dance belts in the rear of the costume. The costume and dance created a 'lift-up-over sound-ing' effect, overlapping the voices. Audience members packed the house and crowded the dance floor. Attendants stood behind and to the side of the dan-cers to light them with resin torches.

Ko:luba songs consist of a refrain and verses. The refrain repeats a melody and text; this alternates with the verses, which consist of a second melody whose text slightly varies with each repetition. In the Kaluli language the

190

refrain is called the *mo:*, meaning 'trunk' or 'base', and the verses are called *dun*, 'branches'. *Ko:luba* songs could thus be said to 'branch' out in verses from their 'trunk' or refrain. Here we see how a forest image is poeticized, bringing the sense of locale together with the sensuousness of vocal and dance performance.

Bifo composed his song in the weeks prior to the ceremony at Sululeb; at the ceremony he sang it paired with Wasio, in the 'lift-up-over sounding' fashion where the first voice is echoed and overlapped by the second, singing the exact same melody and text. During the song's very first voicing, while dancing at the rear house position, a man named Hasele loudly burst into tears and continued to cry periodically throughout the song's performance. He cited the names of his brothers as a text to his melodic wept vocalizations. Finally he rushed out to the dance floor with a resin torch, and as the song continued, burned Bifo's back in retaliation for the pain and grieving the song had caused him.

Hasele's intense grief derived from the personal poignancy of Bifo's song. In 1971 Hasele and his two brothers Seligiwo: and Molugu left Bosavi and went to work on a labor contract near Rabaul, a colonial center far from Bosavi, off the New Guinea mainland on the outlying island of New Britain. Hasele returned to Bosavi the following year, but his brothers stayed near Rabaul. They have never returned to Bosavi, nor have they been heard from again.

mo:	'*trunk*'
uwo:lo:	riflebird (*Ptiloris magnificus*) calling
Bolekini uwo:lo:	calling from Bolekini
uwo:lo:	uwo:lo: bird is calling
wo: wo:	crying out

dun	'*branches*'
Go:go:bo: nabe	could I eat at Go:go:bo:?
ne sago:lomakeya	I have no cousin (there)
ni imolobe	I'm starving
wo: wo:	crying out

With each rendition the song would go through four or five repetitions. Successive 'branches' from the 'trunk' poetically create both a physical map and a social one by the use of alternate place-names and relationship terms. The place-names Mosbi (Pt Moresby), Rabal (Rabaul), and Medi (Mendi) alternate in the first line of successive branches, substituting for Go:go:bo:. These are far city places known to few Kaluli. In parallel, the relationship terms *no:* (mother), *nao* (brother), and *ada:* (older sister/younger brother) alternate in the second line, substituting for *sago:* (cousin). The poetics of the 'branches' thus play on an ironic parallelism, where successively named places become further distant and hence more dangerous and lonely, as successively named social relations become closer and hence more familial and secure. Food is the idiom and medium par excellence of Kaluli hospitality, sharing, sociability and relationship, as discussed in Bambi B. Schieffelin's 1990 ethnography, *The Give and Take of Everyday Life*. Food is central to these poetic 'branches' as well; spatial distance and social loss are equated with the pain of starving.

This parallelism of place and social relationship in the song's 'branches' plays off the central 'trunk' image, the longhouse site of Hasele's family, where a lone riflebird (*Ptiloris magnificus*), the spirit bird of the singer, calls in the bird sound words of its onomatopoeic name, *uwo:lo:*. As the 'branches' travel further and further away, the 'trunk' brings the song back and holds it in a familiar lived-in place. This way the song's form becomes one with its content, producing an image of a lifeworld that is both spatial, with places reaching out and coming back, and temporal, with duration creating a journey of loss.

While Bifo's song was the only one in this particular *ko:luba* that cited place-names from the world beyond Bosavi, the technique was hardly new in 1982. I had heard similar songs in the mid 1970s, songs including names deriving from the first experiences of labor contracts, when Bosavi men left the area in the mid to late 1960s. None the less, Bifo's song was clearly startling and instant in its powers of evocation, and its performance illustrates how singing names of remote places can be as powerfully charged as singing those that are intimately familiar. They also indicate how Kaluli were quick to extend their song maps to include new worlds both gained and lost.

Listening to tape playback of this song with me in August 1992, Hasele nodded his head and smiled gently as he heard himself cry for his brothers. When the song finished, he shrugged his shoulders, swallowed, and said, *sowo: o:ngo: emele mo:mieb ko:lo:*, 'they're like the dead, they won't come back'.

192

This song's text, performance, and impact speak to local memories of Australian colonial practices of importing rural and remote laborers to coastal plantations in the former territories of Papua and New Guinea. In Bosavi these practices arrived within 30 years of first contact, 15 years of the first colonial census, and almost immediately upon the building of a first local airstrip in 1964. The places whose names locally signify the colony beyond are intensely poeticized, made to evoke the connection between labor and loss, distance and distress. History, region, and remote worlds beyond everyday experience are made local, and take on the sense of being close by, palpably immediate. The sound world of Bosavi becomes the entire space and time of a remote region encapsulated within a colonial territory. As the territory absorbs the Kaluli world, the Kaluli absorb the territory by poetically appropriating its place-names into their language, song and singing. Once voiced, these place-names are committed to memory. Local voices know these places; they have heard and felt them resonating through their bodies and through their land. Like water through land and voice through the body, names 'flow', and in so doing they signal how local knowledge is memorially embodied as vocal knowledge.

What are your names?

Bifo's song arose in the male-centered world of Kaluli ceremonies, the part of Kaluli life most strongly associated with male ritual expression. But in laments and in songs for work and leisure Kaluli women voiced similar concerns with place and social memory. In August 1990, Ulahi, the featured composer of the *Voices of the Rainforest* compact disk (CD), invited me to Wo:lo creek, one of her favorite singing spots, to record some of her new songs. At the conclusion of one of her songs, a *gisalo*, Ulahi spontaneously launched into a fragment that was improvised in the moment (heard on *Voices of the Rainforest*, track 6, song 2).

wo: wo:	calling out
ni America kalu-o-e	my America men
gi wi o:ba-e	what are your names?
ni Australia gayo-o-e	my Australia women
gi wi o:ba-e	what are your names?

193

ni America kalu-o-e	my America men
wo: wo:	(calling out)
ni America kalu-o- wo: wo:	my America men (calling out)
gi wi o:ba-e	what are your names?
ni Australia gayo-e	my Australia women
gi wi o:ba-e	what are your names?
ni America kalu-o-wo:	my America men
o wo:-- wo: wo:	calling on and on
gi wi o:ba-e	what are your names?
ni Australia gayo-e	my Australia women
ni America kalu-o-e	my America men
a:-ye- wo: wo:	calling out, wondering

I was stunned by this song, but before I could say a word Ulahi continued with a brief reflective apology, here rather literally translated:

> Well, myself, thinking about it, speaking sadly, I won't see your place but you see mine, I don't know your names, who are you? I'm wondering, thinking like that, you people living in far away lands, listening to me, I haven't heard your land names so who are you? That's what I'm saying. Steve, having come before you can say 'my name is Steve, American man' but all the others, what are your names? 'Many people will hear your Bosavi songs', you said like that to me before, but thinking about it, singing by myself I'm thinking what are your names? That's what I was thinking. I don't really know the land names, just America, Australia, so I'm sadly singing like that so that they can hear it.

The background to this remark was a conversation Ulahi and I had as we walked together from Bolekini, our village, to the spot on Wo:lu creek where she sang her songs that day. Ulahi, with whom I had worked often since 1976, asked why I wanted to record her songs again (Figure 3). I replied that many new people would hear her voice because a song man from my own place (Micky Hart of Grateful Dead rock band fame) was helping me to make a new recording of Bosavi sounds. I could not really explain how *Voices of the Rainforest* was to be a serious departure from the academic recordings I'd previously made for scholarly ethnomusicological audiences. And the world of Bosavi had never heard names like Grateful Dead. So I just told Ulahi that with

FIGURE 3. Ulahi, listening to playback of her songs from *Voices of the Rainforest.*

the help of my friend, many people in Australia and in America would some-
day hear her sing.

What stayed in Ulahi's mind, obviously, was the thought of her voice resonating through America and Australia. But to whom? Who would be listening in
this world beyond? And what would they possibly understand of her world
within? Ulahi's improvised song takes up this theme, appropriating the place-
names of the largest imaginable worlds beyond, and delicately juxtaposing
them with the mystery of personal names. Imagining her listeners in this way,
Ulahi acknowledges both our presence and absence in her sound world. But
placing names in performance, voicing those names poetically, makes them her
own in the moment and from then on. Here Ulahi both anticipates and recipro-
cates the gesture of each distant listener who might hear her recorded voice,
speak her name, or speak the name of her place.

One world or several?

As a final example I turn to a song I recorded late in 1994. It features a different
kind of sound, one that has penetrated all of the cities as well as the interior of
Papua New Guinea. It is a sound that carries with it the intertwined histories of
missionization and Western choral harmony, the spread of guitars and ukuleles
throughout the world. It is the sound of Pan-Pacific acoustic string band popular music. But of course this very urban Papua New Guinea sound, one that

developed tremendous momentum and local cassette market appeal around the time of the country's independence in 1975, has a way of sounding incredibly local when taken on by Kaluli.

Like many other local string band performances the text below, 'Papamama', was sung by a group of Kaluli men and women comprising lead and backup vocals, lead guitar, rhythm guitar, bass guitar and ukulele. The song is sung first in Tok Pisin, a Papua New Guinea lingua franca of cities and towns, and then in Kaluli. The group's leader, Odo Gaso, heard the song from a non-Kaluli pastor; he then translated it and set it to the style of string band music he learned as a student at Tari High School.

papamama	father and mother
tanim bel, nau tasol,	change your thoughts, now,
i no tumora	not tomorrow
bratasusa	brother and sister
tanim bel, nau tasol,	change your thoughts, now,
i no tumora	not tomorrow
i no yumi tasol	not only us
olgeta hap Papua Nugini	all places in Papua New Guinea
tanim bel pinis	have already repented
dowo: no:wo:	father, mother
asugo: nodoma o:g wemaka:	turn your thinking, here and now
alibaka:	not tomorrow
nao nado	brother, sister
asugo: nodoma o:g wemaka	turn your thinking, here and now
alibaka:	not tomorrow
ni ko:mbaka:	not only us
Papua Nugini sambo	everyone in Papua New Guinea
asugo: nodolo:	has turned their thoughts

FIGURE 4. Odo Gaso, leader of the string band movement in Bosavi.

Tok Pisin, while still relatively little heard locally, became part of the linguistic repertory known in Bosavi through the return of laborers, through increasing government presence, and, of course, through missionization, all dating to the early 1970s. Guitars and ukuleles began to appear in the hands of young men returned from labor contracts around the same time. Returnees from provincial high schools, and students at the local mission and government schools also received some encouragement to take up the instrument, although there was little in the way of formal lessons. Throughout the 1970s and well into the 1980s I never heard a guitar or ukulele that was tuned or played as a melody instrument. Young men played them to accompany Tok Pisin songs heard from radio or cassette or pastors. But they were always played like a seed pod rattle and sometimes together with one, the strum always providing more of an isometric rhythmic texture, 'lift-up-over sounding' with voices.

The string band sound developed by Odo Gaso and his friends from the late 1980s celebrates some very new skills and practices (Figure 4). First of course is the beginnings of some mastery of guitar band styles and the skills in tuning and playing guitar, ukulele and bass. To this is added some mastery of the harmony introduced by Christian mission hymns and church singing. These musical skills, however, are never completely separate from their articulation in a naturalized Kaluli way. The instrumental part relationships, the vocal part relationships, and the interplay of the two, are given voice as a density of 'lift-up-over sounding'.

In the realm of social organization of musical activities, all indigenous Kaluli vocal practices and musical contexts were formerly gender separate. Only through Christian missionization and schooling did Bosavi boys and girls, men and women, begin to sing together and learn to create a 'lift-up-over sounding' blend of vocal registers. The string band format developed by Odo takes this a step further. Here, as in several other Bosavi bands, the lead voices are a married couple, here Odo and his wife Sibalame, and the 'lift-up-over sounding' is organized by gendered voice register.

Another interesting dimension to these songs is that the lyrics are typically sung both in Tok Pisin and Bosavi. This is actually quite difficult because of the inevitable prosodic awkwardness of trying to fit the Bosavi word forms into the cadences and number of rhythmic beats of the Western popular song form. None the less, singing the song first in Tok Pisin then in Bosavi works both to demystify, and to appropriate, to make local, language and meaning indexed to places beyond.

Innovations not withstanding, this new generationally based, gender-mixed, multilingual, and often Christian-inspired or Christian hymn text-based song form consistently indicates tremendous sonic continuities with other kinds of Bosavi song. There is, for example, a dense and layered mix of 'lift-up-over sounding' voices and instruments, indicating the Kaluli aesthetic preference for overlapping and echoing layers of sound. At the same time these songs do not typically map a sequence of either forest or distant places. None the less they almost always have a place name, and it is either a regional center, or, as in this case, Papua New Guinea. The imagined province, or the nation, a Christian nation, is a placed totality, a stringband sound world that connects remote Kaluli to Papua New Guinea through the idea that the nation is constituted by church, school and radio.

Sound worlds as embodied histories

All three of these songs, Bifo's ceremonial song, Ulahi's improvised reflection, and Odo's string band innovations, illustrate some of the many intensely local ways specific 'sounds of the world' intertwine with the 'world of sounds' to constitute a Kaluli sound world and locate it within the world and the music of 'world music'. This is not just about Bosavi life becoming 'commoditized' on cassette or CD, or about the tensions between musical loss and musical innovation. It is about the way local difference embodies history in sound.

The world of the Bosavi rainforest, of 'lift-up-over sounding' voices singing 'flowing' song 'paths', articulates the encounter of locality with colonialism, labor contracts, Christian missionization, visiting foreign anthropologists, the nation state and record companies. This is a sound world where these sensibilities have collided, and where they now rebound in 'circulable' cultural representations that embody and express musical histories; that is, histories lived musically. This is a sound world where not only is musical life socially and historically grounded, but social life is itself experienced and made significant musically.

The lived experience of Bosavi song joins the sounds of the forest, the poetics of place and the voicing of song in a memorial cartography. Acts of making and hearing sounds are cartographically imagined and practiced as the making and hearing of a world. Musicking then is clearly, for Bosavis as for many other people, a bodily mode of placing oneself in the world, taking the world in and expressing it out as an intimately known and lived world, a world of local knowledge that is articulated as vocal knowledge. Kaluli songs map the sound world as a space–time continuum of place, of connection, of exchange, of travel, of memory, of fear, of longing and of possibility. It is a sound world whose acoustemology voices an ongoing poetic dialogue, a dialogue where emplacement and displacement embody geographies of local and global difference.

FURTHER READING AND LISTENING

Barlow, S. and Banning, E., *Afropop! An Illustrated Guide to Contemporary African Music*. Edison: Chartwell Books, 1995.

Broughton, S. et al., *World Music: The Rough Guide*, London: The Rough Guides/ Penguin, 1994.

Chambers, I., *Urban Rhythms: Pop Music and Popular Culture*, London: Macmillan, 1985.

Feld, S., *Sound and Sentiment: Birds, Weeping, Poetics, and Song in Kaluli Expression*, Philadelphia: University of Pennsylvania Press, 1982 (2nd edition 1990).

Feld, S., *Voices of the Rainforest*, Boston: Rykodisc, 1991 (compact disc).

Foucault, M., *The Archeology of Knowledge*, translated by A. M. Sheridan Smith, New York: Pantheon, 1972.

Frith, S., *Sound Effects: Youth, Leisure, and the Politics of Rock*, London: Constable, 1983.

Frith, S. (ed.), *World Music, Politics, and Social Change*, Manchester: Manchester University Press, 1989.

Steven Feld

Ihde, D., *Listening and Voice: A Phenomenology of Sound*, Athens, OH: Ohio University Press, 1976.

Merleau-Ponty, M., *Phenomenology of Perception*, London: Routledge and Kegan Paul, 1962.

Middleton, R., *Studying Popular Music*, Milton Keynes: Open University Press, 1990.

Mitchell, T., *Popular Music and Local Identity: Rock, Pop and Rap in Europe and Oceania*, London: Leicester University Press, 1996.

Schafer, R. M., *The Tuning of the World*, New York: Knopf, 1977.

Schieffelin, B. B., *The Give and Take of Everyday Life: Language Socialization of Kaluli Children*, Cambridge: Cambridge University Press, 1990.

Schieffelin, E. L., *The Sorrow of the Lonely and the Burning of the Dancers*, New York: St Martin's Press, 1976.

Sharma, A., 'Sounds oriental: the (im)possibility of theorizing Asian musical cultures', in *Dis-orienting Rhythms: The Politics of the New Asian Dance Music*, ed. S. Sharma, J. Hutnyk and A. Sharma, pp. 15–31, London: Zed Books, 1996.

Shepherd, J., *Music as Social Text*, Cambridge: Polity, 1991.

Sweeney, P., *The Virgin Directory of World Music*, New York: Henry Holt, 1991.

Taylor, T., *Global Pop: World Music, World Markets*, New York: Routledge, 1997.

9 Audio-Vision and Sound

MICHEL CHION

Although sound cinema has existed for several decades (since about the late twenties and early thirties), theoreticians and historians who have given the issue of sound on screen the importance it deserves are still few and far between. I can cite the remarkable articles by Rick Altman in the USA, or Claude Bailblé in France, but I should also mention my own works. Indeed, in parallel with my activities as a composer and a filmmaker, I have devoted the last 20 years or so to the study and teaching of the relationships between sound and image. In this chapter, I propose to give an overview of my personal theorization which has led me to forge a whole new vocabulary.

My approach does not involve studying the sound of films or television programs in isolation from the image. Rather, as I have demonstrated in numerous analyses and experiments, film sound cannot be studied separately from its image, and vice versa. It is their very combination which produces something entirely new and specific, in the same way as a chord or an interval in music.

Since this field of study is new and as yet 'non-coded', I have had to coin numerous expressions to refer to audiovisual effects that have been known and used for a long time, but intuitively, as 'figures' deprived of specific names. This is why I still use the term 'effects', which has lost some of its meaning today, whereas in the past it was commonly found in articles and reviews on opera, theatre or music – in short those arts which, like cinema, are based on performance.

The question is whether these effects make up, or will make up, a rhetorical

Translated from the French by Patricia Kruth and David H. Jones. The terminology used in this chapter – when already existing in English – is from *Audio-Vision: Sound on Screen* translated by Claudia Gorbman.

Although originally written for this volume, this chapter has also appeared in French in Michel Chion's book *Le Son* (Nathan, Paris) in 1998.

system consciously known to the public, or whether they will remain 'effects'. But this is no different from musical effects, such as harmonic progressions or diminished seventh chords, which have long been received by audiences who could feel them without being able to identify and understand them. This is still true for most music listeners today.

I should stress that I work within a descriptive logic where it is never a case of all or nothing, and where exceptions do not disprove the rule.

Audio-vision, added value, illusion of redundancy

I have named ***audio-vision*** the perceptive process by which sound in cinema, television, and video modifies and influences the perception of what is seen. Indeed, audiovisual combination does not work as an addition of similar or opposed components but as a mixture in which sound is rarely taken into account. (In a similar way, to continue the musical comparison suggested above, listeners who have no formal musical training will not be able to distinguish between the overall emotion created by the melody, and the chords that 'accompany' it. They may therefore attribute solely to the melodic line – and in the case of audio-vision, to the image – the emotion or meaning that actually derives from the combination and association of all the musical components.)

Very frequently, when sound adds meaning to the image, the meaning seems to emanate from the image itself. This is what I call ***added value*** (i.e. value added by sound to the image). Added value is at the basis of most 'audiovisual effects', and may be defined as a sort of simultaneous 'Kuleshov effect' between sound and image. (In cinema this effect is named after the Russian director who, in an experiment, juxtaposed the same shot of an actor with a neutral expression and shots of other subjects like a baby, a bowl of soup, a dead body, and the like. Each time the actor's face seemed to register the appropriate emotion.) This value – be it sensorial, informative, semantic, narrative, structural, or expressive – which a sound heard in a scene leads us to project onto the image, can create the impression that we view what in fact we 'audio-view'. Added value is a widely used effect, most of the time experienced unconsciously. To become aware of it and analyze its mechanism, it is necessary to separate out the audiovisual mix by observing the sound and the image of a given sequence independently. Only then do we appreciate how, in different ways, sound never ceases to influence what we see.

Added value is partly bilateral – the image likewise influences our perception of sound. Yet, because of the conscious focusing of the spectator of a film or a television program towards the screen and what is visible, it is ultimately onto the image that the overall product of the mutual influences between sound and image is most often reprojected. On the other hand, in a cultural situation such as a concert – what I call a situation of 'visu-audition' – where conscious attention is projected by cultural tradition onto listening, added value functions mainly the other way round. For example, if we see a player make a vigorous gesture we will 'hear' a more powerful sound.

To come back to cinema, is it appropriate to speak of *audiovisual* effects? These effects do indeed have an audiovisual *cause*, but the result of the combination does not consist in perceptions of sounds and images as such, but rather in perceptions of space, matter, volume, meaning, expression, and organization of space and time. This is why I prefer to speak of **audiovisiogenic effects**, i.e. effects generated by sounds and images. The peculiarity of these effects, as mentioned, is not to be detectable as such, but rather for the most part to create the illusion that sound only duplicates what the image would already say 'by itself'. The relationship between the audio and the visual is therefore based on a fundamental misperception: the belief in a **redundancy** between sound and image.

The most banal and seemingly least questionable example of redundancy one might think of is a dialogue in a film; but it is precisely not a redundancy. Indeed, sound, as a general rule, cannot be inferred from the image, and neither can a spoken text be deduced from what is seen, or just barely, except for a deaf person trained to lip-read (and besides, only in the original language with the actors facing the audience!). Symmetrically, the characters' faces, the way they are dressed and move, or the setting where they evolve can only rarely be deduced from the sound alone. Audiovisual redundancy is therefore impossible.

Sound/image: a skewed symmetry

My theory of audio-vision in the cinema contrasts with the lazily symmetrical model prevalent in a number of film courses, which describes sound on the one hand, and image on the other. On the contrary, audio-vision rests on a dissymmetrical model of description – a model in which sound and image are not two complementary and well-balanced elements. I have demonstrated how the (visible) frame of the image is also the frame in relation to which sound locates itself in space, and onto which sounds project their effects.

If sounds are easily projected by the spectator onto the film image, it is because the image is circumscribed by a frame that can be located in space, whereas sound lacks a frame. The visual frame is therefore the support of a double projection on the 'audio-spectator's' part – the projection of images (since he or she reprojects onto one image the previous ones in the film), and that of sounds.

Cinema indeed depends on the principle of *a visual frame for images*, an all but unique frame that pre-exists their random, sweeping succession. At the same time, it is the frame that allows one to speak of 'the image' in the singular, since images never extend beyond the frame. On the other hand, it can be said that *there is no sound frame for sounds*. Possibly, sounds are only framed by the image which grounds them (through spatial magnetization, see below), anchors and binds them – or not – to an object defined in space; conversely, if sounds are not incorporated into the image, they are made to exist on another invisible stage or in a contiguous (offscreen) space. Furthermore, contrary to the image that is enclosed within a frame, film sounds can be layered on top of one another without any limit of quantity or complexity, and they are free from all laws of realism. Film music, voice-over narration, dialogues or realistic atmospheric noises can all be mixed.

The absence of a sound frame is one of the main reasons which, for a long time, has led me to assert that *there is no soundtrack*. By this I mean that the different sounds which are present in a film (words, noises, diverse musics and sounds) and contribute to its meaning, its shape and its effects do not by themselves, by the sheer virtue of their all being sound elements, make up a comprehensive entity that is interdependent and homogeneous. In other words, in the cinema the relations of meaning, contrast, concordance or divergence that words, noises and musical elements are likely to entertain with one another are much weaker, even non-existent, in comparison with the relations each of the sound elements, on its own, has with a given visual or narrative element present simultaneously in the image. I refer you to my previous books on sound for detailed demonstrations of this assertion which allows few exceptions (see Further reading).

How audiovisiogenic effects originate

Audiovisual relationships are largely cultural and historical but, in everyday life as well as in the audiovisual arts, they rely also on relatively little-known universal psycho-physiological phenomena. (This is probably due to the increasing specialization of scholars, which has led them to pay less attention to the connections between the senses and focus their study on one of them.) First among these phenomena is the effect of **synchresis**.

'Synchresis' – a Lewis Carroll-style word I have forged (from synchronism and synthesis) – is the name I give to a spontaneous and reflex psycho-physiological phenomenon that depends on our nervous and muscular connections. It consists in perceiving as one and the same phenomenon – which manifests itself both on the visual and sound levels – the 'concomitance' of a precise sound event with a precise visual event on the sole and only condition that they happen simultaneously.

Through this phenomenon, which literally cannot be controlled, we are led instantaneously to establish a tight link of interdependence between sounds and images that are often quite unrelated in reality, and to assign them a common origin even if they are of completely different natures and sources. Synchresis therefore allows for the use of almost any sound effect for the footsteps of a character on the screen, in total freedom of expression.

Synchresis also permits effects based on contradiction and discrepancy (like a disproportion between voice and body in cartoons, or a gender inversion in certain comic or fantastical stories), and without it the 'audio' would purely and simply break away from the 'visual'. In brief, without synchresis, sound would have to mimic reality and its range of possibilities of expression would be much smaller. (It should be specified that film sound bears only a very remote resemblance to the sound in real situations.)

The word 'synchresis' is possibly ambiguous; it is not really a synthesis in the sense that no difference is 'transcended' or resolved; the image remains the image, and the sound remains the sound; what they have come to represent exists beyond them, like a projected shadow. If there is such a thing as an **audio-image** – an expression I occasionally use – then, *it is not the image which is on the screen*. It is a mental image, like the space created in a mise-en-scène through cutting and editing.

The second psycho-physiological condition, which is universal (i.e.

non-cultural) and permits audiovisual relations, is what I call *spatial magnetization*, i.e. magnetization of sound by the image. This is the process whereby when we visually locate a sound source (a human being, an animal, a machine, an object, etc.) in a certain place in space, and when for diverse reasons (the sound is electrically amplified, it bounces off the walls . . .) the associated sound comes mainly from another direction, we can still 'hear' the sound come from what we see as its source. Consequently, during the projection of a film on an airplane, the sound of the actors' voices seems to come from the screen whereas we hear the sound through earphones. An important counter-example is when sound really originates from different sources in space (for instance coming out of one loudspeaker, and then out of the other in the case of Dolby cinema) and therefore, for psycho-physiological reasons, our attention is reminded of its real acoustic location. Spatial magnetization has made possible classical talking pictures in which we accept that in mono sound the characters' voices do not really move about, especially when we see the characters walk across the screen. In the same way, sounds which are located 'offscreen' are only mentally so, in the minds of spectators who project onto the sound of a scene movements they have witnessed with their eyes. (This is a case of 'added value' in which value is added by the image to sound.)

Spatial magnetization works all the better when sounds are synchronized with images, and in many cases it implies synchresis. In the case of auditoriums equipped with Dolby, and so with multiple tracks, reflex spatial magnetization may be strengthened or on the contrary weakened by the *real* sources of the sound that is broadcast, depending on the positioning of the loudspeakers (i.e. whether they are more or less distant from one another and located outside the axis of the screen) and the position of the spectators themselves in the auditorium.

Why conscious hearing attention is hierarchical

The analysis of audiovisual relations must also take into account the fact that a human being's conscious hearing attention is not directed indifferently towards all types of sound. It is structured and hierarchical, and in particular *voice-centered*.

I call *voice-centering* the process by which, in a sound environment, the voice attracts and centers our attention, in the same way as the human face in the image of a film. Voice-centering can be obliterated or toned down by specific procedures: this is what happens, for example, in the films of Jacques Tati. The director introduces fluctuations in the sound level and the intelligibility of the text, while he also carefully establishes that the dialogues are not essential to the action proper, and at the same time, of course, puts the characters at a distance with his camera; these are all devices destined to 'prevent' our attention from focusing on the voices.

This does not mean that in the classical voice-centered cinema other sounds, noises and music, are 'unimportant'. On the contrary their role is as important, only at a less conscious level, just like the 'inner parts' (those of the tenor and alto which sound neither above nor below) in a string quartet or mixed four-voice choir. It is only when these parts are missing or different that one can feel that 'something has changed', even though the melody to which one consciously pays attention remains the same.

In sound cinema, voice is also the main, if not the exclusive, vehicle for the text. I have therefore suggested the term *audio(logo)visual* – instead of 'audiovisual' – to highlight the fact that most of the time in cinema the presence of language is central. It is a determining and privileged component, whether as a written text (intertitles in silent films, titles and subtitles in talking pictures, etc.) or as an oral text (dialogues, interior monologues, voice-over, etc.), and in these different forms language can determine, regulate and justify the overall structure of a film. By using the term audio(logo)visual one can avoid reducing cinema to a mere question of 'sounds' and 'images'.

Words, indeed, are not only the center of conscious attention but also frequently the key to audiovisual structuring; in some cases they even completely guide and organize the other elements around them. *Le Roman d'un tricheur* (1936) by Sacha Guitry uses this effect in a particularly conspicuous way. This film, which was very much admired by Orson Welles and the French New Wave, is indeed 'told' from beginning to end by a voice-over narrator-protagonist who 'comments' on the pictures, and even interprets the different voices of the characters on the screen. In the case of classical films with dialogues – which we call 'voice-centered' – this is more insidious and implicit. The whole film is then conceived and structured so as to justify and help the hearing of dialogues and to treat them as action, while at the same time the perception of the dialogue as such is obliterated. The – willing – spectator of classical voice-centered films does not realize that he is really listening to a flow of dialogues around which everything is organized; he is convinced that he is witnessing a complex action whose dialogues make up only what he considers to be an almost negligible part. This is what happens in the films of Hitchcock.

Other films, on the contrary, can be called *logo-decentered*. They correspond to the apparently paradoxical cases where dialogues are abundant and import-ant but instead of being 'dissimulated' or 'absorbed' by the mise-en-scène, their abundance is perceived as such because the other filmic elements do not encourage us to listen to them. Logo-decentered films range from the works of Fellini, where multilingual dialogues abound, to those of Tarkovsky, where the characters chatter away as they are confronted with their lack of power in the face of life and nature's mysteries. Also belonging to this category are cases where the audiovisual style renders speech relative and treats it like one noise among others. As already mentioned, this is the case in the films of Tati.

Effects of rendering and matter

Let me start with the notion of *rendering*, which I defined in my book *Audio-Vision* (Figures 1 and 5). We can speak of rendering when 'the film spectator recognizes sounds to be truthful, effective, and fitting not so much if they *repro-duce* what would be heard in the same situation in reality, but if they *render* (i.e. convey, express) the feelings associated with the situation'. The use of sound as a means of rendering (and not of reproduction) is facilitated because of the almost endless range of causes with which it can be associated. In other words, sound is easily justifiable, or, if you prefer, the spectator is very tolerant of the fact that a sound does not resemble what one would hear in reality; as I have demonstrated in other writings (e.g. *Le Promeneur écoutant*), there is no rigid law linking a sound to its cause(s).

Examples of 'rendering', i.e. of a sound which does not express another sound but rather a sense of speed or strength, would include the sound effects that punctuate action scenes (like the hissing of various swords, which conveys agil-ity in kung fu movies), the noises of falling bodies that impart the violence inflicted upon the characters (whereas the same fall in real life might not make any noise) or the sound of blows in boxing films. Other examples include sounds meant to give an impression of matter or non-materiality, of fragility or

FIGURE 1. Jean-Jacques Annaud's *L'Ours* (*The Bear*, 1988). The sound of the animal's footsteps, created in a studio, are not aimed at reproducing the often faint noises made by a bear walking on the soles of its feet on the ground, but at *rendering* its massive power.

resistance, of hollowness or plenitude, of weight or lightness, of having been used or being brand new, of luxury or misery. This is why sounds are generated – rather than to reproduce the real sound of a given object or character. *A rendering is always the rendering of something.* Besides, we must not forget that the issue of rendering is part of an audiovisual context. The effect of rendering is thus projected onto the image and falsely perceived as directly expressed by it (hence an illusion of redundancy).

Another means of audiovisual expression, dealing in this case with perception of matter, is the variable use of ***materializing sound indices (m.s.i.s)***. This expression refers to any aspect of a sound which reflects with more or less precision the material nature of its source and the concrete history of its production. M.s.i.s will reveal the nature of the source – which may be solid (woody, metallic), ethereal, gooey, grainy, liquid – its material consistency, the accidents occurring while it progresses, and so on. A sound may contain a certain number of materializing sound indices, or ultimately none at all. These m.s.i.s often consist of *unevennesses*, or slight or more pronounced irregularities, which reveal the material conditions of the sound source. In a specific listening situation such as a film or a piece of 'musique concrète', a voice, footsteps or a note may contain a variable number of materializing indices. These include throat clearing and breathing noises in the sound of a voice; crunching, squeaking or hissing noises in footsteps; slight accidents in the attack, the resonance or the tuning of a musical sequence caused by an out-of-tune piano or instruments that do not attack together. In the sound conception of a film, m.s.i.s are variously apportioned, particularly through the production of sound effects that either totally erase them (which creates an abstract, dematerialized universe) or on the contrary accentuate them (which foregrounds matter and bodies) with every possible combination in between. They are all important means of rendering in the cinema.

Materializing indices do not only concern noises but also play a part in the sound of dialogues. Voices in films may be more or less 'materialized' by details such as slight oral clicks, breathing noises between sentences and words, coughing or hoarse voices, or on the contrary be more or less dematerialized. Voice-over narration, especially, is often intentionally purified of its m.s.i.s so as not to attract attention to the physical body emitting the sound.

Scenographic effects

Other audiovisiogenic effects contribute to what I call **audiovisual scenography.** By this I mean everything that, in a combination of sounds and images, has to do with the construction of a narrative scene. This is done especially through ways of entering and exiting the sound frame (characters and vehicles entering and exiting the visual frame, and announced or followed by sound), through the contrast or identity between 'extension of sound space' (see below) and visual framing, through the comparison of the sizes of the screen characters and, acoustically, through the proximity or distance of their voices and more generally of the sounds they produce. It can be stressed right away that only rarely does 'sound perspective' reproduce and strictly redouble 'visual perspective', or if it happens it is in an approximate and tentative manner.

Here are two examples of audiovisual scenography borrowed from well-known films. In Ridley Scott's *Blade Runner* (1982), the setting and the characters are often shown in close shots while their surroundings are acoustically portrayed or suggested by sounds that evoke wide open spaces. This results in a sort of complementarity and compensation between vision in close-up and hearing in long shot. In Fellini's *Satyricon* (1969), on the contrary, several scenes combine visual scenography based on an empty space and the decentering of characters (often shown in long shot and at the bottom of a gigantic cinemascope screen) with fantasy sound scenography: the voices of the characters in question, which are not at the same distance as the bodies who 'emit' them, have an invading intimacy and speak into our ears as if in a dream.

Extension of sound space is one of the effects concerned with construction of space through the combination of sounds and images (Figure 2). By this I mean the concrete, more or less wide open space that the sonic environment defines beyond the screen, which constructs the geographical, human and natural framework from which the image on the screen is extracted. Let us consider the case where the setting of the action is confined to the inside of an apartment from which the camera does not escape. Extension of sound space will be *restricted* if the sound heard are only those made within the apartment; it will be *wider* if one can hear noises coming from the landing and the adjoining apartments offscreen, even wider if street noises are included, and wider still if distant noises such as foghorns or train whistles are perceived. All these choices are left to the director and the sound editor and depend on the scene and what

211

Michel Chion

FIGURE 2. The courtyard set of Alfred Hitchcock's *Rear Window* (1954). Through sound, in this famous film, Hitchcock freely plays with *extension*. He focuses our attention onto the courtyard, the street, other apartments, or on the contrary makes us forget all that is not the inside of James Stewart's character's apartment.

needs to be expressed. All the above possibilities will be accepted as 'natural' by the viewer. Extensions of an interior set will for instance make us feel 'nature' (with the wind blowing outside the house in John Huston's *Key Largo* [1948]) or 'solitude' (through a dog barking in the distance), or on the contrary crowds and promiscuity (with the noises of a Vietnamese street in the love scenes of Jean-Jacques Annaud's *The Lover* [1992]); they will also direct the attention of the spectator or of a character, and create an effect of meaning or contrast.

In this chapter, I can mention only briefly the contributions of Dolby to audiovisual scenography, and I would particularly like to stress the notion of **superfield** which I developed in *Audio-Vision*. 'I call "superfield" the space created, in multitrack films, by ambient natural sounds, city noises, music, and all sorts of rustlings that surround the visual space and that can issue from loudspeakers outside the physical boundaries of the screen.' (This is the case for instance in *Blade Runner*.) By virtue of its acoustic precision and relative stability, this ensemble of sounds takes on a kind of quasi-autonomous existence in

212

FIGURE 3. François Périer and Giulietta Masina in Federico Fellini's *Le notti di Cabiria* (1957). The *suspension* of natural sounds in this idyllic scene gives us a premonition that the couple's happiness is just an illusion.

relation to the visual field, in that it does not depend moment by moment on what we see onscreen, but neither does it acquire the autonomy and pregnancy of sound relations amongst themselves which would justify speaking of a *soundtrack.*

In a fictional scene in which our audiovisual habits call for (urban or natural) ambient noises, **suspension** is the dramatic audiovisiogenic effect which consists of interrupting these noises or even eliminating them from the start, while the causes of these sounds are still present in the action and even in the image. This often results in a feeling of mystery or threat, and sometimes in a sort of poetic suspension where the world loses some of its reality. For example, at the end of Fellini's *The Nights of Cabiria* (1957) during the romantic walk through the scenery of an enchanted wood, no bird song can be heard and the atmosphere is one of the impending doom. We soon learn that the man who has taken Cabiria to the edge of the cliff wants to kill her (Figure 3).

213

Effects concerning time and phrasing

After space, I now turn to time. The question of time is often neglected in the study of cinema and I have taken a particular interest in the way in which sound – by definition a temporal element – contributes to its construction, in general through added value.

One can call **audiovisual phrasing** everything that in a film sequence concerns the construction of time and rhythm through devices including phrasing, punctuations and pauses, freeze frames, anticipation and release. Sound is an important means of audiovisual phrasing because in editing one can easily incorporate sudden punctuating sounds (a honking horn, the cry of an animal) or sounds evolving in time (a passing car, gusts of wind) which help to cut up, enliven and build time. One can also speak of phrasing because sound is an important means of *temporalization*.

Temporalization is an audiovisiogenic effect – a case of added value – in which sound either influences and 'contaminates' the duration which images already have, or endows images with a duration they do not have in themselves (e.g. the completely static shots in Chris Marker's *La Jetée* (1962) or shots of an empty scene or motionless characters). Sound can, in particular, impose a linear and chronological succession to a sequence of images whose relationship does not presuppose temporal succession; this is what I have called **linearization** of images through sound. For example, at the beginning of *Citizen Kane* (Orson Welles, 1941), the first shots of Xanadu are *linearized* by Bernard Herrmann's music, and a similar effect is achieved at the end of *L'Eclisse* (Michelangelo Antonioni, 1962) by the music of Giovanni Fusco. Sound can also 'vectorize' individual shots, i.e. orient them in time by imparting a sense of expectation, of progression, of a movement forward or an imminent action that they do not convey by themselves; this is what I have called **vectorization**. A good example is the sound crescendo, from pianissimo to fortissimo, created by Bergman over some of the shots in the silent prologue sequence of *Persona* (1966). I refer you to my analysis of this sequence in *Audio-Vision: Sound on Screen*. Also, some of the static shots showing no movement in the sequence of the crop-duster attack in Hitchcock's *North by Northwest* (1959) are *vectorized* by the crescendo or decrescendo of the airplane's engine (Figure 4).

Audiovisual phrasing in the cinema also relies on the existence of what I have called 'points of synchronization'. A **point of synchronization**, or **synch point**,

FIGURE 4. Two photograms of a scene from Alfred Hitchcock's *North by Northwest* (1959). In this famous scene, the plane attacking Cary Grant is not always visible, but the sound of the plane, which keeps evolving, coming and going, creates a sense of time and suspense even in the most static shots.

215

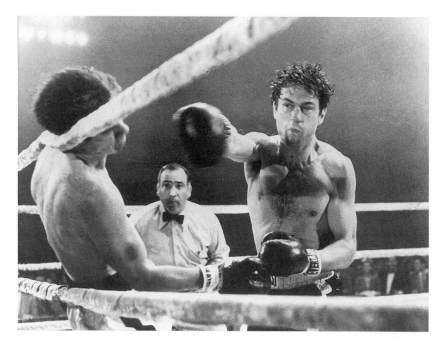

FIGURE 5. Martin Scorsese's *Raging Bull* (1980). The sound of the blows given and received by Robert De Niro (recreated in a studio by the sound editor Frank Warner) is used to *render* physical violence, but also to create *points of synchronization* and build the rhythm of the sequence.

is a salient moment in an audiovisual sequence when a sound event and a visual event meet in synchrony. In other words, it is a point where the effect of synch-resis is particularly prominent. The frequency and distribution of synch points within a sequence contribute to its phrasing and rhythm, and they also provide meaning and emphasis. A point of synchronization can occur between an image and a sound *within a shot*, between a visual cut (followed by another shot) and a sound cut, as well as between a visual cut and a line from the dialogue (Figure 5).

To obtain a synch point, synchronism is necessary but not sufficient. This means that a scene of filmed dialogue with much lip synch does not necessarily contain points of synchronization. Synch points correspond to particularly sali-ent and meaningful moments linked to varied criteria, such as the impact of a break in perception (when sound and image are cut simultaneously), the pres-ence of an emphasis which is both visual (a close-up) and acoustic (a particularly close or powerful sound), a synchronous detail that has a dramatic or emotional value. The context is also meaningful: therefore the first synchronous meeting between a sound and an image after a long absence of synchronism (for example, after a series of long takes of someone listening to a character offscreen) becomes a point of synchronization. The latter synch point may often also have been prepared and arranged as a meeting of temporal vanishing lines (see below). One can for example speak of a synch point when the camera shows the face of an actor at the very moment he says 'Yes' after his hands have been shown for 30 seconds while he was speaking off camera; the 'reunion' between the movement of the lips and the voice is a typical point of synchronization.

A very simple experiment may be performed by starting a piece of music taken at random (from a record) together with a sequence of a film (from a video cassette with the original sound cut out), thereby creating an aleatory audiovisual superposition. This highlights the way in which the spectator, who is 'eager for synchronism', is on the lookout for the slightest synch points, even to the absurd, and uses any pretext to make them up. The experiment confirms the need for a form of scansion and punctuation in an audiovisual sequence, and the tendency for the spectator to find meaning in any concomitance, whether intentional or fortuitous.

One can speak of **temporal vanishing lines** when a certain number of sound and/or visual elements are superimposed and arranged in a way leading to the anticipation that they will cross, meet or collide within a more or less predictable time span. This anticipation is then either realized or 'disappointed' and this crossing may occur sooner or later than expected. Let us take the example of a character (filmed by a static camera) walking towards us at a certain pace while a musical theme with its melodic line can be heard on the soundtrack. We have here two temporal vanishing lines: one based on the anticipation of the 'collision' between the character and the camera, and the other on the conclusion – the 'cadence' – of the musical phrase. This intuitive feeling of anticipation, which leads spectators to project themselves forward in time, does not require any technical knowledge, on their part, of the language of music or film.

Two simultaneous temporal vanishing lines can be found within a single image, for example when a character is walking towards a certain point while the camera is moving diagonally or perpendicularly in relation to him or her. The same is true of course within a sequence of sounds when for example a sentence in a dialogue (in which the object comes after the verb) and a musical phrase (with its cadential flow) heard simultaneously build two temporal vanishing lines.

Audio-division, phantom audio-vision and audiovisual dissonance

I have so far dealt with the cases where sound and image are mutually compounded and result in what is generally experienced as an 'effect of the image'. I should now point out that audiovisual relationships are also based on shortcomings where sound brings out what is missing in the image, or the image what is missing in sound, as in the above-mentioned example of 'suspension'. I would therefore be tempted to make a play on words and speak of **audio-division**.

The term audio-division does not describe audio(logo)visual relationships as complementary and self-contained recreations of an imaginary natural entity; rather, it suggests a concomitance which, as well as generating audiovisionic effects of association, of added value pertaining to rendering or audiovisual phrasing and scenography, also develops new shortcomings, 'phantom' effects (see below) and diverse divisions. In other words, even if sound is 'realistic', it does not answer the question raised by the image; sound divides the image, and vice versa.

For instance, in an audiovisual sequence a **phantom sound** is a sound suggested by the image but not heard, while other sounds associated to the scene are audible. If, in a Fellini film, one can hear the characters constantly talking while they are walking at a brisk pace without hearing their footsteps, the sound of the footsteps becomes a *phantom sound* in the context of the other sounds heard. However, we hear the sound mentally, we imagine it, it does not seem to be missing but rather contributes to a feeling of lightless and fluidity. We find another example in a scene at the beach in *Mr Hulot's Holiday* (1952) by Tati: the sound of the sea, which is visible in the background, cannot be heard whereas one can make out the shouts of the bathers. The distinction we can make between a *phantom sound* and *suspension* is that *suspension* specifically concerns sounds whose absence evokes something similar to a lull before a storm. On the other hand, a **phantom image** is a precise image, suggested by a sound but not visible. For example, the sound of the sea accompanying the close-up of a character's face creates a phantom image of the sea.

Finally, *audiovisual dissonance* is an effect of contradiction between sound and image at a precise moment in a story, or between a realistic sonic environment and the setting with which it is associated. Examples can be found in Godard's *First Name Carmen* (1983), when cries of seagulls and sounds of waves are heard over shots of the Austerlitz Bridge by night, or in the gender inversion between the hero and the heroine's voices in Patrick Schulmann's fantastical comedy *Rendez-moi ma peau* (1980) or also in the contrast between a harsh and booming voice and a tiny body as in Tex Avery's cartoon *The Cat That Hated People*. When contradiction concerns size, the effect does not seem to be of dissonance, but rather of monstrosity.

The term 'dissonance' seems to me more appropriate here than the often misused term 'counterpoint' (which in music concerns a superposition of lines). It can be noted that the effect of audiovisual dissonance is almost always limited to pre-coded rhetorical cases such as gender opposition, contrast between voice and body, city versus nature in Godard's films, nature versus culture in Paolo and Vittorio Taviani's *Padre Padrone* (1977) or past versus science fiction with the *Blue Danube* waltz in Stanley Kubrick's *2001: A Space Odyssey* (1968). Furthermore, audiovisual dissonance is difficult to obtain because of the lack of demand on the spectator's part for a sonic 'verisimilitude' of the image, and also because of the power of the process of synchresis that compounds sounds with images.

Conclusion

In this chapter I have highlighted a selection of the audiovisual effects I have studied and I have provided a basis for their description. Many questions remain: 'How did these effects come about? Can they be assimilated to a "code"? Will the new multitrack technique now widespread in the cinema (what is called Dolby) transform them altogether?' These are three questions, among many others, to which I will provide a very brief and general answer.

The genesis and history of these different effects is a fascinating field of study which I have just barely opened up in my own work. It seems to me that one should take two precautions: first, cinema must be resituated within the history of theatre, music, ballet, pantomime, radio and opera, from which it has borrowed extensively. A history of sound in the cinema separate from the history of sound in audiovisual arts in general is as absurd as telling the history of France without reference to that of the countries with which it was involved.

Second, I do not think that these effects can be approached as a 'code', in the exact sense that there exist codes of visual editing with a fixed meaning (e.g. the use of a shot/reverse shot). It seems to me that it is necessary to have a theory of the audiovisual effect, and of the filmic effect in general – a notion that needs to be rehabilitated. The contributions of scholars such as Christian Metz have very significantly advanced this cause.

Third, I do not expect a complete 'revolution' to take place overnight because of a new technique. Film language, like an individual or a species, is constructed layer by layer and through partial reconfigurations of an overall structure. What is called sound cinema has developed from a structure that was partially dictated by the requirements of silent cinema – a structure it has always retained, as is very well shown by David Bordwell and Kristin Thompson in their study of classical Hollywood cinema. In the same way, the different types of sound cinema in existence today accumulate effects and practices linked to different stages in the evolution of cinema in general. A truly historical approach is necessary to study this evolution, and an exciting task awaits historians who wish to pursue such research.

FURTHER READING

Altman, R. (ed.), *Sound Theory Sound Practice*, New York, London: Routledge, American Film Institute, 1992.

Bailblé, C., 'Pour une nouvelle approche de l'enseignement de la technique du cinéma: programmation de l'écoute', four-part article in *Cahiers du Cinéma*: nos. **292** (September 1978), 52–9; **293** (October 1978), 4–12; **297** (February 1979), 45–54; **299** (April 1979), 16–27.

Bordwell, D., Staiger, J. and Thompson, K., *The Classical Hollywood Cinema*, London: Routledge and Kegan Paul, 1985.

Chion, M., *Guide des objets sonores*, Paris: INA/Buchet-Chastel, 1982.

Chion, M., *La Voix au cinéma*, Paris: Cahiers du Cinéma, 1982. [*The Voice in Cinema* (translated by Claudia Gorbman),] New York: Columbia University Press, 1999.

Chion, M., *Le Son au cinéma*, Paris: Cahiers du Cinéma, 1985.

Chion, M., *La Toile trouée ou La Parole au cinéma*, Paris: Cahiers du Cinéma, 1988.

Chion, M., *L'Audio-vision: Son et image au cinéma*, Paris: Nathan, 1990.
[*Audio-Vision: Sound on Screen* (translated by Claudia Gorbman, foreword by Walter Murch), New York: Columbia University Press, 1994.]
Chion, M., *Le Promeneur écoutant*, Paris: Plume, 1993.
Chion, M., *La Musique au cinéma*, Paris: Fayard, 1995.
Chion, M., *Le Son*, Paris: Nathan, 1998.
Schaeffer, P., *Traité des objets musicaux*, Paris: Seuil, 1967.

Notes on Contributors

Jonathan Ashmore is Bernard Katz Professor of Biophysics at University College London. He completed a Ph.D. in theoretical physics at Imperial College London before moving into biology to work as an experimental physiologist in the visual system and then in hearing when at the University of Bristol. He was elected a Fellow of the Royal Society in 1996.

Michel Chion is a writer, researcher, composer of *musique concrète*, film-maker, and an Associate Professor at the University of Paris III. His 20 books of theory, history and aesthetics devoted to cinema, music and sound have been translated into many languages. He was awarded the Grand Prix du Disque 1978 for his *Requiem*, the Prix Jean-Vigo for best short film in 1985, the Prix du Meilleur livre de cinéma 1995 and the 1996 City of Locarno Grand Prize for his video *La Messe de terre*.

Steven Feld is Professor of Anthropology at New York University. His publications include *Sound and Sentiment* (1982/1990), *Voices of the Rainforest* (1991), *Music Grooves* (with Charles Keil, 1994), *Senses of Place* (edited with Keith Basso, 1996), and *Bosavi-English-Tok Pisin Dictionary* (with Bambi B. Schieffelin, 1998). He also maintains an active career as a trombonist, performing and recording jazz and new music.

Brian Ferneyhough is a composer and Professor of Music at the University of California, San Diego. His compositions have been performed at numerous venues ranging from the Venice Biennale to the London Proms. He lectures and teaches composition widely and is currently engaged in research into computer-assisted composition at IRCAM, Paris. His *Collected Writings* were published in 1996.

Patricia Kruth is a researcher in Film and a *professeur agrégé* of English. She is a former Fellow of Darwin College and Director of the French Cultural Delegation in Cambridge. Her current work is on cinematic figures in the New York City films of Martin Scorsese and Woody Allen. She has also curated several photography exhibitions.

Peter Ladefoged is Emeritus Professor of Phonetics at the University of California, Los Angeles. His books include *Elements of Acoustic Phonetics* (1962), and *A Course in Phonetics* (third edition, 1993). Together with Ian Madison, with whom he co-authored *The Sounds of the World's Languages* (1996), he is currently engaged in a project to study the phonetics of endangered languages.

Christopher Page is Reader in Medieval Music and Literature at the University of Cambridge, presenter of *Spirit of the Age* (BBC Radio 3), and director of Gothic Voices. His books include *Voices and Instruments of the Middle Ages* (1987), *The Owl and the Nightingale* (1989), *Summa Musice* (1991), *Discarding Images* (1993) and *Songs of the Trouvères* (1995).

Philip M. Peek is Professor of Anthropology at Drew University in New Jersey, USA. He has published widely on African visual and verbal arts and has edited *African Divination Systems: Ways of Knowing*. Currently, he is co-editing an encyclopedia of African folklore and is co-curating an exhibition on the arts of the Niger Delta.

Peter J. B. Slater is Kennedy Professor of Natural History and Dean of the Faculty of Science at the University of St Andrews. He was educated at Edinburgh University, and was then Lecturer in Biology at the University of Sussex before taking up his present position. He is a past President of the Association for the Study of Animal Behaviour and is editor of the series *Advances in the Study of Behavior* published by Academic Press. He was elected a Fellow of the Royal Society of Edinburgh in 1991.

Henry Stobart is Lecturer in Ethnomusicology at the Royal Holloway, University of London, and former Adrian Research Fellow of Darwin College. His principal research and publications focus on the music of the Bolivian Andes. As a member of the Early Music ensemble Sirinu, he has toured widely and recorded five CDs.

Charles Taylor is Emeritus Professor of Physics in the University of Wales, and former Professor of Experimental Physics at the Royal Institution. In 1986 he became the first holder of the Royal Society's Michael Faraday Award for contributions to the Public Understanding of Science. He gave the Royal Institution Christmas Lectures on BBC television in 1971 (*Sounds of Music*) and in 1989 (*Exploring Music*).

Acknowledgements

Cover image: Photograph by Alain Willaume, *Near Pointe St Mathieu* (detail), France, 1994. From his series *Études pour objets sonores (profanes et sacrés)*.

INTRODUCTION

FIGURE 1: Photograph by Henry Stobart.

CHAPTER 1

The author extends his sincere appreciation to colleagues at Drew University (Lillie Johnson Edwards, David Kohn, John Lenz, and Merrill Skaggs) and the volume editors, Henry Stobart and Patricia Kruth, and Janine Bourriau for insightful recommendations.

FIGURE 1: Photograph by Paul Gebauer.

FIGURE 2: Photograph by Doran H. Ross.

FIGURE 3: Photograph by Lorentz Homberger, Museum Rietberg, Zürich.

FIGURE 4: Detail from photograph. Courtesy of Library Services, American Museum of Natural History.

FIGURE 5: Photograph by Philip Peek.

CHAPTER 2

FIGURES 1, 2, 3 and 9: Courtesy of Charles Taylor.

FIGURES 4, 5 and 6: From *Sounds of Music* by Charles Taylor, London: BBC, 1976 (Figures 5.1, 5.2 and 5.6). Reproduced with permission from BBC Worldwide Ltd.

FIGURES 7 and 10 to 14: From *Exploring Music* by Charles Taylor, Bristol: Institute of Physics, 1992 (Figures 3.7, 2.32, 2.34, 3.3, 3.6 and 3.11). Reproduced with permission.

FIGURE 8: From *Sound* by J. Tyndall, London: Longmans, Green and Co., 1883.

225

CHAPTER 3

FIGURES 1, 6 and 7: Courtesy of Jonathan Ashmore.

FIGURE 2: From Ganong, W. F., *A Review of Medical Physiology*, 13th edition, Norwalk, CT: Appleton and Lange, 1987, with permission of the McGraw-Hill Companies.

FIGURE 3: Redrawn with permission from Dr Paul Kolston, University of Bristol.

FIGURE 4: Reprinted from *Current Opinion in Neurobiology* **4**, J. F. Ashmore and P. J. Kolston, 'Hair cell based amplification in the cochlea', pp. 503–8 (1994), with kind permission from Elsevier Science Ltd, The Boulevard, Langford Lane, Kidlington, OX5 1GB, UK.

FIGURE 5: All images courtesy of Dr Andy Forge, Institute of Otolaryngology, University College London, except top right, which is courtesy of the Wellcome Institute Biomedical Archive.

FIGURE 8: Reprinted from *Current Biology* **3**, J. F. Ashmore, 'The ear's fast cellular motor', pp. 38–40 (1993), with kind permission from Elsevier Science Ltd, The Boulevard, Langford Lane, Kidlington, OX5 1GB, UK.

CHAPTER 4

TABLE 1: Modified after Alcock, J., *Animal Behavior: An Evolutionary Approach*, Sunderland, MA: Sinauer, 1989.

TABLE 2: Modified from data in Catchpole, C. K. and Slater, P. J. B., *Bird Song. Biological Themes and Variations*, Cambridge: Cambridge University Press, 1995.

FIGURE 1: After Suthers, R. A., Goller, F. and Hartley, R. S., 'Motor dynamics of sound production in mimic thrushes', *Journal of Neurobiology* **25** (1994), 917–36. Copyright © 1994 John Wiley & Sons, Inc. Reprinted by permission of John Wiley & Sons, Inc.

FIGURE 2: After Krebs, J. R., 'Song and territory in the great tit *Parus major*', in *Evolutionary Ecology*, ed. B. Stonehouse and C. Perrins, pp. 47–62, London: Macmillan, 1977.

FIGURE 3: Data collected by the author.

FIGURE 4: After Todt, D. and Hultsch, H., 'Acquisition and performance of song repertoires: ways of coping with diversity and versatility', in *Ecology and Evolution of Acoustic Communication in Birds*, ed. D. E. Kroodsma and E. H. Miller, pp. 79–96, Ithaca and London: Comstock Publishing Associates, 1996. Copyright © 1996 by Cornell University. Used by permission of the publisher, Cornell University Press.

FIGURE 5: (*a*) After Catchpole, C. K., 'Temporal and sequential organisation of song in the sedge warbler (*Acrocephalus schoenobaenus*)', *Behaviour* **59**

(1976), 226–46. (*b*) Reprinted with permission from *Nature*: After Catchpole, C. K., 'Sexual selection and the evolution of complex songs among warblers of the genus *Acrocephalus*', *Behaviour* **74** (1980), 149–66. (*c*) Catchpole, C. K., Dittami, J. and Leisler, B., 'Differential responses to male song repertoires in female songbirds implanted with oestradiol', *Nature* **312** (1984), 563–4. Copyright 1984 Macmillan Magazines Limited.

FIGURE 6: (*a*) After Slater, P. J. B., 'Bird song learning: causes and consequences', *Ethology, Ecology and Evolution* **1** (1989), 19–46. (*b*) Kindly provided by Katharina Riebel. (*c*) After Slater, P. J. B., 'The development of individual behaviour', in *Animal Behaviour*, vol. 3 *Genes, Development and Learning*, ed. T. R. Halliday and P. J. B. Slater, pp. 82–113, Oxford: Blackwell Science Ltd, 1983.

FIGURE 7: Kindly provided by Patrice Adret. Data from Adret, P., 'Operant conditioning, song learning and imprinting to taped song in the zebra finch', *Animal Behaviour* **46** (1993), 149–59.

FIGURE 8: After Handford, P., 'Trill rate dialects in the rufous-collared sparrow, *Zonotrichia capensis*, in northwestern Argentina', *Canadian Journal of Zoology* **66** (1988), 2658–70.

CHAPTER 5

TABLES: Some of the material in the tables has been published in Ladefoged, P., *A Course in Phonetics*, 3rd edition, Orlando, FL: Harcourt Brace, 1993.

ALL FIGURES: Courtesy of Peter Ladefoged.

CHAPTER 6

FIGURE 1: Facsimile reproduced from *Firenze, Biblioteca Mediceo-Laurenziana, Pluteo 29, 1*, Part 1, Fascicles I-VI, ff. 1–262, ed. L. Dittmer, New York: Institute of Mediaeval Music, Ltd. Score courtesy of Christopher Page.

FIGURE 2: © National Gallery, London.

FIGURE 3: From Michael Praetorius, *De Organografia*, 2nd book of *Syntagma Musicum*, 1619.

CHAPTER 7

FIGURE 1: Colfranc Music Publishing Corporation, New York, 1966/7.

FIGURE 2: © 1954 by Universal Edition (London) Ltd, London. Final version: 1975 by Universal Edition (London) Ltd, London. Reproduced with permission.

FIGURE 3: © Moeck Verlag und Musikinstrumentenwerk, D-Celle. Reproduced with permission.

FIGURE 4: © 1969 Musikverlage Hans Gerig, Köln. Assigned to Breithopf and Härtel, Wiesbaden 1980. Reproduced with permission.

FIGURE 5: Denkbare Musik, DuMont Schauberg Verlag, Cologne, 1972.

CHAPTER 8

This chapter is dedicated to the memory of Frank X. Magne, who died during fieldwork in Papua New Guinea in March 1994. Frank's pursuits in music and anthropology at the University of Texas at Austin and at the University of Manchester were filled with an eclectic intensity. I know he would have made a remarkable difference to our ability to enter the sound worlds of Papua New Guinea, and to locate them in the world of cultural politics.

I am grateful to Drs Henry Stobart and Patricia Kruth, convenors of the Darwin Lectures, Professor Geoffrey Lloyd, Master of Darwin College, and Drs Ruth Davis, Carole Pegg, and Professor Marilyn Strathern of the University of Cambridge ethnomusicological and anthropological communities, for their generous hospitality during my visit to Cambridge.

FIGURE 1: Courtesy of Piggott Printers, Cambridge.

All other figures courtesy of Steven Feld.

CHAPTER 9

All film stills courtesy of Cahiers du Cinéma, Paris, France.

INDEX

Bold numbers indicate pages with illustrations.

229